SECOND TREATISE OF GOVERNMENT

AND

A LETTER CONCERNING TOLERATION

JOHN LOCKE was the son of John Locke, attorney, and Agnes Keene. He was born on 29 August 1632 at Wrington, Somerset, and attended Westminster School, London (1647–52) and Christ Church, Oxford, graduating BA in 1656 and MA in 1658. He remained in Oxford until 1667, employed as a tutor and lecturer in Greek, rhetoric, and moral philosophy. While at Oxford Locke developed interests in medicine and natural philosophy. In 1667 he moved to London under the patronage of Anthony Ashley Cooper, future Earl of Shaftesbury and Lord Chancellor. He served the earl's interests in colonial 'plantations', helping to draft *The Fundamental Constitutions of Carolina* (1669), and served as secretary to Charles II's short-lived Council for Trade and Plantations (1673–4). He spent the years 1675–9 in France, and returned to embroilment in the Whig movement which Shaftesbury now led against Charles II and his Catholic brother and heir James. The earl fled to Holland in 1682, and Locke followed in 1683, remaining until 1689. Locke returned to England after the Glorious Revolution, which overthrew James II and installed William III and Mary II.

Locke now rapidly became much published and famous. The *Two Treatises of Government*, *Letter Concerning Toleration*, and *Essay Concerning Human Understanding* all appeared in 1689. Later there followed *Some Thoughts Concerning Education* (1693), *The Reasonableness of Christianity* (1695), and a series of economic tracts. In 1696 he became one of the state's most senior servants as a founder member of the Board of Trade and Plantations, attempting to govern America. He divided his time between public duties in London and scholarly seclusion at Oates in Essex, the home of Lady Damaris Masham, herself a published philosopher. He died in her company on 28 October 1704, and is buried at the parish church of High Laver.

MARK GOLDIE is Professor of Intellectual History at the University of Cambridge, where he is a Fellow of Churchill College. He has written extensively on British political, religious, and intellectual history in the seventeenth and eighteenth centuries, and is currently working on an intellectual biography of Locke's final, post-Revolution, years.

OXFORD WORLD'S CLASSICS

*For over 100 years Oxford World's Classics have brought
readers closer to the world's great literature. Now with over 700
titles—from the 4,000-year-old myths of Mesopotamia to the
twentieth century's greatest novels—the series makes available
lesser-known as well as celebrated writing.*

*The pocket-sized hardbacks of the early years contained
introductions by Virginia Woolf, T. S. Eliot, Graham Greene,
and other literary figures which enriched the experience of reading.
Today the series is recognized for its fine scholarship and
reliability in texts that span world literature, drama and poetry,
religion, philosophy, and politics. Each edition includes perceptive
commentary and essential background information to meet
the changing needs of readers.*

OXFORD WORLD'S CLASSICS

JOHN LOCKE

Second Treatise of Government

and

A Letter Concerning Toleration

Edited with an Introduction and Notes by
MARK GOLDIE

OXFORD
UNIVERSITY PRESS

OXFORD
UNIVERSITY PRESS

Great Clarendon Street, Oxford, ox2 6DP
United Kingdom

Oxford University Press is a department of the University of Oxford.
It furthers the University's objective of excellence in research, scholarship,
and education by publishing worldwide. Oxford is a registered trade mark of
Oxford University Press in the UK and in certain other countries

First Edition published in 2016

Impression: 4

Published in the United States of America by Oxford University Press
198 Madison Avenue, New York, NY 10016, United States of America

British Library Cataloguing in Publication Data
Data available
Library of Congress Control Number: 2015953859

ISBN 978-0-19-873244-0

Printed in Great Britain by
Clays Ltd, Elcograf S.p.A.

CONTENTS

INTRODUCTION

AFTER the fall of Soviet Communism a journalist wrote that the Cold War had been about whether John Locke or Karl Marx was right.[1] The remark attests Locke's eminence as the philosopher of liberalism. His vocabulary of liberty, equality, rights, and consent is ours, and his accent on property chimes with the primacy of economics in modern politics. But Locke has been lucky. His *Two Treatises of Government* was published in the year of the English Revolution and was lauded in the year of the American Revolution. For as long as the Anglo-American version of modernity continues to prevail, Locke has a secure buttress for his canonical status. Locke made his own luck too. He was skilful at rendering political ideas, inherited from the classical and medieval past and familiar among his contemporaries, into plain and resonant prose which made his truths seem self-evident, and self-evidently his.

Locke's Life

John Locke was a child of the Reformation and an inspiration of the Enlightenment. During his lifetime (1632–1704) England changed dramatically. When he was young, royal absolutism was a doctrine in fashion and the Church of England the only lawful religion. By the time he died, parliamentary monarchy and party politics were the new norms, and Protestant Dissenters worshipped freely. Twice, a revolution overthrew Stuart monarchy: Charles I was executed in 1649 and his son James II was expelled in 1688. Twice, Anglicanism was restrained: abolished in the 1640s and its restored monopoly of 1662 curtailed by the Act of Toleration in 1689. The first revolution, and the brief republic of the 1650s, collapsed; the second, the so-called Glorious Revolution of 1688, endured.

In thought and action, Locke participated in these transformations. The son of a village attorney in Somerset, his talents took him to Westminster School and Christ Church, Oxford. A conventional career beckoned, as a university tutor, to be followed by

---

[1] Peregrine Worsthorne, *Guardian*, 14 Sept. 1996.

clerical ordination. He was deflected by public service, and joined the household of King Charles II's minister Lord Ashley, future earl of Shaftesbury. But in the 1670s Shaftesbury turned against the crown and led the Whig movement which rocked the foundations of the Restoration settlement in church and state. Fearing that royal power was again menacing, that Protestant Dissenters were destined for destruction, that the king appeased the French superpower, and that the Catholicism of the king's brother and heir, James, was incompatible with the Reformation, the Whig movement campaigned against 'popery and arbitrary government' and tried to alter the succession. The Whigs won general elections but were outmanoeuvred and crushed by Charles, supported by loyalists who came now to be called Tories. A savage reaction ensued, with the executions of leading Whigs and mass repression of Dissent. Shaftesbury and Locke fled to the Netherlands, where the earl died. James acceded to the British thrones in 1685, but speedily alienated the political nation. A series of risings, and Dutch military intervention led by Prince William of Orange, cut short his reign. In February 1689 a Convention declared the throne vacant and invited William and his consort Mary to become monarchs.

Locke had followed Shaftesbury into opposition, confrontation, and exile. In 1689 he returned to England. While before the Revolution he was obscure and unpublished, afterwards he was famous and prolific. A great trilogy of books appeared in 1689, prepared in earlier years. The *Essay Concerning Human Understanding* reorientated philosophy towards epistemology: the problem of the nature and limits of human knowledge. The *Two Treatises of Government* assailed absolutism and urged that no government is legitimate which does not have the consent of the people. The *Letter Concerning Toleration* argued that religious truth should never be imposed by force. Locke continued to write, in self-vindication, and in new treatises on economics, education, and theology. His *Two Treatises* and *Toleration* appeared anonymously, but rumours of their authorship were sufficient for commentators to begin to applaud or denounce his entire oeuvre. His enemies called him an atheist and republican who shook the foundations of Christianity, morality, and political stability. His admirers began to excerpt the *Second Treatise* in pamphlets, speeches, and even sermons. By the time of his death it was deployed in manifold ways, such as in William Molyneux's *Case of Ireland*

(1698), which insisted Ireland was not subordinate to England; and in John Somers's *Jura Populi Anglicani* (1701), which held that parliament was bound to listen to the sovereign voice of the people.

Locke's Critique

Locke's Preface made clear his intention in publishing the *Two Treatises*:

> to establish the Throne of our great Restorer, Our present King William; to make good his Title, in the Consent of the People, which being the only one of all lawful Governments, he has more fully and clearly, than any Prince in Christendom; and to justifie to the World the People of England, whose love of their just and natural Rights, with their Resolution to preserve them, saved the Nation when it was on the very brink of Slavery and Ruin.

The book's first task was to contribute to the controversy over allegiance to King William and Queen Mary that followed the Revolution. Locke dogmatically insists that Whig doctrine alone should legitimate the new regime: the community makes governments, and tyrants may be forcibly deposed. He was dismayed that Tories, who had earlier argued for royal absolutism, and who now, in fright at James II's rule, reluctantly accepted the Revolution, were trying to justify allegiance to William as a merely *de facto* and not *de jure* ruler. Tories also argued that James had not been deposed, but had abdicated, and that his daughter, Mary, now reigned by hereditary right. Locke's dramatic counter claim was that the old regime had dissolved, and that the community was free to choose a new form or new persons: the Convention was a constituent assembly of the sovereign people. Even so, he handled his thesis paradoxically. Its form is radical, yet he thought his countrymen were prudent to recur to the 'Ancient Constitution', the balanced polity of king, lords, and commons. Revolutionary theory underpinned a moderate constitutional outcome.

Locke's Preface is misleading about the origins of his book, for most of it was written between 1679 and 1683, between the apogee of the first Whig movement and its destruction. His fellow Whig, Algernon Sidney, was executed in 1683 for a similar work, *Discourses Concerning Government* (posthumously published in 1698), and Locke kept his own book secret until after the Revolution. The three most profound Whig works, Locke's, Sidney's, and James Tyrrell's *Patriarcha non Monarcha* (1681), were counterblasts against the ideological flagship of Toryism, Sir Robert Filmer's *Patriarcha, or, the Natural Power of Kings*. Drafted probably in the 1620s and excerpted in tracts for the royal cause during the Civil Wars, *Patriarcha* was published posthumously in 1680. Locke responded to the immediate needs of the Whig movement, but he also incorporated self-contained essays on larger themes, notably on property, the family, and legislative power.

The *Second Treatise* almost never refers to other theorists, friend or foe. But Locke's book comprises not one but two treatises, and the *First Treatise* is a rebarbative line-by-line critique of Filmer. By separating the *Second* from the *First*, Locke—and we—exaggerate its detachment from the fray.[2] Refuting Filmer was necessary to the Whig cause. If today it is Hobbes's *Leviathan* which is considered the pre-eminent English defence of absolute sovereignty, Filmer's patriarchalism was far more characteristic of Royalism and Toryism. Hobbes and Filmer both believed that royal supremacy was unimpeachable and armed resistance impermissible. But Filmer claimed that a theory of sovereignty grounded, as Hobbes's was, in the natural equality and liberty of individuals, was a house built on sand, because the idea of a *total* alienation of our powers to a sovereign under a social contract was unsustainable. Filmer denounced the premise of natural liberty, promoted alike by Hobbes, Calvinist and Catholic enemies of monarchy, Civil War Parliamentarians, and Whigs. Political authority, he insists, cannot derive from the individuals who make up communities.

Filmer argued that Adam's dominion, in the Book of Genesis, was the archetype of all human authority, familial, domestic, and civil. His case is scriptural but naturalistic too. By nature we are born unfree, subject to a father. The wild hypothesis of natural liberty and equality is anarchic, and violates the truth of the Christian Bible. The sovereign is a patriarch like Adam, so that rebellion is a parricidal denial of natural hierarchy. Filmer attempts to argue that modern kings derive their right by lineal descent from Adam, but he is on safer ground in regarding Adamic authority as paradigmatic of all human dominion.

---

[2] The *First Treatise* is important for professional scholars but unrewarding for first-time readers of Locke. It is omitted here, and was omitted early on, in the French translation, *Du Gouvernement civil* (Amsterdam, 1691).

He invigorated the Royalist and Tory doctrine of divine-right monarchy and the duty of 'non-resistance and passive obedience'. Locke remarked that he would not have bothered with Filmer had not the pulpit lately preached his doctrine. One purpose of Locke's *Two Treatises* was educative. It is a handbook of intellectual hygiene, for cleansing the minds of an ideologically corrupted generation. Absolutism, he held, was a recent and aberrant doctrine, whereas his own argument was ancient—which is why he regularly quoted Richard Hooker, the sixteenth-century voice of Christian natural law and natural liberty.

The *Second Treatise* summarizes the case against patriarchalism. Locke holds that Filmer is guilty of a profound category error. Familial relations are not political relations, and the family is not the microcosm of the state. Commonwealths and families are distinct. Every human community is built upon its *telos*, or end: our different purposes generate a plurality of communities, each regulated by laws and duties bounded by those ends. It is true that commonwealths may historically have arisen from kin groups, but the patriarch's *political* authority depends on the consent of adult descendants, who are, on attaining their majority, at liberty to secede. Similarly, while it is true that children owe gratitude and respect to their parents, in perpetuity, these are not *political* duties. Locke shows how Filmer's mistakes multiply. It is misguided to exalt fatherly power rather than to stress the duties of parents to nurture and educate their children. It is wrong to demean the role of wives and mothers. And it is false to ignore the difference between the dependence of pre-rational children and the autonomy of every adult child.

A Philosophy of Right

Locke offers a theory of justice, a philosophy of right. Though often curious about, and speculating upon, empirical facts about the exercise of power in human societies, he is fundamentally concerned with moral philosophy, and not political sociology. Often enough people are coerced, whether by naked force, or more usually by inducements, threats, or unyielding conventions. To live always thus is to be unfree, to be a slave, to suffer under tyranny. No great physical suffering need be entailed (a slave may be cosseted): the crime consists rather in being subjected to the arbitrary will of another, the loss of autonomy, of reasoned agency. Political justice is certainly about material comfort, because it is about human flourishing, but it is at root about preventing the violation of human personality, the evil of being banished from the realm of right. Locke constantly abjures 'force without right'. Often his language is of bestiality: to renounce right is to descend from humanity to the realm of beasts. The moral evaluation of empirical human circumstances is constantly at issue. In particular, submission is not the same as consent: both involve acceptance, but only the latter is valorized by free agency. I might submit to an armed robber—or a rapist—and do his bidding; but it is not consent. A whole society might submit to a dictator or a domineering foreign empire; but it is not consent.

None of this, however, is to say that legitimate rule can do without force. Quite the contrary. The state is necessarily an instrument of coercion. It exists to protect us, vigilantly, forcibly. The state is the collectivized embodiment of every individual's fund of physical force. Enforcement is the corollary of law, and the rule of law is empty without penalties. Indeed, for Locke, the majesty of the state is encapsulated in its right to take our life, whether in capital punishment, or in sending us to die in war. Locke's conception of justice is punitive. Those who exercise just power have the right to visit retribution on the unjust, on violators. Authority is right armed with power—or power infused with right. The philosophy of right, therefore, has the task of redeeming coercion.

To suppose that coercion can be redeemed may seem perverse, though Locke is not guilty of the naivety of supposing that coercion can be dispensed with. We constantly inhabit two realms, the brute facts of power relations, and the domain of rectitude, striving to unite them whenever we use the word 'ought'. In a strict sense, Locke is idealist: he holds that in thought and moral volition we strive to bend the realm of *is* to that of *ought*. But he is no utopian. He stands at a distance from Plato's *Republic* or More's *Utopia*. While social peace and freedom from injustice are viable aspirations, we can expect no idyll of harmony. Locke is keenly aware that societies are arenas of competing visions of the good, and that the goods that we are capable of agreeing upon, and embodying in our communities, are limited. A society of strenuous and sincere strivers towards a consensual vision of the good is the height of his ambition. He is also emphatic that commonwealths comprise a plurality of associations, among which the *political* association is but one, albeit supreme. As we would now express it, 'civil society' is not the same as the state. He is no less aware that individuals and groups compete for advantage amidst limited material resources: justice is largely about managing scarcity, and there would be no need of it in a land of cornucopias.

Another sense in which Locke's is a philosophy of right is that his method is juridical. He construes the relations between human agents, one among another, and with the state, in terms of law. Individuals are bearers of rights and obligations; human associations and states are the makers of binding rules that protect rights, enforce duties, and police the commensality pertinent to each association. Furthermore, public procedures are macrocosms of the law-like conduct involved in the self-rule of every individual person. Virtuous agency in individuals, as ancient moralists had taught, comprises rational deliberation, which is given substance through action by well-motivated volition. The morally competent person succeeds in having a *will* to do what *ought* to be done. In this sense, each of us should embody right reason in our outward actions: activity in the world should be the executive arm of right. The continuum between good conduct in individuals and in rulers is visible, Locke holds, if we consider that everyone exercises office, whether a widow governing a household, a constable a village, or a 'supreme magistrate' the commonwealth. 'Office' pertains to any of our duties, however modest, and office is a trust, it is 'fiduciary', exercised on behalf of communities, small and large. When we fail in our trust, we betray it, and morally desert it. Though Locke has much to say about political institutions, it is not procedural mechanics that are of the essence, but the moral quality of the conduct of office. "True politicks I looke on as a Part of Moral Philosophie.'[3]

Locke's approach is juridical in that he follows the broad character of medieval 'scholastic' political and moral philosophy, which fused Aristotle's analysis of the purposes and affinities which bind human associations with a Roman Law analysis of the formal legislative character of those associations, of which the state and its legislative and adjudicative power is the supreme instance. Affinities bind us emotionally, but justice formalizes the ties that bind. Justice implies courts: we stand before the court of conscience, before the king's courts, and before the court of God's judgement.

[3] Locke to Carey Mordaunt, Countess of Peterborough, *c.*1697: in Locke, *Selected Correspondence*, ed. Mark Goldie (Oxford, 2002), 253.

Locke does recognize that inclination brings people together in societies, but the *Treatise* offers a thin account of sociability. In part this is because the state is not the primary locus of sociability. Locke is far from supposing that the state, politics, engulfs all moral and affective agency. There are many spheres of activity and obligation, of need and rapport, which are not the state's immediate concern. Relations like love and friendship, and virtues like gratitude and charity, are not civil relations. In Locke, religious affiliation, bargaining in the marketplace, disputing philosophy, assisting the needy, and nurturing children are not political. They subsist outwith the political sphere, and the public sphere by no means engulfs the private. Of course there is a complex web of overlap, and resort to public adjudication often arises, but there are essential distinctions to be made. Consider, for example, the distinction between debt and gift. My obligation to repay a debt is enforceable in a public court of law; but my charitable giving cannot be enforced. (Locke was rigorous in extracting rent from his tenants, but generous in distributing gifts to them when needy and deserving.)

The Law of Nature

The *Second Treatise* is secular in a precise sense. Locke refuses to turn to Adam for guidance on politics. The Bible teaches the path to salvation, but not the pattern of temporal government. The groundwork of politics lies elsewhere, in reason and nature. There was nothing modern about this claim. It is an ancient theology which holds that God speaks through his Works as well as his Words. Reason is God's natural revelation. Political philosophy, Locke holds, belongs to theology, but not via Scripture. Just as public right mirrors the virtuous conduct of the self, so also it is a microcosm of God's conduct towards humanity. The deity (and only the deity) achieves the perfect union of right reason (an understanding of what ought to be done) and will (the promulgating of binding commands). To speak of divine, transcendent imperatives, law-like axioms of right, is to speak of a law of nature. Human legislation ought always to conform to this higher law of nature. Our personal self-legislation, and even God's self-acting, are governed by natural law.

Philosophers disagreed about what constituted the law-like quality of nature. Nature might be construed as providing rationally deducible norms, rules by which we can best flourish as natural organisms. But we might demur at the thought that such axioms amount, strictly speaking, to law, for law surely must be the command of somebody authorized to give rules, and punish their breach, which, in the case of nature, prior to the state, can only mean God. Thus perhaps law resolves into command rather than into nature or reason. Place too much emphasis on rationally discernible axioms, and God and his commands become ciphers. On the other hand, place too much emphasis on imperative command, and rules begin to look devoid of rational content beyond the legislator's arbitrary will. The perfect harmony of reason and will begins to look philosophically precarious. In his early *Essays on the Law of Nature* (1663–4) Locke grappled with this profound dilemma. In his *Essay Concerning Human Understanding* he seems to doubt our capacity to arrive at knowledge of natural law. But in the *Second Treatise* he blithely pronounces that the law of nature is 'writ in the Hearts of all Mankind', as if innately discernible (§ 11).[4] There is no satisfactory resolution of this ambiguity. Suffice to say, in the *Treatise* the law of nature stands as a sturdy roadblock in the way of unlimited human, and especially state, action. Whatever the 'supremacy' of human legislatures and rulers, it is an *earthly* supremacy, always limited by eternal laws. Human rulers are answerable before a higher court. None of Locke's contemporaries would have disagreed with him on this, but he adds that a ruler's actions are also justiciable here on earth, answerable to human communities: for many, that was a shocking conclusion.

In the modern world, we have taken hold of a secular version of Locke's train of thought. We speak of human rights as generating a system of law-like obligations that transcend the laws of particular states. By the twenty-first century it became possible to bring to court even heads of state, notwithstanding that they are, or have been, sovereign within their own territories. We have built a system of transcendent natural law, bereft of theology, but still armed with an Aristotelian sense that what is natural and right is what is universally conducive to human flourishing, and we have armed it with quasi-judicial procedures in the court of humanity.

For Locke, because we are bound by natural law, our natural liberty

---

[4] Compare the famous second sentence of the American Declaration of Independence: 'we hold these truths to be self-evident, that all men are created equal, that they are endowed by their creator with certain unalienable rights . . .'

is not licence, a freedom to do whatever we wish. The point of a free state is not to liberate us to follow our whims and desires, but to provide us with a secure arena within which to strive to perfect ourselves within the mould of God's making. Because we are God's creatures, there are strict limits on our freedom. In particular, nobody is free to take their own life, because that violates God's creation of us. We are God's property, and property should not be violated. Locke's 'suicide taboo' shows the distance between his Christian natural jurisprudence and modern secular libertarian values.

Origins of Civil Society

The sense of 'origin' is ambiguous. It can mean priority in time, or priority in concept. For Locke it is both. Conceptually deconstructed, civil societies comprise individuals who may be understood to join together to meet their natural needs and interests. Imagined outside their social and institutional settings, in a 'state of nature', these individuals are said to be free and equal, and in need of having security for their lives, liberties, and properties. These are the things that pertain to their personhood, both their subsistence as physical beings and their dignity as moral beings. In the state of nature individuals judge that they are better off under a common umpire of their disputes, for they find their natural state of independency unstable and liable to tip into a state of war, which is a condition in which right cannot prevail against the anarchy of rival arbitrary wills and unjust violence. Such individuals therefore sanction an agreement by which they are bound together and prescribe a regime for making rules. They are not obliged unless they so sanction by their free consent. Locke is accordingly commonly called a 'social contract' theorist, although he tends rather to use the word 'compact'. The agreement may be construed as a contract because it involves reciprocal, enforceable obligations. Such a system is nugatory without the means of enforcement, and the compact entails transference to the society of the right to use force which each person naturally has in the state of nature. In nature we have what Locke called the 'Executive Power of the Law of Nature' (§ 13), which is a right not only of self-defence but also to punish invasions of others' rights. The relationship of contract exists only among individuals: there is no contract with the ruler, who is merely a designated executive, entrusted with common power.

Objectors to this model standardly complained that it is grounded in a delusion, for nobody is born in a state of nature, free or equal. It is, they said, empirically false, because failing to recognize the necessarily social and organic character of the human self, and it is blasphemous too, for the Book of Genesis gives a quite different account of the origins of human society and authority. But since the Lockean model involves conceptual origins, and does not deny sociable affinities, the empirical objection may be said to miss the point. Yes, states may have arisen from kin groups, or from conquest. But any type of empirical origin of social power can be made good, if its service of the public good is recognized by individuals as worthy of their consensual allegiance. Furthermore, by being conceptually prior, the state of nature, and its lurking potential to become a state of war, is always immanent, here and now, constantly present beneath the carapace of the social order, erupting whenever public trust is violated—or whenever somebody attacks me in an alleyway.

Precisely because social facts are so diverse, Locke does also envisage empirical circumstances in which commonwealths are formed *de novo*. Anciently, and in the present day, communities leave their old allegiances, migrate, and establish new commonwealths. Thus, the fifth-century Venetians did so in their Adriatic lagoon, and Europeans do so in settling new societies in America. Locke's world was one which assumed there were empty lands available to migrants. Today we preserve a version of his thought, when we hold that one criterion of a free society is that it allows its citizens to emigrate. Locke further held that contemporary anthropological writings reported forms of community among native peoples, notably in America, which scarcely had states at all. Chieftains are chosen in time of war, to galvanize against external threat, but otherwise their societies are sufficiently simple as not to generate the kinds of rivalries which, in more complex economic and social conditions, make law-governed states imperative. The state, with its web of legislation and adjudication, is largely the child of developed property relations.

Property

Locke's fifth chapter, 'Of Property', has been more intensively construed than any other. His emphatic view is that states exist to protect property. The right of property is prior to government: it is that which, naturally arising but being vulnerable, stands in need of protection. Locke follows his contemporaries in holding that God gave the earth to humankind in common, but that God's purpose, the rendering of his natural gifts fruitful, is rightly fulfilled by dividing nature into individuated parcels. Nature is no use to us without a means of appropriation and exploitation. Thus original common property becomes legitimately privatized, but only if the guiding criterion of 'improvement' is fulfilled. Most seventeenth-century theorists asserted that privatization arose from a combination of occupation and mutual tacit consent. By contrast, Locke places tremendous emphasis on labour, the workmanship that makes nature fructify. Property is that which a person 'hath mixed his *Labour* with' (§ 27). Through labour we make a portion of the material world ours. It supplies subsistence, and, if we are industrious and skilful, produces wealth and civilization too. The invention of money, he contends, and hence the possibility of trade, whereby I can exchange my surpluses for yours, allows a leap from subsistence to growth economies. Under the market regime possessions become disproportionate and some people become rich: entrepreneurship creates expanding economies with unparalleled power to enrich, though at the cost of greater inequality. Locke holds that it is rational to accept this inequality, because *everyone* is richer in post-primitive societies. His remark that even an English labourer 'feeds, lodges, and is clad' better than an Indian chief points towards the modern capitalist's 'trickle-down' argument (§ 41). In simple economies there are limits to growth, and to inequality, and thus to envy and contention, which is why they have limited need of governance. In complex commercial societies the protective, regulatory, and adjudicative roles of government become pressing.

Locke's is, of course, a theory that justifies *private* property. It rules out both communistic and absolutist theories which license collective ownership or taxation by royal edict. To be free is to have a right to dispose of our property as we choose, through consumption, sale, or gift. Governments, in protecting these rights, have consequential duties, such as to extract only a portion of our property for communal purposes, and with our collective consent. The American Revolutionaries would turn this into a slogan: 'No taxation without representation.'

However, property right is always bounded by the higher requirements of natural law. No property claim can obliterate the right of every human person to subsistence, the means of self-preservation (hence Locke speaks of us as having a property in our person and our labour, as well as in things). Nor can it license a feckless failure of industriousness that betrays the purpose of individuated property, which is the creation of wealth for the common good. Thus private property right is not absolute but provisional; it, too, is a trust, or stewardship. On this ground, governments are entitled to intervene to regulate property arrangements, to ensure that the prior conditions are met. Although communism is ruled out, communalism is not: the community has a right of use and access, a 'usufructory' right, whereby its members can fulfil the imperatives of subsistence and improvement. Locke asserts, concerning the well-off, that a 'needy Brother [has] a Right to the Surplusage of his Goods'.[5] Villages may maintain their 'commons', for shared benefit. There may even be 'squatters' rights', where needy and industrious tillers may make use of undeveloped landed estates (§ 36). At the same time, Locke holds that it is an economic truth that enclosed land, when properly husbanded, is vastly more productive than unenclosed, and that everyone will benefit, in the long run, from an advanced agrarian economy. To enclose, and cultivate, the commons is to add, and not to detract, from the common stock; it is to be a benefactor of mankind.

In highly populated European countries most of the land had been enclosed. In underpopulated regions, notably North America, there is, Locke believed, a vast surplus of land that is unimproved waste. Famously, he remarked that: 'In the Beginning all the World was *America*' (§ 49). Native Americans are mostly transhumant hunter-gatherers. They have property in what they catch, but not in untilled land. (Consider a parallel: I have property in the fish I catch, but the oceans remain a great common.) Hence it is no injustice for European settlers to appropriate unimproved 'waste' land and cultivate it. This is Locke's 'agriculturist argument', and it would sustain later European justifications for empire by settlement.

Constitutions

It is not Locke's ambition to specify in detail desirable constitutional arrangements, but their rudiments do pertain to the 'extent

---

[5] See note to § 25.

and end' of civil government. The essence of the state is supreme legislative power, the making of binding and enforceable rules which achieve our purposes in joining civil society, the protection of our lives, liberties, and estates. Laws must be made by majority rule. Becoming a member of the society requires unanimity, for we are not members unless each individual consents, but the law-making procedure which we sanction must be majoritarian, because that is the only practicable mechanism. In a sense, every law is unanimous, because we all approve the (majoritarian) rule-making mechanism. But caveats apply. Since liberty is not licence, legislatures are not unlimited. There is here no *carte blanche* for democratic supremacy, for the tyranny of the majority. (Our modern elision, 'liberal democracy', obscures a deep tension.) Accordingly, we are warned that even elected legislatures are prone to act in breach of their trust, just as an absolute monarchy, or *any* political institution, might. Next, the legislature need not (should not) be a mirror-image of the people. The franchise should be weighted toward property, although Locke is anxious that new forms of property be enfranchised, in an increasingly commercial society. He is no universal-suffrage democrat. Furthermore, he accepts the form of the traditional English legislature, which comprises monarch, lords, and commons. He is no republican. It is unclear how this notion comports with the majoritarian principle, unless one assumes that the commons must be paramount and that the monarchic and aristocratic elements provide wisdom rather than decision, so that decision-making is *reasonable* volition. While civil societies are entitled to choose any form of government that suits them, Locke favours, as a good Whig, the English (and European) 'Gothic' constitution, grounded in the ideal of a 'mixed polity' inherited from classical sources: namely, that the best polity is a mixture of monarchy, aristocracy, and democracy. This does not entail an idea of shared or distributed sovereignty: legislative supremacy remains a singularity, but it lies with a hybrid parliamentary body.

For Locke, a prerequisite of a free society is a separation of powers. He identifies three such powers: legislative, executive, and 'federative'. The more familiar distinction is legislative, executive, and judicial, but Locke regards judicial as a form of executive power, tasked with administering and enforcing the law. Federative power concerns foreign policy and war-making, which we would now regard as part of executive power. Locke's 'separation' is readily misunderstood. He draws a conceptual distinction, not necessarily requiring strict placement of powers in distinct hands. He does not demur at the English system in which the crown is both chief executive and a member of the legislature. But a degree of separation is necessary, so that, for example, the crown must not be in a position to manipulate elections or bribe or bully members of parliament, or suborn the judiciary. (His attack on such practices is the closest he gets to direct commentary on the Stuart despotism of the 1680s: §§ 20, 210, 222.) Above all, it must be understood that the executive is subordinate to the supreme legislative power. Monarchs are merely chief executives or civil servants. And the determination of who shall be the monarch lies with the legislature. Thus monarchy, while a legitimate form of regime, is fundamentally elective, even if habitually hereditary, and the hereditary line may be altered. That was a core claim for the Whig movement, and it was sufficient to ensure that Whigs were denounced as 'republicans' by their Tory enemies.

Although an enemy of arbitrary government, Locke is remarkably sanguine about executive power. So long as it is bounded and limited by law, the 'supreme magistrate' ought to have a broad ambit of discretionary prerogative power. Once we are free of the dangerous mistake of absolutists that prerogatives inhere naturally, and without accountability, in monarchs, we can see the practical benefits of executive freedom of action, especially when lodged in a wise and trusted prince. The defence of the realm pre-eminently requires quick action. Moreover, law-making is, Locke imagined, a part-time occupation, and there is no need of permanent parliaments. Most everyday government consists in executive action, whether the county magistrate managing the Poor Laws or the crown building a navy. Locke is remarkably uninterested in programmes for the devolution and distribution of central power. On the contrary, he wishes to promote 'the great Art of Government', which requires sophisticated governmental activism to enhance commercial growth and national resilience. After the Revolution England became a fiscal-military state, wielding global power, with a powerful navy to protect trade, strong public credit, and high taxes underwritten by parliament. Locke was one of its senior managers, engaging in that 'art of government' as a member of King William's Board of Trade and Plantations.[6]

---

[6] See the passage on this theme which Locke added to § 42 in 1698 or later.

Tyranny and Revolution

The revolutionary Locke had turned apparatchik of the post-Revolution state. But that is to glance ahead, and to forget that the *Second Treatise* was written before the Revolution. The culmination of his book is a justification of a right of resistance against tyranny. The people retain an unalienable reserve power of self-defence. Resistance is not against a monarch as such: the office is unassailable. But a monarch who has become systemically despotic ceases to be a monarch, he 'unkings' himself, and becomes a private individual, acting like a common marauder. The tyrant divests himself of the moral character of his office and abdicates it. The carapace of government falls away; the people have returned to a condition in which they assume the power they had in the state of nature to protect themselves against an attacker. Resistance is thus not rebellion, for it is the tyrant who has rebelled, against law and public good. Tyrannical rebellion unhinges the order of right, whereas resistance is the executive instrument of a violated people which restores the rule of right.

Construed another way, despotism is the transmutation of the free citizen's relationship to rulers into the categorically different relation of a slave to a master. The master–slave relation is by definition a despotic one. The slave has no property in his goods or person, no liberty to direct his own agency. He is a tool at the disposal of his master. The thought that a slave might live comfortably, but never freely, provided an important argument against absolutists, who insisted that European, and especially English, monarchy, although absolute, is also limited and benign. England, they held, is replete with popular liberties, representative institutions, and the rule of law, so that the equation of absolutism with despotism was a Whig caricature. To square this circle, absolutists relied on the idea of *concessio* (concession): liberties were the historic grants or franchises of generous princes. And this was the rub, according to their critics. However practically and contingently free I may be, and comfortable under benevolent despots, such liberty cannot have the moral, juridical, or psychological character of true liberty if it exists at the mere will of the ruler. Freedom must be grounded in transcendent right, not in grace and favour.

In Locke's time, the aberrant ruler was characteristically a monarch. Kings and queens are susceptible to unbridled ambition, and to the flattery of corrupt courtiers and perverse ideologues. Yet, as we have seen, Locke insists that parliaments, and republics, can be tyrannical too. He may be thinking of the Cavalier Parliament (1661–79), which imposed coercive religious legislation and succumbed to royal blandishments; or the parliaments of 1649–60, which imposed an unwanted republic and military rule. The kernel of his thesis about tyranny is classical: with the Greeks and Romans, he insisted that tyranny is not a type of regime, but a pathological distortion of any regime, defined by pursuit of sectional interest over the *salus populi*, the public good. The common weal becomes a private fiefdom.

Locke's defence of resistance is no licence for anarchy. The people will put up with governmental mistakes and partial injustices, acting only against a sustained and manifest pattern of aggressive misrule. The healthy constitution supplies avenues for legal redress. It is the systematic preclusion of redress that marks tyranny. 'Where-ever Law ends, Tyranny begins' (§ 202).

Locke addresses an obvious objection. Who is to be judge of 'tyranny'? It was commonly said that to allow private judgement, or even the judgement of public 'lesser magistrates', against the supreme magistrate, is a recipe for civil war, and violates the principle that every state must have an unchallenged locus of final adjudication. Locke grants there can be no judge *within* the constitution: resistance occurs only when the constitution is dissolved. The right of revolution is a natural and not a civil right: it is a right of self-defence. The tyrant enters into a state of war with his people, and the people may save themselves. The right of natural judgement, in the court of conscience, is never rescinded. The contract that creates government is a revocable transfer of power, and when government dissolves, power devolves to its original constitutive body. The ultimate instance of a philosophy of right's redemption of coercion is its legitimation of the right of taking up arms against misrule. Terrorism is sometimes what states do, so that violence against such states is morally justified. Locke's account of tyranny and the right of resistance is fundamental to modern theories of revolution, from the American and French to the Irish, Russian, and Chinese.

The mechanics of the exercise of resistance do not detain Locke. Though armed struggle may prove necessary, he does not glorify it. Some regimes spontaneously crumble amid a universal collapse of their legitimacy; others through humanitarian intervention from outside. Jephtha intervened to rescue ancient Israel; William of Orange rescued England.[7] The outcome of a war of liberation is uncertain, which is why Locke calls it an appeal to heaven. An oppressed people may choose whichever they judge the safer option: submission, enduring enslavement and bare existence, for the time being; or resistance, if they judge there is a fair chance of success. The outcome is in the hands of providence, which shall determine whether we die or find liberation.

Toleration

Locke's *Letter Concerning Toleration* is an assault upon those who persecute in the name of religion. Religious persecution is a virulent species of tyranny. Christian history offered a dismal scene of religious violence, whether internal inquisitions or wars between confessional states. Religious coercion was not the child of unreflective bigotry, but of a considered belief in its legitimacy. In the fourth century, St Augustine had called upon the secular powers of the Roman Empire to serve true religion by suppressing heresy and schism. His interpretation of Christ's words in St Luke's Gospel, 'Compel them to come in', was read as an injunction on behalf of the unity of the church, and remained commonplace in seventeenth-century pulpits. The 'godly magistrate' should wield the temporal sword as a helpmeet to spiritual censures. The case for intolerance was both theological and prudential. There was a duty to bend people's minds to embrace divine and saving truth; and no society could survive the anarchy of religious sectarianism. Schism and sedition were thought to be twins, and tolerance looked like indifference to both eternal truth and temporal peace.

In 1685 King Louis XIV of France revoked the Edict of Nantes, which had given freedom to Protestants, the Huguenots. Vicious persecution ensued; thousands fled; and the word 'refugee' entered the language. Living among the diaspora in the Netherlands, Locke and Pierre Bayle—and in Germany, Samuel Pufendorf—penned treatises in shocked response. Yet Locke's native England was religiously coercive too. The Restoration era saw the final attempt to enforce membership of the Church of England. The Puritans who had flourished

---

[7] Besides Adam, Jephtha is the biblical figure who appears most often in the *Second Treatise*.

during the Civil Wars and under Oliver Cromwell—Presbyterians, Congregationalists, Baptists, and Quakers—were now victims, in danger of annihilation. The Revolution prevented their destruction. The publication of Locke's *Letter* coincided with the Act of Toleration, which legalized a plurality of Protestant denominations, although toleration of Catholics had to wait another century.

Locke's argument for tolerance has several strands. The first is evangelical, an answer to the question: what are the valid means of evangelizing? He writes as a Christian, enquiring about the proper ways to spread the Gospel. Christ enjoined the putting aside of the sword, and forswore a temporal kingdom. Teaching and persuading, by word and example, are the true means of conversion. The opening lines of the *Letter* assert that meekness and charity are a 'mark', a defining characteristic, of the true church. Yet Locke does not privatize religious life: Christians have a duty to evangelize.

The second is theological. The essence of Christianity is virtue and holy living, not punctiliousness about ceremony and liturgy, nor creedal dogmatism in speculative and abstruse matters where Scripture is silent. God requires that he be worshipped, but whether it is done kneeling or facing east is unimportant. Christ is God's presence in the world, but the precise nature of his unity with the Father in the Trinity is not illuminated by applying metaphysics to Scripture, still less by imposing dogma by force. While Locke is no sceptic, he does tend toward a minimalism, which holds that there is a wide ambit of indeterminacy about doctrine, liturgy, and ecclesiastical governance. Liturgies and hierarchies are largely the child of culture, tradition, and human convention, and hence are inessentials. To enforce such things is pharisaic formalism. Put another way, Locke belongs to the Protestant *sola scriptura* tradition: that which is not incontrovertibly prescribed by Scripture is not necessary to salvation. Finding religious truth is difficult, and power gives no special access to truth. An effortful society of sincere searchers after truth, even if, for now, it remains mired in disagreement, is more valuable than the happenstance and hollow husk of enforced or merely habitual conformity.

Third, Locke has a philosophical—an ontological—objection to coercion. Force cannot convince the mind of anything. We can enforce outward behaviour, but not inward conviction. Any scheme for 'coercion of belief' is therefore based on a simple error about the relationship between mind and body. Torture can produce compliant dissemblers, or non-compliant martyrs, but not true believers. Locke's claim here is, however, problematic, and it became central to his quarrel with the Oxford High Churchman Jonas Proast, pursued for several years through the *Second*, *Third*, and unfinished *Fourth Letter*. Proast countered, subtly, that coercion, though not directly able to persuade the mind, can be used indirectly, because people, locked within unreflective inherited ideas, can be brought to reconsider by being made to listen. The mind–body relationship is complex: physical trauma can jolt spiritual enlightenment and conversion. That was St Paul's experience on the road to Damascus.

Fourth, Locke turns to political philosophy. He draws a sharp distinction between church and state. This has been read as a manifesto for 'separation' of church and state, and disestablishment of official religions. But Locke is making a conceptual more than an institutional point. The *telos*, or purpose, of church and state are fundamentally different: one exists to bring us to eternal salvation, the other to protect our temporal well-being. Rational agents, in authorizing government and laws, would not authorize a right in the temporal ruler to enforce a particular path to heaven, for the official path might prove abhorrent to conscience and endanger salvation. Here the argument parallels the *Second Treatise*. The care of our soul is not written into the social compact. A church is one among many associations, like guilds, colleges, or clubs, which make up civil society. It is not the state's alter ego. We may wish that our rulers are godly, but, strictly speaking, there is no such thing as 'godly rule' or a 'Christian commonwealth'. With some exaggeration, we may say that Locke here broke with a millennium of 'godly rule'.

Based on these principles, for Locke the aperture of toleration is wide indeed, far beyond Protestantism. Pagans, Muslims, Jews, and 'heathen' natives in America are entitled to toleration. Conversely, the aperture of those guilty of intolerance is also wide: not only Catholics and Anglicans, but Calvinists in Massachusetts, Scotland, and Geneva, even Quakers in Pennsylvania. Arresting, then, are Locke's apparently abrupt exclusions from toleration: Catholics, atheists, and antinomians. Catholics are inadmissible not because their creeds are superstitious—thinking somebody absurd is never a ground for intolerance—but because they held doctrines incompatible with citizenship and morality, namely that popes can depose heretic princes and authorize breaches of trust with 'heretics'. Atheists, Locke held, had no motives for keeping promises and other basic ethical principles, having no fear of divine punishment. Antinomians are any sort of people who invoke the deity to trump the laws of reason and nature, fatally pitting God's Word against his Works. Antinomians assert either their own unique divine right to rule, or their special divine warrant to ignore earthly rules. Here the state may indeed 'interfere' in religion, for every state has a duty to protect its people from physical harm by those whose beliefs license mayhem.

Locke's *Letter* has subsidiary themes besides. It voices a vigorous anticlericalism. Religious coercion is typically an instrument for securing the worldly power of priests, and churches are often engines of clerical domination. The clergy tend to preach up the divine right of kings, expecting, as a *quid pro quo*, that kings will empower the church. Thus the court and the pulpit form an oppressive alliance. The clergy and its institutions claim to be *the* Church, whereas the Gospel tells us it is the community of all believers. Some of Locke's by-arguments are pragmatic, or *politique*. He offers an argument from reciprocity. Truth, he archly remarks, is different on each side of the Alps, since 'every Prince is Orthodox to himself' (p. 148): hence it cannot be prudent to license the state to enforce 'truth', because the same argument will serve any regime that believes *it* has the truth. An argument used in Protestant London can be used in Catholic Paris or Islamic Constantinople. Finally, Locke suggests that intolerance is economically disastrous, since religious minorities are often socio-economically distinct communities. This is not as utilitarian as it seems, for those who industriously improve God's natural gifts live a life that is more godly than those who police ceremonial or censor theology.

Universalism

Political philosophers sometimes seek Olympian detachment, deliberately abstracting their arguments from circumstances. This can simply be a rhetorical idiom, but it can also derive from philosophical premises. This is so where the aim is to discover what is true of humanity *per se*, the irreducible needs, duties, and rights of any person, at any time. Locke is a universalist. He grounds polities in the rational choices of apparently universal persons. His rights-bearing individuals are not defined or limited by ethnicity, religion, language, culture, or history. The liberal holds that local cultural norms and particular identities cannot trump claims that are unconditionally human. It is tempting to see here the spirit of the Enlightenment, but it is rooted in ancient natural jurisprudence: the Stoics and the medieval Scholastics appealed to human nature, to a putatively timeless and placeless humanity that lies behind the artifices of culture and history. Modern liberal political philosophy has, for persuasive and unpersuasive reasons, detached Locke from ancient jurisprudence, and from theology, and finds valuable his universalizing principles concerning what should constitute justice in any human community, and has entrenched 'human rights' in the political vernacular.

There is a line of descent from Locke (via Rousseau and Kant) to such modern classics as John Rawls's *Theory of Justice* (1971) and Robert Nozick's *Anarchy, State, and Utopia* (1974). The former offers a yet more abstracted thesis about what people need simply as humans and what rights their needs generate. Humans are conceived as standing behind a 'veil of ignorance', not knowing any aspect of their contingent human identity, and they are asked what they would rationally choose by way of just laws. Would I consent to a law by which men are paid and promoted more than women, if I knew only that I was human and not whether I was female or male? Rawls concludes that, behind the veil, no such person would consent to such a law, so that such a law is unjust. Nozick's derivation is very different, wherein universal humans have such a minimum of collective aspirations, affiliations, and values that they have no wish for a state to do anything other than provide law-and-order umpirage. It is therefore wrong to tax us to support any human collective endeavour other than to pay judges, policemen, and soldiers.

Locke's universalist ambition is vulnerable to the charge that it is naive, deceptive, perhaps even manipulative, in obscuring, brushing aside, our profound particularities, whether of culture, ethnicity, religion, gender, or class. In his own time and terms, there were three patent vulnerabilities. First, the logic of universalizability, as Kant would see, points to a world state. If the relations between individuals in nature are insecure, and require agreed and competent adjudication, so do relations between states. But Locke took for granted mutually competitive states, which remain in a state of nature one with another, and hence potentially or actually in a state of war. His concept of compact-formation, to establish an umpire among us, is not activated at the international level. On the contrary, a primary function of a state is martial. Next, while Locke's formulation is secular, in the sense that our religious interests are not within the remit of temporal rule, his Protestant preconceptions are only thinly disguised. Catholics, he holds, cannot be proper citizens; and a ruler who favours a religion not of the people is a presumptive instance of a tyrant.[8] Third, it is unclear how many human beings constitute persons. Locke speaks not of 'free men' but 'freemen', a category, in Roman Law, which is set off against 'slave'. Locke holds that slavery may be legitimate. It can arise from a just war, where the vanquished forfeit their lives but where the victors may reprieve them as slaves. Or it may arise in temporary form from a contract of service as indentured labour. Locke does not hold a theory of slavery based on natural (racial) difference, or from the biblical curse of Ham, but he does presume a juridical status of slave. Similarly, the language of 'freemen' is gendered, and it is unclear whether 'man' stands for 'person'. A source of difficulty here, in the world of early modern Europeans, is the immense weight of the household-family, and the notion that wives, children, servants, and, in some places, slaves were 'included in their masters'. Locke's society was a federation of heads of households, and, for all that he critiques patriarchalism, he concedes much to the household-family.[9]

Reputation Today

The conundrums of Enlightenment universalism ensure that, today, Locke's reputation is badly bifurcated. He is both applauded and denounced with inordinate enthusiasm—inordinate because he tends to become simply an icon or emblem for impassioned causes. Ironically, more attention is paid to him in the United States, where he is an honorary Founding Father, than in his native England. On the political Right he is commonly lionized as a celebrant of private property and free markets, and correspondingly as a libertarian enemy of interference and of the 'demoralizing' welfare state, a theorist of minimal government, of the umpire state, in which the state

---

[8] For today's debate about whether Locke would think there are religious groups ineligible for citizenship, see Explanatory Notes at p. 189, 'Mahumetan' and 'Oracles'.

[9] See Explanatory Note to § 85, 'Family of his Master', p. 174.

has no substantive role beyond dispute resolution and defence. The gun lobby takes to heart his irrevocable right of self-defence.

This reading of Locke is depressingly fixated upon a vision of the state as inimical to liberty and property. It seems oblivious to the extent to which Locke's insistence on the state's purpose as guarantor of the right ordering of property is expansive and inclusive. If property is the expression of human personality, as much as, and wrapped up in its role as, our means of subsistence and flourishing, then every person has an irreducible entitlement, which the polity must underwrite. Locke argued that if 'every Man [has] a Title to the product of his honest Industry', so equally, 'every Man [has] a Title to [the] means to subsist'; and nobody can 'justly make use of another's necessity, to force him to become his Vassal' (*First Treatise*, § 42).

If Locke remains a hero for defenders of liberal constitutionalism and the free market, in the past few decades a quite different and negative set of evaluations of him has arisen. Critics pursue the thought that his putative universalism is a deceptive mask for a particularist leaning in favour of one or other section of humanity. In these accounts, his notion of free and equal rights-bearing individuals masks an ethnic, class, or gender bias. In particular, the fact that liberalism, imperialism, and slavery historically developed together, that Locke was involved in American colonial enterprise, that he defends the priority of European agrarian cultivation, are grounds for indictment of him as an ideologist of the expropriation or enslavement of native peoples. This postcolonial critique has been the loudest. Post-liberal feminists, meanwhile, hold that Locke confines women to the private sphere, and that the Lockean state is limited to consenting men in public. These attacks, which followed in the wake of the Marxian unmasking of Locke as a theorist of 'possessive individualism', who served 'bourgeois capitalism', commonly take the form of elevating Locke into a surrogate of 'the Enlightenment project', doubtful though such a construct is. These are views which hold that liberalism and Enlightenment produced oppression rather than liberation. Ironically, such critiques echo a theory of tyranny which Locke himself inherited from Plato and Aristotle: tyranny is the perversion of 'the public' to private, sectional advantage. Hence liberalism is seen as a kind of tyranny, because an ostensive public good masks, and ideologically serves, the private advantage of a single class, race, or gender.

An intriguing new development has occurred among theologians, who argue that liberalism's putatively even-handed tolerance of religious plurality, and separation of church and state, is in practice a dogmatic secularist exclusion of faith from the public realm. For the liberal, the universalized human person must not exhibit any particular faith when adopting the persona of citizen: hence, for example, a crucifix or headscarf may not enter public space or adorn a public person.

All these critics enthusiastically offer toxicology, accounts of how 'Enlightenment rationalism' produced poisonous effluents. But, if they are to offer remedies too, they find themselves in a bind. Either they reject universalism, in which case there is little more on offer than mutually exclusive and antagonistic visions of how humans should live together. Or they must embrace at least a modest universalism: principles of justice and equity recognizable among all those who, here and now, are thrown into social and civil contact with each other.

NOTE ON THE TEXT

THIS edition offers the texts in original dress. In the case of texts written in the late seventeenth century, doing so offers few obstacles to modern readers. While we today read Locke's works as transhistorical classics, valuable for our own reflection, it is worthwhile also appreciating that he wrote and published in a different era and in a distinctive style.

Second Treatise of Government

Locke continued to correct and augment the *Two Treatises* between the time of the first edition in 1689[1] and his death in 1704, and his amendments appear in the second edition of 1694, the third of 1698, and the belated fourth edition of 1713. The last was faithfully reproduced in the following year in the first edition of *The Works of John Locke*. In the preface to the *Works*, Locke's publisher announced: 'As to this Edition of all his Works together, I have this to advertise the Reader, that most of them are printed from Copies corrected and enlarg'd under Mr. LOCKE's own Hand; and in particular, that the *Two Treatises of Government* were never till now, publish'd from a Copy corrected by himself.' This is a striking claim to textual authority, and it follows some preceding humility, for earlier in the same page he quotes from Locke's will, in which Locke, listing his anonymous works to which he now admitted authorship, and referring to the *Two Treatises*, complained that 'Mr. *Churchill* has publish'd several Editions, but all very incorrect'. Taking the two remarks together, it is evident that Churchill now avowedly undertook that he had at last accurately printed the text as Locke wished it.[2]

Locke must have left behind a master-copy which contained his final textual intentions, presumably a printed copy marked up with amendments. This document has not survived, but there are three pieces of independent evidence for its having existed. First, Pierre

---

[1] It carries the date 1690 but was published in November 1689.

[2] In fact there were two Churchills, brothers Awnsham and John, long in business together. The 1713 *Two Treatises*, the first to have Locke's name on the title-page, and the *Works* were issued under John's name.

Coste, Locke's French translator, who lived with him at Oates in Essex, wrote in the rear endpaper of a copy of the *Two Treatises*, concerning an amendment: 'This is how Mr. L. corrected this passage in the exemplar [from] which he wishes his book to be reprinted after his death.' Second, Charles de la Motte, an Amsterdam literary agent, in his memoir of Coste, referred to a package which Locke, at his death, left for Coste, which 'contained the Book on Civil Government, with various Additions and Corrections, which Mr Coste then handed over to Churchil for reprinting'. And third, Jean Barbeyrac, a Huguenot jurist, writing from Berlin in 1709, enquired after the most up-to-date edition, which 'incorporated the corrections which were in the exemplar left to Mr Coste', though such an edition had not yet appeared.[3]

In light of this evidence, I have chosen to base the present edition on the version in the *Works* of 1714. Nonetheless, the decision to do so is today unusual. In 1960 the Cambridge historian Peter Laslett transformed Locke scholarship with his edition of the *Two Treatises*.[4] He showed that previous editors had been slack in failing to recognize the variations which Locke had introduced in the several early editions. More importantly, he judged that Locke's final (surviving) textual intentions were embodied in the handwritten marginalia in a copy of the third edition of 1698 which had come to light in the library of Christ's College, Cambridge, the copy in which Coste penned the remark quoted above. This was a major discovery, and today the marginalia can be viewed online.[5]

There are, however, some difficulties with Laslett's claim for the pre-eminence of the Christ's Copy. First, it is doubtful that Locke's hand in penning the marginalia, as opposed to Coste's, extends beyond the first few paragraphs of the *First Treatise*. Second, it is probable that a main purpose of the Christ's Copy was to prepare the ground for a better translation of the *Treatises* into French. The

---

[3] Copy in Christ's College, Cambridge, of the *Two Treatises* (3rd edn., 1698), shelf-mark Bb. 3. 7a; Charles de la Motte, 'Vie de Coste', in Locke, *Que la religion chrétienne est très-raisonnable, telle qu'elle nous est représentée dans l'Ecriture sainte, [et autres textes]* [an edition of Coste's translation of Locke's *Reasonableness of Christianity*], ed. Hélène Bouchilloux and Maria-Cristina Pitassi (Oxford, 1999), 243; Barbeyrac is reported in De la Motte to Pierre Desmaizeaux, 5 Nov. 1709: British Library, Add. MS 4286, fo. 91. The quotations, all originally in French, are translated by Delphine Soulard.

[4] John Locke, *Two Treatises of Government*, ed. Peter Laslett (Cambridge, 1960). This is the version used in the current series Cambridge Texts in the History of Political Thought.

[5] <http://issuu.com/christsbooks/docs/bb37alocke?e=3803189/2905437>.

translation of Locke's books into French was one of Coste's roles at
Oates (he also acted as a tutor), and we know both that Locke was dis-
satisfied with the 1691 translation, *Du Gouvernement civil*, and that,
as de la Motte tells us, he asked Coste to make a new translation—
de la Motte's testimony was unknown to Laslett.[6] Third, there are
sometimes tangles in the marginalia, and Laslett himself had occasionally to turn to the 1713/14 editions to clarify the text.[7] Fourth,
Laslett conceded that there must have been a separate master-copy,
for the Christ's Copy is not it; and even that 'there is a possible case
for supposing that the 4th edition [of 1713] was indeed a printing of
the other "exemplaire" referred to by Coste, . . . and that a critical edition should be based on this text . . . and not on the Christ's Copy'.[8]
Fifth, there is evidence that, in the case of another of Locke's works,
The Reasonableness of Christianity, the *Works* of 1714 follows a master-
copy prepared by Locke.[9] Finally, it is worth noting that the textual
scholar Peter Nidditch, who prepared the authoritative edition of
Locke's *Essay Concerning Human Understanding*, which is abridged in
the Oxford World's Classics series, wrote privately to take issue with
Laslett's decision to use the Christ's Copy: 'it seems overwhelmingly
probable . . . that the 1713 edition is based on a more authoritative
amended copy.'[10] For all these reasons, I rest my choice of copy-
text on the veracity of Churchill's claim in 1714.

All this said, there are scarcely any material differences between
the Christ's Copy and the 1713/14 editions: they are much closer
to each other than to the first, second, and third editions, and it is
probable that they both derived from the lost master-copy. I point out
the most significant variations in the Explanatory Notes. The main
changes between the Christ's Copy and the 1713/14 editions were to

---

[6] For these points see Delphine Soulard, 'The Christ's Copy of John Locke's *Two
Treatises of Government*', *Historical Journal*, 58 (2015), 25–49; J. R. Milton, 'Pierre Coste,
John Locke, and the Third Earl of Shaftesbury', in Sarah Hutton and Paul Schuurman
(eds.), *Studies on Locke: Sources, Contemporaries, and Legacy* (Dordrecht, 2008), 195–223;
S.-J. Savonius, 'Locke in French: The *Du Gouvernement civil* of 1691 and its Readers',
Historical Journal, 47 (2004), 47–79.

[7] See Explanatory Note to § 50. In § 45 the 1713/14 versions place a bracket correctly,
where the Christ's Copy does not. Equally, occasionally the Christ's Copy offers a better
reading: see Explanatory Note to § 94.

[8] Locke, *Two Treatises*, ed. Laslett, 149. At p. 10 he called the 1713 edition 'definitive'.

[9] Locke, *The Reasonableness of Christianity*, ed. John C. Higgins-Biddle (Oxford,
1999), Introduction, pp. cxxv–cxxix; and 25 n., 82 n.

[10] Letter, 16 July 1975: Cambridge University Library, Add. MS 9995, Box 26.

punctuation, of which there were several hundred. While capitalization varied too, the italicization remained almost identical.

The title of Locke's book merits comment. The full title is: *Two Treatises of Government: in the Former, the False Principles and Foundation of Sir Robert Filmer, and his Followers, are Detected and Overthrown. The Latter is an Essay Concerning the True Original, Extent, and End of Civil-Government.* There is some confusion about what, in fact, to call the *Second Treatise*. The lifetime editions carry a separate title page, 'An Essay Concerning the True Original, Extent, and End of Civil-Government', but the text itself is headed simply 'Book II'. The 1714 edition has no separate title-page for the *Second Treatise*, and the text is misleadingly headed 'Of Civil-Government. Book II' (rather than the other way about), which, being repeated in later editions of the *Works*, has sponsored a habit of referring to Locke's 'Second Treatise of [*or* on] Civil Government', which is a misnomer. The usual title today is *Second Treatise of Government*, but there is good reason to call it either 'An Essay Concerning Civil Government' or 'A Treatise Concerning Civil Government'. To add to the confusion, nowhere in the *Second Treatise* does Locke refer to it as a 'treatise', 'book', or 'essay', but rather as a 'discourse'.

My text follows the spelling, punctuation, capitalization, and punctuation of the 1714 *Works* edition. I have occasionally inserted words in square brackets to clarify an obscure passage, and made silent emendations to a handful of printing errors. References to pounds sterling have been modernized (e.g. £5 rather than 5 *l.*); numerals in §§ 40 and 43 have been spelt out; and indicators for Locke's footnotes have been rendered as numbers.

A Letter Concerning Toleration

Locke wrote this tract in Latin in 1685, and it was first published at Gouda in the Netherlands in 1689 as *Epistola de Tolerantia*. Later in the same year an English translation appeared in London. Both versions were anonymous, and Locke did not formally admit his authorship until his death. The translator was William Popple, who made some amendments and improvements in a second edition in 1690, and this is the edition used here. It is the version by which Locke's tract has chiefly been known in the anglophone world ever since. Popple, a former wine merchant, pamphleteer on behalf of toleration, and later a civil servant, took some liberties with the Latin. The effect was to make Locke's case starker and livelier. He adjusts the Latin to clarify, to emphasize, and to make more intimate. Thus, for example, 'vices' becomes 'enormous vices'; 'to demonstrate' becomes 'abundantly to demonstrate'; 'superstition' becomes 'credulous superstition'; 'you' sometimes becomes 'we'. Popple provided more specific examples than had Locke, mainly to English but also to French circumstances. The translation shifts Locke's stiffer scholastic style into a more informal conversational format, which sometimes obscures the classical and biblical allusions. Popple was strongly anticlerical: where, for instance, Locke writes 'the religion established', the translation has 'the Religion, which either Ignorance, Ambition, or Superstition had chanced to establish'. In the Explanatory Notes I have recorded some of the more significant changes. My text follows the spelling, punctuation, capitalization, and italicization of the original. Scriptural citations which appeared in the margins have been inserted in brackets at the appropriate points in the text, given in modern form, and occasionally corrected.

There are two modern editions which offer new translations of the Latin.[11] These can offer a gain in literal accuracy, but are apt to lose something in literary and historical authenticity. Popple's prose is vivid and of the seventeenth century. It is unlikely that Locke was involved in the translation, for in his will he said it was done 'without my privity', meaning 'without my authorization'. However, when he came to defend his arguments against his adversary, the Oxford clergyman Jonas Proast, he was happy to base his defence on Popple's English text. He remarked that, while the *Epistola* might have been translated 'more literally . . . yet the Translator is not to be blamed, if he chose to express the Sense of the Author, in words that very lively represented' his meaning.[12]

---

[11] Ed. Raymond Klibansky and J. W. Gough (Oxford, 1968); ed. Richard Vernon and Michael Silverthorne (Cambridge, 2010). There is also a parallel Latin/Popple edition: ed. Mario Montuori (The Hague, 1963). I have constantly benefited from these editions.

[12] Locke, *A Second Letter Concerning Toleration* (1690), 10.

SELECT BIBLIOGRAPHY

The Clarendon Edition of the Works of John Locke

This project by Oxford University Press, which began publishing in 1975, will eventually amount to thirty-five volumes. Most volumes are available in paperback.

An Essay Concerning Human Understanding, ed. Peter H. Nidditch (1975).
The Correspondence of John Locke, 8 vols., ed. E. S. de Beer (1976–89).
A Paraphrase and Notes on the Epistles of St Paul, 2 vols., ed. Arthur W. Wainright (1987).
Some Thoughts Concerning Education, ed. John W. Yolton and Jean S. Yolton (1989).
Drafts for the Essay Concerning Human Understanding and Other Philosophical Writings, vol. 1, ed. Peter H. Nidditch and G. A. J. Rogers (1990).
Locke on Money, 2 vols., ed. Patrick Hyde Kelly (1991).
The Reasonableness of Christianity, ed. John C. Higgins-Biddle (1999).
An Essay Concerning Toleration and Other Writings on Law and Politics, 1667–1683, ed. J. R. Milton and Philip Milton (2006).
Vindications of the Reasonableness of Christianity, ed. Victor Nuovo (2011).

Other Editions of Works by Locke

Epistola de Tolerantia: A Letter on Toleration, ed. Raymond Klibansky and J. W. Gough (Oxford, 1968).
An Essay Concerning Human Understanding, abridged edn., ed. Pauline Phemister (Oxford: World's Classics, 2008).
A Letter Concerning Toleration and Other Writings, ed. Mark Goldie (Indianapolis, 2010).
Locke on Toleration, ed. Richard Vernon, trans. Michael Silverthorne (Cambridge, 2010).
Locke's Travels in France, 1675–1679, ed. John Lough (Cambridge, 1953).
Political Essays, ed. Mark Goldie (Cambridge, 1997).
Selected Correspondence, ed. Mark Goldie (Oxford, 2002).
Two Treatises of Government, ed. Peter Laslett (Cambridge, 1963).
Writings on Religion, ed. Victor Nuovo (Oxford, 2002).

Bibliography and Biographies

A comprehensive bibliography of publications by and about Locke (some 8,000 items) is available online, compiled by John C. Attig: <www.libraries.psu.edu/tas/locke/>.

Cranston, Maurice, *John Locke: A Biography* (Oxford, 1957; 1985).

Goldie, Mark, 'The Life of John Locke', in Sami-Juhani Savonius-Wroth, Paul Schuurman, and Jonathan Walmsley (eds.), *The Bloomsbury Companion to Locke* (London, 2014).

Collections of Essays

Anstey, Peter (ed.), *John Locke: Critical Assessments*, 4 vols. (London, 2006).

Ashcraft, Richard (ed.), *John Locke: Critical Assessments*, 4 vols. (London, 1991).

Chappell, Vere (ed.), *The Cambridge Companion to Locke* (Cambridge, 1994).

Dunn, John, and Harris, Ian (eds.), *Locke*, 2 vols. (Cheltenham, 1997).

Hirschmann, Nancy J., and McClure, Kirstie M. (eds.), *Feminist Interpretations of John Locke* (University Park, Pa., 2007).

Milton, J. R. (ed.), *Locke's Moral, Political, and Legal Philosophy* (Aldershot, 1999).

Yolton, John W. (ed.), *John Locke: Problems and Perspectives* (Cambridge, 1969).

Contexts for Locke's Politics

Armitage, David, *The Ideological Origins of the British Empire* (Cambridge, 2000).

Burns, J. H., and Goldie, Mark (eds.), *The Cambridge History of Political Thought, 1450–1700* (Cambridge, 1991).

Haakonssen, Knud, *Natural Law and Moral Philosophy from Grotius to the Scottish Enlightenment* (Cambridge, 1996).

Kenyon, J. P., *Revolution Principles: The Politics of Party, 1689–1720* (Cambridge, 1977).

Pateman, Carole, *The Sexual Contract* (Cambridge, 1988).

Phillipson, Nicholas, and Skinner, Quentin (eds.), *Political Discourse in Early Modern Britain* (Cambridge, 1993).

Pocock, J. G. A., *The Ancient Constitution and the Feudal Law* (Cambridge, 1957; 1987).

———— *The Machiavellian Moment: Florentine Political Thought and the Atlantic Republican Tradition* (Princeton, 1975).

———— *Virtue, Commerce and History* (Cambridge, 1985).

———— et al. (eds.), *The Varieties of British Political Thought, 1500–1800* (Cambridge, 1993).

Scott, Jonathan, *Algernon Sidney and the Restoration Crisis, 1677–1683* (Cambridge, 1991).

Skinner, Quentin, *The Foundations of Modern Political Thought*, 2 vols. (Cambridge, 1978).

—— *Liberty Before Liberalism* (Cambridge, 1988).

Tuck, Richard, *Natural Rights Theories* (Cambridge, 1979).

Waldron, Jeremy, *The Right to Private Property* (Oxford, 1988).

Contexts for Locke's Toleration

Coffey, John, *Persecution and Toleration in Protestant England, 1558–1689* (Harlow, 2000).

Grell, O. P., Israel, J. I., and Tyacke, N. (eds.), *From Persecution to Toleration: the Glorious Revolution and Religion in England* (Oxford, 1991).

Israel, Jonathan I., *Enlightenment Contested: Philosophy, Modernity, and the Emancipation of Man, 1670–1752* (Oxford, 2006).

Kaplan, Benjamin J., *Divided by Faith: Religious Conflict and the Practice of Toleration in Early Modern Europe* (Cambridge, 2007).

Murphy, Andrew R., *Conscience and Community: Revisiting Toleration and Religious Dissent in Early Modern England and America* (Philadelphia, 2001).

Walsham, Alexandra, *Charitable Hatred: Tolerance and Intolerance in England, 1500–1700* (Manchester, 2006).

Zagorin, Perez, *How the Idea of Religious Toleration Came to the West* (Princeton, 2003).

On Locke's Politics

Arneil, Barbara, *John Locke and America* (Oxford, 1996).

Ashcraft, Richard, *Revolutionary Politics and Locke's Two Treatises of Government* (Princeton, 1986).

Corbett, Ross J., *The Lockean Commonwealth* (Albany, NY, 2009).

Dunn, John, *The Political Thought of John Locke* (Cambridge, 1969).

—— *Locke* (Oxford, 1984).

Forster, Greg, *John Locke's Politics of Moral Consensus* (Cambridge, 2005).

Franklin, J. H., *John Locke and the Theory of Sovereignty* (Cambridge, 1978).

Harris, Ian, *The Mind of John Locke* (Cambridge, 1994).

Grant, Ruth, *John Locke's Liberalism* (Chicago, 1987).

Harrison, Ross, *Hobbes, Locke, and Confusion's Masterpiece* (Cambridge, 2003).

Josephson, Peter, *The Great Art of Government: Locke's Use of Consent* (Lawrence, Kan., 2002).

Kendall, Willmoore, *John Locke and the Doctrine of Majority Rule* (Urbana, Ill., 1941, 1959).

Kramer, Matthew H., *John Locke and the Origins of Private Property* (Cambridge, 1997).

McClure, Kirstie, *Judging Rights: Lockean Politics and the Limits of Consent* (Ithaca, NY, 1996).

Macpherson, C. B., *The Political Theory of Possessive Individualism* (Oxford, 1962).

Marshall, John, *John Locke: Resistance, Religion, and Responsibility* (Cambridge, 1994).

Parker, Kim Ian, *The Biblical Politics of John Locke* (Waterloo, Ont., 2004).

Parry, Geraint, *John Locke* (London, 1978).

Schouls, Peter, *Reasoned Freedom: John Locke and Enlightenment* (Ithaca, NY, 1992).

Seliger, M., *The Liberal Politics of John Locke* (New York, 1969).

Simmons, A. John, *The Lockean Theory of Rights* (Princeton, 1992).

———— *On the Edge of Anarchy: Locke, Consent, and the Limits of Society* (Princeton, 1993).

Spellman, W. M., *John Locke and the Problem of Depravity* (Oxford, 1988).

———— *John Locke* (Basingstoke, 1997).

Tarcov, Nathan, *Locke's Education for Liberty* (Chicago, 1984).

Thomas, D. A. Lloyd, *Locke on Government* (London, 1995).

Tully, James, *A Discourse on Property: John Locke and his Adversaries* (Cambridge, 1980).

———— *An Approach to Political Philosophy: John Locke in Contexts* (Cambridge, 1993).

Waldron, Jeremy, *God, Locke, and Equality* (Cambridge, 2002).

Wood, Neal, *The Politics of Locke's Philosophy* (Berkeley, 1983).

———— *John Locke and Agrarian Capitalism* (Berkeley, 1984).

Zuckert, Michael P., *Launching Liberalism: On Lockean Political Philosophy* (Lawrence, Kan., 2002).

On Locke's Toleration

Casson, Douglas John, *Liberating Judgment: Fanatics, Skeptics, and John Locke's Politics of Probability* (Princeton, 2011).

Horton, John, and Mendus, Susan (eds.), *Locke: A Letter Concerning Toleration in Focus* (London, 1991).

Marshall, John, *John Locke, Toleration, and Early Enlightenment Culture* (Cambridge, 2006).

Perry, John, *The Pretenses of Loyalty: Locke, Liberal Theory, and American Political Theology* (Oxford, 2011).

Tuckness, Alex, *Locke and the Legislative Point of View: Toleration, Contested Principles, and the Law* (Princeton, 2002).

Vernon, Richard, *The Career of Toleration: John Locke, Jonas Proast, and After* (Montreal, 1997).

Locke's Contemporaries on Politics

The following are available in the series Cambridge Texts in the History of Political Thought (Cambridge University Press).

Astell, Mary, *Political Writings*, ed. Patricia Springborg (1996).

Baxter, Richard, *A Holy Commonwealth*, ed. William Lamont (1994).

Bayle, Pierre, *Political Writings*, ed. Sally Jenkinson (2000).

Bossuet, Jacques-Bénigne, *Politics Drawn from Holy Scripture*, ed. Patrick Riley (1990).

Filmer, Robert, *Patriarcha and other Writings*, ed. Johann Sommerville (1991).

Fletcher, Andrew, *Political Works*, ed. John Robertson (1997).

Harrington, James, *The Commonwealth of Oceana*, ed. J. G. A. Pocock (1992).

Hobbes, Thomas, *Leviathan*, ed. Richard Tuck and Michael Silverthorne (1991).

Hooker, Richard, *Of the Laws of Ecclesiastical Polity*, ed. A. S. McGrade (1989).

James VI and I, *Political Writings*, ed. Johann Sommerville (1995).

Lawson, George, *Politica sacra et civilis*, ed. Conal Condren (1992).

Leibniz, Johann Gottfried von, *Political Writings*, ed. Patrick Riley (1988).

Milton, John, *Political Writings*, ed. Martin Dzelzainis (1991).

Pufendorf, Samuel, *On the Duty of Man and Citizen*, ed. James Tully (1991).

Outwith that series:

[Locke, John], *The Reception of Locke's Politics*, ed. Mark Goldie, 6 vols. (London, 1999).

Sidney, Algernon, *Discourses Concerning Government*, ed. Thomas G. West (Indianapolis, 1990).

Locke's Contemporaries on Toleration

Bayle, Pierre, *A Philosophical Commentary on These Words of the Gospel, Luke 14: 23, 'Compel them to Come In'*, ed. John Kilcullen and Chandran Kukathas (Indianapolis, 2005).

Penn, William, *The Political Writings of William Penn*, ed. Andrew Murphy (Indianapolis, 2002).

Pufendorf, Samuel, *Of the Nature and Qualification of Religion in Reference to Civil Society*, ed. S. Zurbuchen (Indianapolis, 2002).

Spinoza, Benedict de, *Theological-Political Treatise*, ed. Jonathan Israel and Michael Silverthorne (Cambridge, 2007).

Walwyn, William, *The Writings of William Walwyn*, ed. Jack R. McMichael and Barbara Taft (Athens, Ga., 1989).

Williams, Roger, *On Religious Liberty*, ed. James Calvin Davis (Cambridge, Mass., 2008).

A CHRONOLOGY OF JOHN LOCKE

1632 Born at Wrington, Somerset, 29 August; raised at Pensford.

1642 Outbreak of the Civil Wars.

1643 Troops of Col. Popham, Locke's future patron, despoil Wells Cathedral.

1645 Defeat of Charles I at Naseby by Oliver Cromwell.

1647 Enters Westminster School, London.

1648 Treaty of Westphalia putatively ends European wars of religion.

1649 Execution of Charles I; England a republic.

1651 Thomas Hobbes, *Leviathan*.

1652 Elected a Student of Christ Church, Oxford.

1652–67 Usually resident in Oxford.

1656 Graduates Bachelor of Arts; James Harrington, *The Commonwealth of Oceana*.

1658 Graduates Master of Arts; death of Lord Protector Oliver Cromwell.

1660 Restoration of monarchy under Charles II; Royal Society founded.

1660–2 Writes *Two Tracts on Government*, against religious toleration (published 1967).

1661–3 Attends medical and chemical lectures.

1661–4 Lecturer in Greek, rhetoric, and moral philosophy.

1662 Act of Uniformity reimposes Anglicanism; Dissenting worship illegal.

1663–4 Writes *Essays on the Law of Nature* (published 1954).

1665 First extant correspondence with Robert Boyle.

1665–6 Secretary to an embassy to the Elector of Brandenburg at Cleves.

1666 Licensed to practise medicine; granted dispensation to retain Studentship without taking holy orders; Great Fire of London.

1667 Joins Lord Ashley's household; usually resident in London until 1675; writes *An Essay Concerning Toleration* (published 1876).

1668 Oversees a life-saving operation on Ashley; elected a Fellow of the Royal Society; writes a tract on the lowering of interest (published 1691).

1669 Helps draft *The Fundamental Constitutions of Carolina*.

1670 Secret Treaty of Dover: Charles II promises support for Catholicism; Baruch Spinoza, *Tractatus Theologico-Politicus*.

1671 Secretary to the Lords Proprietors of Carolina (until 1675); first drafts of *An Essay Concerning Human Understanding*.

1672 First visit to France; Ashley created Earl of Shaftesbury and Lord Chancellor; Secretary for Ecclesiastical Presentations (until 1673); Samuel Pufendorf, *On the Law of Nature and Nations*.

1673 Secretary and Treasurer of the Council of Trade and Plantations (until 1674); joins Bahamas Adventurers; the king's brother and heir, James, Duke of York, converts to Catholicism; Test Act excludes Catholics from public office; Shaftesbury ousted from office; begins to lead opposition; Samuel Pufendorf, *On the Duty of Man and Citizen*.

1674 Invests in the Royal African Company, trading in slaves to America.

1675 Helps write Shaftesbury's manifesto, *A Letter from a Person of Quality*; graduates Bachelor of Medicine; to France; chiefly resident at Montpellier until 1677; then mainly Paris.

1676 Translates parts of Pierre Nicole's *Essais de Morale* (published 1712).

1677 Marriage of Prince William of Orange to Princess Mary of England; repeal of writ *De haeretico comburendo*, abolishing burning for heresy; Andrew Marvell, *An Account of the Growth of Popery and Arbitrary Government*.

1678 The Popish Plot revealed; executions of Catholics (until 1681).

1679–81 Exclusion Crisis; Whigs seek to exclude the Catholic heir from the throne; Whig victories in three general elections, but outmanoeuvred.

1679 Returns to England from France; Habeas Corpus Act.

1680 Signs London's 'monster petition' demanding sitting of parliament; Sir Robert Filmer, *Patriarcha, or The Natural Power of Kings* (posthumous).

1679–83 Resides in Oxford, London, and Oakley (James Tyrrell's home); writes *Two Treatises of Government*.

1681 Writes a defence of toleration against Edward Stillingfleet; rumoured
      to be author of (Robert Ferguson's) *No Protestant Plot*; assists
      Shaftesbury at the Oxford Parliament; Oxford Parliament dismissed;
      Charles summons no more parliaments; beginning of Tory backlash
      against Whigs and Dissenters; Shaftesbury charged with treason
      (charge dismissed by Whig grand jury); Whig satirist Stephen
      College executed for treason; Scottish Succession Act declares her-
      editary succession inviolable; William Petty, *Political Arithmetic.*

1682 First extant correspondence with Damaris Cudworth (later Lady
      Masham); royal coup against Whig leadership in the City of London;
      flight of Shaftesbury to Holland; a spy reports Locke's reticence in
      Oxford, 'now his Master is fled'.

1683 Death of Shaftesbury in Holland; Locke attends funeral in Dorset;
      Whig Rye House Plot to assassinate the king revealed; execution of
      Lord William Russell and Algernon Sidney; Earl of Essex's suicide
      in the Tower (Whigs suspect royal murder); *Judgment and Decree of
      Oxford University* against seditious doctrines.

1683–9 Exile in Holland; lives mainly in Utrecht, Amsterdam, and
      Rotterdam.

1684 Rumoured to be author of tracts on the 'murder' of the Earl of Essex;
      expelled *in absentia* from Studentship of Christ Church; begins cor-
      respondence with Edward Clarke concerning education; first extant
      correspondence with Philip van Limborch, Dutch Remonstrant.

1685 Death of Charles II; accession of James II and VII; abortive rebel-
      lion of the Whig Duke of Monmouth, followed by his execution;
      Louis XIV revokes the Edict of Nantes; persecution of Huguenots;
      English envoy seeks Locke's extradition; in hiding in Amsterdam;
      writes *Epistola de tolerantia* (*A Letter Concerning Toleration*).

1686 *An Essay Concerning Human Understanding* substantially finished;
      first extant correspondence with Jean Le Clerc, Amsterdam pub-
      licist; Pierre Bayle, *Philosophical Commentary on 'Compel them to
      Come In'.*

1687 James II issues Declaration of Indulgence (prerogative edict of
      toleration); Catholics and Protestant Dissenters free to worship;
      reviews books for Le Clerc's *Bibliothèque Universelle*; Isaac Newton,
      Principia Mathematica (which Locke reviews).

1688 Culmination of resistance to James II's Catholicizing policies;
      'Glorious Revolution'—intervention in England by William of
      Orange; James II flees to France (abdication or deposition?); pub-
      lishes *Abrégé* (summary) of the *Essay* in *Bibliothèque Universelle.*

1689 National Convention installs King William III and Queen Mary II; Declaration of Rights (statutory as Bill of Rights); Nine Years War against Louis XIV commences; Toleration Act—freedom of worship for Protestant Dissenters; returns to England in February; client of Lord Mordaunt; declines an ambassadorship; appointed Commissioner of Appeals in Excise; publication of *Epistola de tolerantia / A Letter Concerning Toleration*; publication of *Two Treatises of Government* (imprint 1690); publication of *An Essay Concerning Human Understanding* (imprint 1690); first extant correspondence with John Somers, future Whig leader.

1690 Battle of the Boyne: William defeats Jacobites in Ireland; *Letter Concerning Toleration* attacked by Jonas Proast; publication of *A Second Letter Concerning Toleration*; first extant correspondence with Isaac Newton.

1691 Settles at Oates in Essex in Lady Damaris Masham's household; publication of *Some Considerations of the . . . Lowering of Interest.*

1692 Publication of *A Third Letter for Toleration*; prepares Robert Boyle's *General History of the Air* for publication; first extant correspondence with William Molyneux, Dublin philosopher; memorandum on the general naturalization of immigrants.

1693 Publication of *Some Thoughts Concerning Education.*

1694 Founding of the Bank of England; invests £500; first letter in 'College' series, advising Whig Members of Parliament; Triennial Act—regular parliamentary elections; Mary Astell, *A Serious Proposal to the Ladies.*

1695 Advises on the ending of press censorship and the recoinage; sermon preached in Oxford against the *Two Treatises*: publication of *The Reasonableness of Christianity*; *The Reasonableness* attacked by John Edwards; publishes *Vindication*; publication of *Further Considerations Concerning . . . Money*; appointed a Commissioner for Greenwich Hospital; Damaris Masham, *A Discourse Concerning the Love of God.*

1696 Member of the Board of Trade and Plantations (to 1700); the *Essay* attacked by Bishop Edward Stillingfleet; John Toland, *Christianity not Mysterious*; Pierre Bayle, *Historical and Critical Dictionary.*

1697 Treaty of Ryswick—temporary peace with France; publication of *Second Vindication of the Reasonableness of Christianity*; publication of two replies to Stillingfleet in defence of the *Essay*; composes *An Essay on the Poor Law* (published 1789); composes a report on the government of Virginia; composes *The Conduct of the Understanding* (published 1706); Huguenot Pierre Coste settles at Oates, to translate Locke's books.

1698 Molyneux's *Case of Ireland* cites *Two Treatises* in defence of Ireland; Algernon Sidney, *Discourses Concerning Government* (posthumous).

1699 Publishes third and final reply to Stillingfleet in defence of the *Essay*; François Fénelon, *Telemachus*.

1700 Composes 'Some Thoughts on Reading and Study' (published 1720); Pierre Coste's French translation of the *Essay* published; resigns from the Board of Trade and Plantations.

1701 Act of Settlement, ensuring Protestant (Hanoverian) succession; renewal of war against France.

1702 Final visit to London; composes *A Discourse on Miracles* (published 1706); death of William III; accession of Queen Anne; world's first daily newspaper, in London.

1703 Sends *Aesop's Fables* (primer for children) to press; Oxford College heads discourage study of the *Essay*; first major published critique of *Two Treatises*, by Charles Leslie.

1704 Battle of Blenheim: Marlborough's victory over France; capture of Gibraltar ensures British Mediterranean naval presence; completes *A Paraphrase and Notes on the Epistles of St Paul* (published 1705–7); begins (incomplete) *Fourth Letter on Toleration* (published 1706); dies at Oates, 28 October; buried in High Laver churchyard, Essex; Edward Hyde, Earl of Clarendon, *History of the Rebellion* (posthumous).

1705 Damaris Masham, *Occasional Thoughts [on] a Vertuous or Christian Life.*

1706 Publication of *Posthumous Works of Mr John Locke.*

1707 Treaty of Union between England and Scotland effected.

1708 Publication of *Some Familiar Letters between Mr Locke and his Friends.*

1710 Publication of *Oeuvres diverses de Monsieur Jean Locke.*

1713 Treaty of Utrecht ends war with France; Anthony Collins, *Discourse of Freethinking.*

1714 Publication of the first edition of the *Works of John Locke*; Hanoverian succession—accession of George I.

1720 Publication of *A Collection of Several Pieces of Mr John Locke.*

TWO
TREATISES

OF

GOVERNMENT.

In the Former,

The false PRINCIPLES and FOUNDATION of

Sir ROBERT FILMER, and his FOLLOWERS

Are *Detected* and *Overthrown.*

The Latter, is an

ESSAY

Concerning the

True ORIGINAL, EXTENT, and END of

CIVIL-GOVERNMENT.

[*Quasi-facsimile title-page of the* Two Treatises *in Vol. ii of* The Works of John Locke *(London, printed for John Churchill at the Black Swan in Pater-noster-Row. MDCCXIV.)*]

AN ESSAY
CONCERNING THE TRUE
ORIGINAL, EXTENT, AND END
OF CIVIL-GOVERNMENT

CHAP. I.

*The Introduction.**

1. It having been shewn in the foregoing Discourse.

(1) That *Adam** had not either by natural Right of Fatherhood, or by positive Donation from God, any such Authority over his Children, or Dominion* over the World as is pretended.

(2) That if he had, his Heirs, yet, had no Right to it.

(3) That if his Heirs had, there being no Law of Nature nor positive Law* of God that determins, which is the Right Heir in all Cases that may arise, the Right of Succession, and consequently of bearing Rule, could not have been certainly determined.

(4) That if even that had been determined, yet the knowledge of which is the eldest Line of *Adam*'s Posterity, being so long since utterly lost, that in the Races of Mankind and Families of the World, there remains not to one above another, the least pretence to be the eldest House, and to have the Right of Inheritance.

All these premises having, as I think, been clearly made out, it is impossible that the Rulers now on Earth, should make any benefit, or derive any the least shadow of Authority from that, which is held to be the Fountain of all Power, *Adam's private Dominion and paternal Jurisdiction*; so that, he that will not give just occasion, to think, that all Government in the World is the product only of Force and Violence, and that Men live together by no other Rules but that of Beasts, where the strongest carries it; and so lay a Foundation for perpetual Disorder and Mischief, Tumult, Sedition and Rebellion, (things that the followers of that Hypothesis so loudly cry out against) must of necessity find out another rise of Government, another original of Political

Power, and another way of designing and knowing the Persons that have it, than what Sir *Robert F.** hath taught us.

2. To this purpose, I think it may not be amiss, to set down what I take to be political Power. That the Power of a *Magistrate** over a Subject, may be distinguished from that of a *Father* over his Children, a *Master* over his Servant, a *Husband* over his Wife, and a *Lord* over his Slave.* All which distinct Powers happening some-times together in the same Man, if he be considered under these different Relations, it may help us to distinguish these Powers one from another, and shew the difference betwixt a Ruler of a Common-wealth,* a Father of a Family, and a Captain of a Galley.

3. *Political Power*, then I take to be a *Right* of making Laws with Penalties of Death, and consequently all less Penalties, for the Regulating and Preserving of Property, and of employing the force of the Community, in the Execution of such Laws, and in the defence of the Common-wealth from foreign Injury, and all this only for the publick Good.

CHAP. II.

Of the State of Nature.

4. To understand political Power, right, and derive it from its Original, we must consider, what State all Men are naturally in, and that is, a *State of perfect Freedom* to order their Actions, and dispose of their Possessions, and Persons as they think fit, within the bounds of the Law of Nature, without asking leave, or depending upon the Will of any other Man.

A *State* also *of Equality*, wherein all the Power and Jurisdiction is Reciprocal, no one having more than another; there being noth-ing more evident, than that Creatures of the same species and rank, promiscuously born to all the same advantages of Nature, and the use of the same Faculties, should also be equal one amongst another without Subordination or Subjection, unless the Lord and Master of them all, should by any manifest Declaration of his Will set one above another, and confer on him, by an evident and clear Appointment, an undoubted Right to Dominion and Sovereignty.

5. This *equality* of Men by Nature, the Judicious *Hooker** looks upon as so evident in it self, and beyond all question, that he makes it

the Foundation of that Obligation to mutual Love amongst Men, on which he builds the duties they owe one another, and from whence he derives the great Maxims of *Justice* and *Charity*. His words are.

The like natural inducement, hath brought Men to know that it is no less their Duty, to Love others than themselves, for seeing those things which are equal, must needs all have one Measure; if I cannot but wish to receive good, even as much at every Mans hands, as any Man can wish unto his own Soul, how should I look to have any part of my desire herein satisfied, unless my self be careful to satisfie the like desire, which is undoubtedly in other Men, being of one and the same Nature; to have any thing offered them repugnant to this desire, must needs in all respects grieve them as much as me, so that if I do harm, I must look to suffer, there being no reason that others should shew greater measure of love to me, than they have by me, shewed unto them; my desire therefore to be lov'd of my equals in Nature, as much as possible may be, imposeth upon me a natural Duty of bearing to themward, fully the like Affection; from which relation of equality between our selves and them that are as our selves, what several Rules and Canons, natural reason hath drawn, for direction of Life, no Man is Ignorant. Eccl. Pol. Li. I.*

6. But though this be *a State of Liberty*, yet *it is not a State of Licence*;* though Man in that State have an uncontrolable Liberty, to dispose of his Person or Possessions, yet he has not Liberty to destroy himself, or so much as any Creature in his Possession, but where some nobler Use, than its bare Preservation calls for it. The *State of Nature* has a Law of Nature to govern it, which obliges every one: And Reason, which is that Law, teaches all Mankind, who will but consult it, that being all *equal and independent*, no one ought to harm another in his Life, Health, Liberty, or Possessions. For Men being all the Workmanship* of one Omnipotent, and infinitely wise Maker: All the Servants of one Sovereign Master, sent into the World by his Order, and about his Business, they are his Property, whose Workmanship they are, made to last during his, not one anothers Pleasure: And being furnished with like Faculties, sharing all in one Community of Nature, there cannot be supposed any such *Subordination* among us, that may authorize us to destroy one another, as if we were made for one another's Uses, as the inferior ranks of Creatures are for ours. Every one as he is *bound to preserve himself*, and not to quit his Station wilfully, so by the like reason, when his own Preservation comes not in Competition, ought he, as much as he can, *to preserve the rest of*

Mankind, and may not unless it be to do Justice on an Offender, take away, or impair the Life, or what tends to the Preservation of the Life, the Liberty, Health, Limb, or Goods of another.

7. And that all Men may be restrained from invading others Rights, and from doing hurt to one another, and the Law of Nature be observed, which willeth the Peace and *Preservation of all Mankind*, the *Execution* of the Law of Nature is in that State, put into every Man's Hands, whereby every one has a Right to punish the Transgressors of that Law to such a Degree, as may hinder its Violation. For the *Law of Nature* would, as all other Laws, that concern Men in this World, be in vain, if there were no Body that in the State of Nature, had a *Power to execute* that Law, and thereby preserve the Innocent and restrain Offenders. And if any one in the State of Nature may punish another, for any evil he has done, every one may do so. For in that *State of perfect Equality*, where naturally there is no Superiority or Jurisdiction of one, over another, what any may do in Prosecution of that Law, every one must needs have a Right to do.

8. And thus in the State of Nature, *one Man comes by a Power over another*; but yet no absolute or arbitrary Power,* to use a Criminal, when he has got him in his Hands, according to the passionate Heats, or boundless Extravagancy of his own Will; but only to retribute to him, so far, as calm Reason and Conscience dictate what is proportionate to his Transgression, which is so much as may serve for *Reparation* and *Restraint*. For these two are the only Reasons, why one Man may lawfully do harm to another, which is that we call *Punishment*. In transgressing the Law of Nature, the Offender declares himself to live by another Rule, than that of common Reason and Equity, which is that measure God has set to the actions of Men, for their mutual Security; and so he becomes dangerous to Mankind, the Tye, which is to secure them from Injury and Violence, being slighted and broken by him. Which being a trespass against the whole Species, and the Peace and Safety of it, provided for by the Law of Nature, every Man upon this Score, by the Right he hath to preserve Mankind in general, may restrain, or where it is necessary, destroy things noxious to them, and so may bring such evil on any one, who hath transgressed that Law, as may make him repent the doing of it, and thereby deter him, and, by his Example others, from doing the like Mischief. And in this Case, and upon this Ground, *every Man hath a Right to punish the Offender, and be Executioner of the Law of Nature*.

9. I doubt not but this will seem a very strange Doctrine to some Men: But before they condemn it, I desire them to resolve me, by what Right any Prince* or State can put to death, or *punish an Alien*, for any Crime he commits in their Country. 'Tis certain their Laws by virtue of any Sanction, they receive from the promulgated Will of the Legislative, reach not a Stranger:* They speak not to him, nor, if they did, is he bound to hearken to them. The legislative Authority, by which they are in Force over the Subjects of that Common-wealth, hath no Power over him. Those who have the supream Power of making Laws in *England, France* or *Holland*, are to an *Indian*, but like the rest of the World, Men without Authority: And therefore, if by the Law of Nature, every Man hath not a Power to punish Offences against it, as he soberly Judges the Case to require, I see not how the Magistrates of any Community, can *punish an Alien* of another Country; since in Reference to him, they can have no more Power, than what every Man naturally may have over another.

10. Besides the Crime which consists in violating the Law, and varying from the right Rule of Reason, whereby a Man so far becomes degenerate, and declares himself to quit the Principles of human Nature, and to be a noxious Creature, there is commonly *Injury* done, [to] some Person or other, some other Man receives Damage by his Transgression, in which Case he who hath received any Damage, has besides the right of Punishment common to him with other Men, a particular Right to seek *Reparation* from him that has done it. And any other Person who finds it just, may also joyn with him that is injur'd, and assist him in recovering from the Offender, so much as may make satisfaction for the Harm he has suffered.

11. From these *two distinct Rights*, the one of *punishing* the Crime *for restraint*, and preventing the like Offence, which right of punishing is in every Body; the other of taking *Reparation*, which belongs only to the injured Party, comes it to pass, that the Magistrate, who by being Magistrate, hath the common Right of punishing put into his Hands, can often, where the publick good demands not the Execution of the Law, *remit* the Punishment of criminal Offences by his own Authority, but yet cannot *remit* the Satisfaction due to any private Man, for the Damage he has received. That, he who has suffered the Damage has a Right to demand in his own Name, and he alone can remit: The damnified* Person has this Power of appropriating to himself, the Goods or Service of the Offender, *by Right of self-Preservation*, as

every Man has a Power to punish the Crime, to prevent its being committed again, *by the Right he has of Preserving all Mankind*, and doing all reasonable things, he can, in order to that end: And thus it is, that every Man in the State of Nature, has a Power to kill a Murderer, both *to deter* others from doing the like Injury, which no Reparation can compensate, by the Example of the Punishment that attends it from every body, and also to secure Men from the attempts of a Criminal, who having renounced Reason, the common Rule and Measure, God hath given to Mankind, hath by the unjust Violence and Slaughter he hath committed upon one, declared War against all Mankind, and therefore may be destroyed as a *Lyon* or a *Tyger*, one of those wild savage Beasts, with whom Men can have no Society nor Security: And upon this is grounded the great Law of Nature, *whoso sheddeth Man's Blood, by Man shall his Blood be shed*. And *Cain* was so fully convinced, that every one had a Right to destroy such a Criminal, that after the Murther of his Brother, he cries out, *Every one that findeth me, shall slay me*;* so plain was it writ in the Hearts of all Mankind.*

12. By the same reason, may a Man in the State of Nature *punish the lesser Breaches* of that Law. It will perhaps be demanded with Death? I answer, each Transgression may be *punished* to that *Degree*, and with so much *Severity*, as will suffice to make it an ill Bargain to the Offender, give him Cause to repent, and terrifie others from doing the like. Every Offence that can be committed in the State of Nature, may in the State of Nature be also punished equally, and as far forth* as it may, in a Commonwealth. For though it would be besides my present Purpose, to enter here into the particulars of the Law of Nature, or its *measures of Punishment*; yet, it is certain there is such a Law, and that too, as intelligible and plain to a rational Creature, and a Studier of that Law, as the positive Laws of Commonwealths; nay possibly plainer; as much as Reason is easier to be understood, than the Phancies and intricate Contrivances of Men, following contrary and hidden Interests put into Words; for so truly are a great part of the *municipal Laws** of Countries, which are only so far right, as they are founded on the Law of Nature, by which they are to be regulated and interpreted.

13. To this strange doctrine, *viz.* That *in the State of Nature, every one has the Executive Power* of the Law of Nature, I doubt not but it will be objected, that it is unreasonable for Men to be Judges in their own Cases, that self-love will make Men partial to themselves

and their Friends: And on the other side, that ill Nature, Passion and Revenge will carry them too far in punishing others; and hence nothing but Confusion and Disorder will follow, and that therefore God hath certainly appointed Government to restrain the partiality and violence of Men.* I easily grant, that *Civil Government* is the proper Remedy for the Inconveniencies of the state of Nature, which must certainly be great, where Men may be Judges in their own Case, since 'tis easie to be imagined, that he who was so unjust as to do his Brother an Injury, will scarce be so just as to condemn himself for it: But I shall desire those who make this Objection, to remember, that *absolute Monarchs* are but Men, and if Government is to be the Remedy of those Evils, which necessarily follow from Mens being Judges in their own Cases, and the State of Nature is therefore not to be endured, I desire to know what kind of Government that is, and how much better it is than the State of Nature, where one Man commanding a Multitude, has the Liberty to be Judge in his own Case, and may do to all his Subjects whatever he pleases, without the least question or controle of those who execute his Pleasure? And in whatsoever he doth, whether led by Reason, Mistake or Passion, must be submitted to? Which Men in the State of Nature are not bound to do one to another:* And if he that judges, judges amiss in his own, or any other Case, he is answerable for it to the rest of Mankind.

14. 'Tis often asked as a mighty Objection, *where are*, or ever were, there any *Men in such a state of Nature*? To which it may suffice as an Answer at present: That since all Princes and Rulers of *Independent Governments* all through the World, are in a state of Nature, 'tis plain the World never was, nor ever will be, without Numbers of Men in that State. I have named all Governors of *Independent Communities*, whether they are, or are not, in League with others. For 'tis not every Compact* that puts an end to the state of Nature between Men, but only this one of agreeing together mutually to enter into one Community, and make one Body Politick;* other Promises, and Compacts, Men may make one with another, and yet still be in the state of Nature. The Promises and Bargains for Truck,* &c. between the two Men in the desert Island, mentioned by *Garcilasso de la Vega*,* in his History of *Peru*; or between a *Swiss* and an *Indian*,* in the Woods of *America*, are binding to them, though they are perfectly in a state of Nature, in reference to one another. For Truth and keeping of Faith belongs to Men, as Men, and not as Members of Society.

15. To those that say, There were never any Men in the State of Nature; I will not only oppose the Authority of the judicious *Hooker, Eccl. Pol. Lib.* I. *Sect.* 10. where he says, *The Laws which have been hitherto mentioned*, i.e. the Laws of Nature, *do bind Men absolutely, even as they are Men, although they have never any settled Fellowship, never any solemn Agreement amongst themselves what to do or not to do, but for as much as we are not by our selves sufficient to furnish our selves with competent store of things, needful for such a Life, as our Nature doth desire, a Life fit for the Dignity of Man; therefore to supply those Defects and Imperfections which are in us, as living single and solely by our selves, we are naturally induced to seek Communion and Fellowship with others, this was the Cause of Mens uniting themselves, at first in politick Societies.* But I moreover affirm, That all Men are naturally in that State, and remain so, till by their own Consents they make themselves Members of some politick Society; and I doubt not in the Sequel of this Discourse, to make it very clear.

CHAP. III.
Of the State of War.

16. The *State of War* is a state of *Enmity* and *Destruction*: And therefore declaring by Word or Action, not a passionate and hasty, but a sedate settled Design, upon another Man's Life, *puts him in a State of War* with him against whom he has declared such an Intention, and so has exposed his Life to the others Power to be taken away by him, or any one that joyns with him in his Defence, and espouses his Quarrel; it being reasonable and just I should have a Right to destroy that, which threatens me with Destruction. For *by the fundamental Law of Nature, Man being to be preserved*, as much as possible, when all cannot be preserved, the safety of the Innocent is to be preferred: And one may destroy a Man who makes War upon him, or has discovered an Enmity to his being, for the same Reason, that he may kill a *Woolf* or a *Lion*; because such Men are not under the ties of the Common Law of Reason, have no other Rule, but that of Force and Violence, and so may be treated as Beasts of Prey, those dangerous and noxious Creatures, that will be sure to destroy him, whenever he falls into their Power.

17. And hence it is, that he who attempts to get another Man into

his Absolute Power, does thereby *put himself into a State of War* with him; It being to be understood as a Declaration of a design upon his Life. For I have reason to conclude, that he who would get me into his Power without my Consent, would use me as he pleased, when he had got me there, and destroy me too, when he had a fancy to it; for no body can desire to *have me in his absolute Power*, unless it be to compel me by force to that, which is against the Right of my Freedom, *i.e.* make me a Slave. To be free from such force is the only security of my Preservation; and reason bids me look on him, as an Enemy to my Preservation, who would take away that *Freedom*, which is the fence to it; so that he who makes an *attempt to enslave* me, thereby puts himself into a State of War with me. He that in the State of Nature, *would take away the Freedom*, that belongs to any one in that State, must necessarily be supposed to have a design to take away every thing else, that *Freedom* being the Foundation of all the rest: As he that in the State of Society, would take away the *Freedom* belonging to those of that Society or Common-wealth, must be supposed to design to take away from them every thing else, and so be looked on as *in a State of War*.

18. This makes it lawful for a Man to *kill a Thief*, who has not in the least hurt him, nor declared any Design upon his Life, any far- ther, than by the use of Force, so to get him in his Power, as to take away his Money, or what he pleases from him; because using Force, where he has no Right, to get me into his Power, let his Pretence be what it will, I have no reason to suppose, that he, who would *take away my Liberty* would not, when he had me in his Power, take away every thing else. And therefore it is lawful for me to treat him, as one who has *put himself into a state of War* with me, *i.e.* kill him if I can; for to that Hazard does he justly expose himself, whoever introduces a State of War, and is aggressor in it.

19. And here we have the plain *Difference between the state of Nature, and the state of War*, which however some Men have con- founded,* are as far distant, as a state of Peace, good Will, mutual Assistance and Preservation; and a state of Enmity, Malice, Violence and mutual Destruction are one from another. Men living together according to Reason, without a common superior on Earth, with Authority to judge between them, is *properly the state of Nature*. But force, or a declared design of Force upon the Person of another, where there is no common Superior on Earth to appeal to for Relief,

is the state of War: And 'tis the want of such an Appeal gives a Man the right of War even against an *Aggressor*, though he be in Society and a fellow Subject. Thus a *Thief*, whom I cannot harm, but by Appeal to the Law, for having stolen all that I am worth, I may kill, when he sets on me to rob me but of my Horse or Coat; because the Law, which was made for my Preservation where it cannot interpose to secure my Life from present Force, which if lost, is capable of no Reparation, permits me my own Defence, and the right of War, a Liberty to kill the Aggressor, because the Aggressor allows not time to appeal to our common Judge, nor the decision of the Law, for Remedy in a Case, where the Mischief may be irreparable. *Want of a common Judge with Authority, puts all Men in a state of Nature: Force without Right, upon a Man's Person, makes a state of War*, both where there is, and is not, a common Judge.

20. But when the actual Force is over, the *state of War ceases* between those that are in Society, and are equally on both Sides* subjected to the fair Determination of the Law; because then there lies open the remedy of Appeal for the past Injury, and to prevent future Harm, but where no such Appeal is, as in the state of Nature, for want of positive Laws, and Judges with Authority to appeal to, *the state of War once begun, continues*, with a right to the innocent Party to destroy the other whenever he can, until the Aggressor offers Peace, and desires Reconciliation on such Terms, as may repair any Wrongs he has already done, and secure the Innocent for the future; nay where an Appeal to the Law,* and constituted Judges lies open, but the Remedy is deny'd by a manifest perverting of Justice, and a barefac'd wresting of the Laws to protect or indemnifie the violence or injur-ies of some Men, or party of Men, *there* it *is* hard to imagine any thing but *a state of War*. For where-ever Violence is used, and Injury done, though by hands appointed to administer Justice, it is still Violence and Injury, however colour'd with the Name, Pretences, or forms of Law, the End whereof being to protect and redress the Innocent, by an unbiassed Application of it, to all who are under it; where-ever that is not *bona fide* done, *War is made* upon the Sufferers, who having no Appeal on Earth to right them, they are left to the only Remedy in such Cases, an Appeal to Heaven.

21. To avoid this *state of War* (wherein there is no Appeal but to Heaven, and wherein every the least Difference is apt to end, where there is no Authority to decide between the Contenders) is one

great *reason of Mens putting themselves into Society*, and quitting the
State of Nature. For where there is an Authority, a Power on Earth,
from which Relief can be had by *Appeal*, there the continuance of
the *state of War* is excluded, and the Controversie is decided by that
Power. Had there been any such Court, any superior Jurisdiction on
Earth, to determine the Right between *Jephtha** and the *Ammonites*,
they had never come to a *state of War*, but we see he was forced to
appeal to Heaven. *The Lord the Judge* (says he) *be Judge this Day
between the Children of Israel, and the Children of Ammon, Judg.* 11.
27. and then Prosecuting, and relying on his *Appeal*, he leads out
his Army to Battle: And therefore in such Controversies, where the
Question is put, *who shall be Judge?* It cannot be meant, who shall
decide the Controversie; every one knows what *Jephtha* here tells us,
that *the Lord the Judge*, shall Judge. Where there is no Judge on Earth,
the Appeal lies to God in Heaven. That Question then cannot mean,
who shall judge? whether another hath put himself in a *state of War*
with me, and whether I may as *Jephtha* did, *appeal to Heaven* in it?
Of that I my self can only be Judge in my own Conscience, as I will
answer it at the great Day, to the supream Judge of all Men.

CHAP. IV.

Of Slavery.

22. The *Natural Liberty* of Man is to be free from any superior Power on Earth, and not to be under the Will or legislative
Authority of Man, but to have only the Law of Nature for his Rule.
The *Liberty of Man*, in Society, is to be under no other legislative
Power, but that established, by Consent, in the Commonwealth; nor
under the dominion of any Will, or restraint of any Law, but what the
Legislative shall enact, according to the Trust put in it. Freedom then
is not what Sir *R. F.* tells us, *O. A.* 55.* *A Liberty for every one to do
what he lists, to live as he pleases, and not to be tyed by any Laws*: But
Freedom of Men under Government, is, to have a standing Rule to live
by, common to every one of that Society, and made by the legislative
Power erected in it; a Liberty to follow my own Will in all things,
where the Rule prescribes not; and not to be subject to the inconstant,
uncertain, unknown, arbitrary Will of another Man: As *Freedom of
Nature* is to be under no other Restraint but the Law of Nature.

23. This *Freedom* from absolute, arbitrary Power, is so necessary to, and closely joyned with a Man's Preservation, that he cannot part with it, but by what forfeits his Preservation and Life together. For a Man, not having the Power of his own Life, *cannot*, by Compact, or his own Consent, *enslave himself* to any one, nor put himself under the absolute, arbitrary Power of another, to take away his Life, when he pleases. No body can give more Power than he has himself; and he that cannot take away his own Life, cannot give another Power over it. Indeed having by his Fault, forfeited his own Life, by some Act that deserves Death; he, to whom he has forfeited it, may (when he has him in his Power) delay to take it, and make use of him to his own Service, and he does him no Injury by it. For, whenever he finds the hardship of his Slavery outweigh the value of his Life, 'tis in his Power, by resisting the Will of his Master, to draw on himself the Death he desires.

24. This is the perfect condition of *Slavery*, which is nothing else, but *the state of War continued, between a lawful Conqueror, and a Captive*. For, if once *Compact* enter between them, and make an Agreement for a limited Power on the one Side, and Obedience on the other, the *state of War and Slavery* ceases, as long as the Compact endures. For, as has been said, no Man can, by Agreement, pass over to another that which he hath not in himself, a Power over his own Life.

I confess, we find among the *Jews*, as well as other Nations, that Men did sell themselves; but, 'tis plain, this was only to *Drudgery, not to Slavery*. For, it is evident, the Person sold was not under an absolute, arbitrary, despotical Power. For the Master could not have Power to kill him, at any time, whom at a certain time, he was obliged to let go free out of his Service; and the Master of such a Servant was so far from having an arbitrary Power over his Life, that he could not at Pleasure, so much as maim him, but the loss of an Eye, or Tooth, set him free, *Exod.* XXI.

CHAP. V.

Of Property.

25.* Whether we consider natural *Reason*, which tells us, that Men, being once born, have a right to their Preservation, and consequently to Meat and Drink,* and such other things, as Nature affords for their

Subsistence; or *Revelation*, which gives us an account of those Grants God made of the World to *Adam*, and to *Noah*, and his Sons, 'tis very clear, that God, as K. *David* says, *Psal.* CXV. xvi. *has given the Earth to the Children of Men*; given it to Mankind in common. But this being supposed, it seems to some a very great Difficulty, how any one should ever come to have a *Property* in any thing: I will not content my self to answer, That if it be difficult to make out *Property*, upon a Supposition, that God gave the World to *Adam*, and his Posterity in common; it is impossible that any Man, but one universal Monarch should have any *Property* upon a Supposition, that God gave the World to *Adam*, and his Heirs in Succession, exclusive of all the rest of his Posterity. But I shall endeavour to shew, how Men might come to have a *Property* in several parts of that which God gave to Mankind in common, and that without any express Compact of all the Commoners.*

26. God, who hath given the World to Men in common, hath also given them reason to make use of it to the best Advantage of Life, and Convenience.* The Earth, and all that is therein, is given to Men for the Support and Comfort of their Being. And though all the Fruits it naturally produces, and Beasts it feeds, belong to Mankind in common, as they are produced by the spontaneous Hand of Nature; and no body has originally a private Dominion, exclusive of the rest of Mankind, in any of them, as they are thus in their natural State: yet being given for the use of Men, there must of necessity be *a means to appropriate* them some way or other, before they can be of any use, or at all beneficial to any particular Man. The Fruit, or Venison, which nourishes the wild *Indian*, who knows no Inclosure, and is still a Tenant in common, must be his, and so his, *i.e.* a part of him, that another can no longer have any right to it, before it can do him any Good for the Support of his Life.

27. Though the Earth, and all inferior Creatures be common to all Men, yet every Man has a *Property* in his own *Person*: This no Body has any right to but himself. The *Labour* of his Body, and the *Work* of his Hands, we may say, are properly his. Whatsoever then he removes out of the State that Nature hath provided, and left it in, he hath mixed his *Labour* with, and joyned to it something that is his own, and thereby makes it his *Property*. It being by him removed from the common State Nature placed it in, it hath by this *Labour* something annexed to it, that excludes the common Right of other Men. For this

Labour being the unquestionable Property of the Labourer, no Man but he can have a Right to what that is once joyned to, at least where there is enough, and as good left in common for others.

28. He that is nourished by the Acorns he pickt up under an Oak, or the Apples he gathered from the Trees in the Wood, has certainly appropriated them to himself. No body can deny but the Nourishment is his. I ask then, When did they begin to be his? When he digested? Or when he eat? Or when he boiled? Or when he brought them home? Or when he pickt them up? And 'tis plain, if the first gathering made them not his, nothing else could. That *Labour* put a Distinction between them and common: That added something to them more than Nature, the common Mother of all, had done; and so they became his private Right. And will any one say, he had no Right to those Acorns or Apples, he thus appropriated, because he had not the Consent of all Mankind to make them his? Was it a Robbery thus to assume to himself what belonged to all in common? If such a Consent as that was necessary, Man had starved, notwithstanding the Plenty God had given him. We see in *Commons*, which remain so by Compact, that 'tis the taking any part of what is common, and removing it out of the state Nature leaves it in, which *begins the Property*; without which the Common is of no use. And the taking of this or that part, does not depend on the express Consent of all the Commoners. Thus the Grass my Horse has bit; the Turfs my Servant has cut; and the Ore I have digg'd in any Place, where I have a Right to them in common with others, become my *Property*, without the Assignation or Consent of any body. The *Labour* that was mine, removing them out of that common State they were in, hath *fixed* my *Property* in them.

29. By making an explicit Consent of every Commoner, necessary to any ones appropriating to himself any part of what is given in common, Children or Servants could not cut the Meat, which their Father or Master had provided for them in common, without assigning to every one his peculiar Part. Tho' the Water running in the Fountain be every ones, yet who can doubt, but that in the Pitcher is his only who drew it out? His *Labour* hath taken it out of the Hands of Nature, where it was common, and belong'd equally to all her Children, and *hath* thereby *appropriated* it to himself.

30. Thus this Law of Reason makes the Deer that *Indian's* who hath killed it; 'tis allowed to be his Goods, who hath bestowed

his Labour upon it, though before[,] it was the common Right of every one. And amongst those who are counted the civiliz'd part of Mankind, who have made and multiplied positive Laws to determine *Property*, this original Law of Nature, for the *beginning of Property*, in what was before common, still takes place; and by vertue thereof, what Fish any one catches in the Ocean, that great and still remaining Common of Mankind; or what Ambergreise any one takes up here, is *by* the *Labour* that removes it out of that common State Nature left it in, *made* his *Property*, who takes that Pains about it. And even amongst us, the Hare that any one is hunting, is thought his who pursues her during the Chase. For being a Beast that is still looked upon as common, and no Man's private Possession; whoever has employ'd so much *Labour* about any of that kind, as to find and pursue her, has thereby removed her from the State of Nature, wherein she was common, and hath *begun a Property*.

31. It will perhaps be objected to this, That if gathering the Acorns, or other Fruits of the Earth, *&c.* makes a Right to them, then any one may *ingross* as much as he will. To which I answer, Not so. The same Law of Nature, that does by this means give us Property, does also *bound* that *Property* too. *God has given us all things richly*, 1 Tim. vi. 12.* is the Voice of Reason confirmed by Inspiration. But how far has he given it us? *To enjoy.* As much as any one can make use of to any Advantage of Life before it spoils; so much he may by his Labour fix a Property in: Whatever is beyond this, is more than his Share, and belongs to others. Nothing was made by God for Man to spoil or destroy. And thus considering the Plenty of natural Provisions there was a long time in the World, and the few Spenders; and to how small a Part of that Provision the Industry of one Man could extend it self, and ingross it to the Prejudice of others; especially keeping within the *Bounds*, set by Reason, *of* what might serve for his *Use*; there could be then little room for Quarrels or Contentions about Property so establish'd.

32. But the *chief Matter of Property* being now not the Fruits of the Earth, and the Beasts that subsist on it, but *the Earth it self*; as that which takes in and carries with it all the rest: I think it is plain, that *Property* in that too is acquir'd as the former. *As much Land* as a Man Tills, Plants, Improves, Cultivates, and can use the Product of, so much is his *Property*. He by his Labour does, as it were, inclose it from the Common. Nor will it invalidate his Right to say, Every body

else has an equal Title to it; and therefore he cannot appropriate, he cannot inclose, without the Consent of all his Fellow-Commoners, all Mankind. God, when he gave the World in common to all Mankind, commanded Man also to labour, and the Penury of his Condition required it of him. God and his Reason commanded him to subdue the Earth,* *i.e.* improve it for the Benefit of Life, and therein lay out something upon it that was his own, his Labour. He that in Obedience to this Command of God, subdued, tilled and sowed any part of it, thereby annexed to it something that was his *Property*, which another had no Title to, nor could without Injury take from him.

33. Nor was this *Appropriation* of any parcel of *Land*, by improving it, any Prejudice to any other Man, since there was still enough, and as good left; and more than the yet unprovided could use. So that in effect, there was never the less left for others because of his Inclosure for himself. For he that leaves as much as another can make use of, does as good as take nothing at all. No Body could think himself injur'd by the drinking of another Man though he took a good Draught, who had a whole River of the same Water left him to quench his Thirst: And the Case of Land and Water, where there is enough of both, is perfectly the same.

34. God gave the World to Men in common; but since he gave it them for their Benefit, and the greatest conveniencies of Life they were capable to draw from it, it cannot be supposed he meant it should always remain common and uncultivated. He gave it to the use of the industrious and rational, (and *Labour* was to be *his Title* to it;) not to the Fancy or Covetousness of the Quarrelsom and Contentious. He that had as good left for his Improvement, as was already taken up, needed not complain, ought not to meddle with what was already improved by another's Labour: If he did, 'tis plain he desired the benefit of another's Pains, which he had no right to, and not the Ground which God had given him in common with others to labour on, and whereof there was as good left, as that already possessed, and more than he knew what to do with, or his Industry could reach to.

35. 'Tis true, in *Land* that is *common* in *England*, or any other Country, where there is plenty of People under Government, who have Money and Commerce, no one can inclose or appropriate any part, without the consent of all his Fellow-Commoners: Because this is left common by Compact, *i.e.* by the law of the Land, which is not

to be violated. And tho' it be common, in respect of some Men, it is not so to all Mankind; but is the joint property of this Country, or this Parish. Besides, the remainder, after such Inclosure, would not be as good to the rest of the Commoners, as the whole was, when they could all make use of the whole; whereas in the Beginning and first peopling of the great Common of the World, it was quite otherwise. The Law Man was under, was rather for appropriating. God commanded, and his Wants forced him to *labour*. That was his *Property* which could not be taken from him where-ever he had fixed it. And hence subduing or cultivating the Earth, and having Dominion, we see are joined together. The one gave Title to the other. So that God, by commanding to subdue, gave Authority so far to *appropriate*: And the Condition of human Life, which requires Labour and Materials to work on, necessarily introduces private Possessions.

36. Nature has well set the *measure of Property** by the extent of Mens *Labour and the Conveniencies of Life*: No Man's Labour could subdue, or appropriate all; nor could his Enjoyment consume more than a small Part; so that it was impossible for any Man, this Way, to intrench upon the Right of another, or acquire to himself a Property, to the prejudice of his Neighbour, who would still have room for as good, and as large a Possession (after the other had taken out his) as before it was appropriated. [This] *Measure* did confine every Man's *Possession*, to a very moderate Proportion, and such, as he might appropriate to himself, without Injury to any Body, in the first Ages of the World, when Men were more in Danger to be lost, by wandring from their Company, in the then vast wilderness of the Earth, than to be straitned for want of room to plant in. And the same *Measure* may be allowed still without Prejudice to any Body, as full as the World seems. For supposing a Man, or Family, in the State they were at [the] first peopling of the World by the Children of *Adam*, or *Noah*; let him plant in some In-land, vacant places of *America**, we shall find that the *Possessions* he could make himself, upon the *Measures* we have given, would not be very large, nor, even to this day, prejudice the rest of Mankind, or give them reason to complain, or think themselves injured by this Man's Incroachment, though the race of Men have now spread themselves to all the corners of the World, and do infinitely exceed the small Number [which] was at the Beginning. Nay, the extent of *Ground* is of so little Value, *without Labour*, that I have heard it affirmed, that in *Spain* it self, a Man may be permitted to

plough, sow and reap, without being disturbed upon Land he has no other Title to, but only his making use of it.* But, on the contrary, the Inhabitants think themselves beholden to him, who, by his Industry on neglected, and consequently waste Land, has increased the stock of Corn, which they wanted. But be this as it will, which I lay no Stress on; this I dare boldly affirm, that the same *rule of Propriety*,* (*viz.*) that every Man should have as much as he could make use of, would hold still in the World, without straitning any Body; since there is Land enough in the World to suffice double the Inhabitants, had not the *Invention of Money*, and the tacit Agreement of Men, to put a Value on it, introduced (by Consent) larger Possessions, and a Right to them; which, how it has done, I shall by and by shew more at large.

37. This is certain, That in the beginning, before the desire of having more than Man needed, had altered the intrinsick value of things, which depends only on their usefulness to the Life of Man; or [men] had *agreed, that a little piece of yellow Metal*, which would keep without wasting or decay, should be worth a great piece of Flesh, or a whole heap of Corn, though Men had a right to appropriate, by their Labour, each one to himself, as much of the things of Nature, as he could use; yet this could not be much, nor to the Prejudice of others, where the same plenty was still left, to those who would use the same Industry. To which let me add,* that he who appropriates Land to himself by his Labour, does not lessen but increase the common stock of Mankind. For the Provisions serving to the support of human Life; produced by one Acre of Inclosed and Cultivated Land are (to speak much within compass) ten times more than those which are yielded by an Acre of Land of an equal richness lying waste in Common. And therefore he that incloses Land, and has a greater plenty of the Conveniencies of Life from ten Acres, than he could have from an hundred left to Nature, may truly be said to give ninety Acres to Mankind. For his Labour now supplies him with Provisions out of ten Acres, which were but the Product of an hundred lying in Common. I have here rated the improv'd Land very low in making its Product but as ten to one, when it is much nearer an hundred to one. For I ask whether in the wild Woods and uncultivated waste of *America* left to Nature without any Improvement, Tillage or Husbandry, a thousand Acres yield the needy and wretched Inhabitants as many Conveniencies of Life, as ten Acres of equally fertile Land do in *Devonshire*, where they are well Cultivated?

Before the appropriation of Land, he who gathered as much of the wild Fruit, killed, caught, or tamed, as many of the Beasts, as he could; he that so imployed his Pains about any of the spontaneous Products of Nature, as any way to alter them, from the state which Nature put them in, *by* placing any of his *Labour* on them, did thereby *acquire a Propriety in them*: But if they perished, in his Possession, without their due Use; if the Fruits rotted, or the Venison putrified, before he could spend it, he offended against the common Law of Nature, and was liable to be punished; he invaded his Neighbour's share, for he had *no Right, farther than his Use* called for any of them, and they might serve to afford him Conveniencies of Life.

38. The same *Measures* governed the *Possession of Land* too: Whatsoever he tilled and reaped, laid up and made use of, before it spoiled, that was his peculiar Right; whatsoever he enclosed, and could feed, and make use of, the Cattle and Product was also his. But if either the Grass of his Inclosure rotted on the Ground, or the Fruit of his planting perished without gathering, and laying up, this part of the Earth, notwithstanding his Inclosure, was still to be looked on as waste, and might be the Possession of any other. Thus, at the beginning, *Cain* might take as much Ground as he could Till, and make it his own Land, and yet leave enough to *Abel's* Sheep to feed on; a few Acres would serve for both their Possessions. But as Families increased, and industry inlarged their Stocks, their *Possessions inlarged* with the need of them; but yet it was commonly *without any fixed property in the ground* they made use of, till they incorporated, settled themselves together, and built Cities, and then, by consent, they came in time, to set out the *bounds of their distinct Territories*, and agree on limits between them and their Neighbours; and by Laws within themselves, settled the *Properties* of those of the same Society. For we see, that in that part of the World which was first inhabited, and therefore like[ly] to be best peopled, even as low down as *Abraham's* Time, they wandred with their Flocks, and their Herds, which was their substance, freely up and down; and this *Abraham* did, in a Country where he was a Stranger. Whence it is plain, that at least, a great part of the *Land lay in common*; that the Inhabitants valued it not, nor claimed Property in any more than they made use of. But when there was not room enough in the same Place, for their Herds to feed together, they by consent, as *Abraham* and *Lot* did, *Gen.* xiii. 5. separated and inlarged their Pasture, where it best liked them. And

for the same Reason *Esau* went from his Father, and his Brother, and planted in *Mount Seir, Gen.* xxxvi. 6.

39. And thus, without supposing any private Dominion, and Property in *Adam*, over all the World, exclusive of all other Men, which can no way be proved, nor any ones Property be made out from it; but supposing the *World* given as it was to the Children of Men *in common*, we see how *labour* could make Men distinct Titles to several parcels of it, for their private Uses; wherein there could be no doubt of Right, no room for quarrel.

40. Nor is it so strange, as perhaps before consideration it may appear, that the *Property of Labour* should be able to over-balance the Community of Land. For 'tis *labour* indeed that *puts the difference of value* on every thing; and let any one consider what the difference is between an Acre of Land planted with Tobacco or Sugar,* sown with Wheat or Barley; and an Acre of the same Land lying in common, without any Husbandry upon it, and he will find, that the improvement of *labour makes* the far greater part of the Value. I think it will be but a very modest Computation to say, that of the *Products* of the Earth useful to the Life of Man nine-tenths are the *effects of labour*: Nay, if we will rightly estimate things as they come to our Use, and cast up the several expences about them, what in them is purely owing to *Nature*, and what to *Labour*, we shall find, that in most of them ninety-nine hundredths are wholly to be put on the account of *Labour*.

41. There cannot be a clearer demonstration of any thing, than several Nations of the *Americans* are of this, who are rich in Land, and poor in all the Comforts of Life; whom Nature having furnished as liberally as any other People, with the materials of Plenty, *i.e.* a fruitful Soil, apt to produce in abundance, what might serve for Food, Rayment, and Delight; yet for *want of improving it by Labour*, have not one hundredth part of the Conveniencies we enjoy: And a King of a large and fruitful Territory there Feeds, Lodges, and is clad worse than a day Labourer in *England*.*

42. To make this a little clearer, let us but trace some of the ordinary provisions of Life, through their several Progresses, before they come to our Use, and see how much they receive of their *value from human Industry*. Bread, Wine and Cloth, are things of daily Use, and great Plenty, yet notwithstanding, Acorns, Water and Leaves, or Skins, must be our Bread, Drink and Cloathing, did not *labour* furnish

us with these more useful Commodities. For whatever *Bread* is more worth than Acorns, Wine than Water, and *Cloth* or *Silk*, than Leaves, Skins or Moss, that is wholly *owing to Labour* and *Industry*. The one of these being the Food and Rayment which unassisted Nature furnishes us with; the other Provisions which our Industry and Pains prepare for Us, which how much they exceed the other in Value, when any one hath Computed, he will then see, how much *labour makes the far greatest part of the value* of things we enjoy in this World: And the ground which produces the Materials, is scarce to be reckon'd in, as any, or at most, but a very small part of it; so little, that even amongst us, Land that is left wholly to Nature, that hath no improvement of Pasturage, Tillage, or Planting, is called, as indeed it is, *Waste*; and we shall find the benefit of it amount to little more than nothing.

This shews* how much numbers of Men are to be preferred to largeness of Dominions; and that the increase of Lands,* and the right employing of them is the great Art of Government: And that Prince, who shall be so Wise and Godlike, as by established Laws of Liberty to secure Protection and Encouragement to the honest industry of Mankind, against the Oppression of Power and Narrowness of Party, will quickly be too hard for his Neighbours; But this by the by: To return to the Argument in Hand.

43. An Acre of Land, that bears here twenty Bushels of Wheat, and another in *America*, which, with the same Husbandry, would do the like, are, without doubt, of the same natural intrinsick Value: But yet the Benefit Mankind receives from the one in a Year, is worth £5 and from the other possibly not worth a Penny, if all the Profit an *Indian* received from it were to be valued, and sold here; at least, I may truly say, not one thousandth. 'Tis *Labour* then, which *puts the greatest part of Value upon Land*, without which it would scarcely be worth any thing: 'Tis to that we owe the greatest part of all its useful Products; for all that the Straw, Bran, Bread, of that Acre of Wheat, is more worth than the Product of an Acre of as good Land, which lies waste, is all the effect of Labour. For 'tis not barely the Plough-man's Pains, the Reaper's and Thresher's Toil, and the Baker's Sweat, [that] is to be counted into the *Bread* we Eat; the Labour of those who broke the Oxen, who digged and wrought the Iron and Stones, who felled and framed the Timber imployed about the Plough, Mill, Oven, or any other Utensils, which are a vast Number, requisite to this Corn, from its being Seed to be sown to its being made Bread, must all be

charged on the account of *Labour*, and received as an effect of that: Nature and the Earth furnished only the almost worthless Materials, as in themselves. 'Twould be a strange *Catalogue of things, that Industry provided and made use of, about every Loaf of Bread*, before it came to our Use, if we could trace them; Iron, Wood, Leather, Bark, Timber, Stone, Bricks, Coals, Lime, Cloth, Dying Drugs, Pitch, Tar, Masts, Ropes, and all the Materials made use of in the Ship, that brought any of the Commodities made use of by any of the Workmen, to any part of the Work, all which, 'twould be almost impossible, at least too long, to reckon up.*

44. From all which it is evident, that though the things of Nature are given in common, yet Man by being Master of himself, and *Proprietor of his own Person, and the Actions or Labour of it, had still in himself the great Foundation of Property*; and that, which made up the great part of what he applyed to the Support or Comfort of his Being, when Invention and Arts had improved the conveniencies of Life; was perfectly his own, and did not belong in common to others.

45. Thus *Labour*, in the beginning *gave a Right of Property*, wherever any one was pleased to imploy it, upon what was common, which remained a long while, the far greater part, and is yet more than Mankind makes use of. Men, at first, for the most part, contented themselves with what un-assisted Nature offered to their Necessities: And though afterwards, in some parts of the World, (where the Increase of People and Stock, with the *Use of Money*, had made Land scarce, and so of some Value) the several *Communities* settled the Bounds of their distinct Territories; and by Laws within themselves, regulated the Properties of the private Men of their Society; and so, *by Compact* and Agreement, *settled the Property* which Labour and Industry began; and the Leagues that have been made between several States and Kingdoms, either expressly or tacitly disowning all Claim and Right to the Land in the others Possession, have, by common Consent, given up their Pretences to their natural common Right, which originally they had to those Countries, and so have, by *positive Agreement, settled a Property* amongst themselves, in distinct Parts and Parcels of the Earth; yet there are still *great Tracts of Ground* to be found, which, (the Inhabitants thereof not having joyned with the rest of Mankind, in the consent of the Use of their common Money) *lie waste*, and are more, than the People, who dwell on it, do, or can make use of, and so still lie in common. Tho' this can scarce

happen amongst that part of Mankind, that have consented to the Use of Money.

46. The greatest part of *things really useful* to the life of Man, and such as the necessity of subsisting made the first Commoners of the World look after, as it doth the *Americans* now, *are* generally things of *short Duration*; such as, if they are not consumed by use, will decay and perish of themselves: Gold, Silver and Diamonds, are things, that Fancy or Agreement hath put the Value on, more than real Use, and the necessary support of Life. Now of those good things which Nature hath provided in common, every one had a Right (as hath been said) to as much as he could use, and *Property* in all that he could affect with his Labour; all that his *Industry* could extend to, to alter from the state Nature had put it in, was his. He that *gathered* a hundred Bushels of Acorns or Apples, had thereby a *Property* in them, they were his Goods as soon as gathered. He was only to look, that he used them before they spoiled, else he took more than his share, and robb'd others. And indeed it was a foolish thing, as well as dishonest, to hoard up more, than he could make use of. If he gave away a part to any body else, so that it perished not uselessly in his Possession, these he also made use of. And if he also bartered away Plumbs, that would have rotted in a Week, for Nuts that would last good for his eating a whole Year he did no injury; he wasted not the common Stock; destroyed no part of the portion of Goods that belonged to others, so long as nothing perished uselessly in his hands. Again, If he would give his Nuts for a piece of Metal, pleased with its Colour; or exchange his Sheep for Shells, or Wooll for a sparkling Peble or a Diamond, and keep those by him all his Life, he invaded not the Right of others, he might heap up as much of these durable things as he pleased; the *exceeding of the bounds of* his *just Property* not lying in the largeness of his Possession, but the perishing of any thing uselessly in it.

47. And thus *came in the use of Money*, some lasting thing that Men might keep without spoiling, and that by mutual Consent Men would take in exchange for the truly useful, but perishable supports of Life.

48. And as different degrees of Industry were apt to give Men Possessions in different Proportions, so this *Invention of Money* gave them the Opportunity to continue and enlarge them. For supposing an Island, separate from all possible Commerce with the rest of the World, wherein there were but an hundred Families, but there

were Sheep, Horses and Cows, with other useful Animals, wholsome Fruits, and Land enough for Corn for a hundred thousand Times as many, but nothing in the Island, either because of its Commonness, or perishableness, fit to supply the place of *Money*: What reason could any one have there to enlarge his Possessions beyond the use of his Family, and a plentiful supply to its *Consumption*, either in what their own Industry produced, or they could barter for like perishable, useful Commodities, with others? Where there is not something, both lasting and scarce, and so valuable, to be hoarded up, there Men will not be apt to enlarge their *Possessions of Land*, were it never so rich, never so free for them to take. For I ask, what would a Man value Ten thousand, or an Hundred thousand Acres of excellent *Land*, ready cultivated, and well stocked too with Cattle in the middle of the In-land Parts of *America*, where he had no hopes of Commerce with other parts of the World, to draw *Money* to him by the sale of the Product? It would not be worth the inclosing, and we should see him give up again to the wild Common of Nature, whatever was more than would supply the conveniencies of Life to be had there for him and his Family.

49. Thus in the Beginning all the World was *America*, and more so than that is now; for no such thing as *Money* was any where known. Find out something that hath the *Use and Value of Money* amongst his Neighbours, you shall see the same Man will begin presently to *enlarge* his Possessions.

50. But since Gold and Silver, being little useful to the Life of Man in proportion to Food, Rayment, and Carriage, has its *Value* only from the consent of Men, whereof *Labour* yet *makes*, in great part, *the Measure*, it is plain, that Men have agreed to a disproportionate and unequal *Possession of the Earth*, they having by a tacit and voluntary Consent, found out a Way how a Man may fairly possess more Land, than he himself can use the Product of, by receiving in Exchange for the overplus Gold and Silver, which may be hoarded up without Injury to any one; these Metals not spoiling or decaying in the hands of the Possessor. This Partage* of things in an inequality of private Possessions, Men have made practicable out of the bounds of Society, and without Compact only by putting a Value on Gold and Silver, and tacitly agreeing in the use of Money. For in Governments, the Laws regulate the right of Property, and the possession of Land is determined by positive Constitutions.*

51. And thus, I think, it is very easie to conceive without any Difficulty, *how Labour could at first begin a title of Property* in the common things of Nature, and how the spending it upon our uses bounded it. So that there could then be no reason of quarreling about Title, nor any doubt about the largeness of Possession it gave. Right and Conveniency went together; for as a Man had a Right to all he could imploy his Labour upon, so he had no Temptation to labour for more than he could make use of. This left no room for Controversie about the Title, nor for Incroachment on the right of others; what Portion a Man carved to himself, was easily seen; and it was useless as well as dishonest to carve himself too much, or take more than he needed.

CHAP. VI.
Of Paternal Power.

52.* It may perhaps be censured as an impertinent Criticism in a discourse of this Nature to find fault with Words and Names, that have obtained in the World: And yet possibly it may not be amiss to offer new ones, when the old are apt to lead Men into Mistakes as this of *paternal Power* probably has done, which seems so to place the power of Parents over their Children wholly in the *Father*, as if the *Mother* had no share in it, whereas, if we consult Reason or Revelation, we shall find, she hath an equal Title. This may give one reason to ask, whether this might not be more properly called *parental Power*. For whatever obligation Nature and the right of Generation lays on Children, it must certainly bind them equal to both the concurrent Causes of it.* And accordingly we see the positive Law of God every where joyns them together, without Distinction when it commands the Obedience of Children, *Honour thy Father and thy Mother*, Exod. 20. 12. *Whosoever curseth his Father or his Mother*, Lev. 20. 9. *Ye shall fear every Man his Mother and his Father*, Lev. 19. 3. *Children obey your Parents*, &c. Eph. 6. 1. is the stile of the Old and New Testament.

53. Had but this one thing been well consider'd, without looking any deeper into the Matter, it might perhaps have kept Men from running into those gross Mistakes, they have made, about this power of Parents; which however it might, without any great Harshness, bear the name of absolute Dominion, and regal Authority, when under the

Title of *paternal Power* it seem'd appropriated to the Father, would yet have sounded but odly, and in the very Name shewn the Absurdity, if this supposed absolute Power over Children had been called *Parental*; and thereby have discover'd, that it belong'd to the *Mother* too; for it will but very ill serve the turn of those Men, who contend so much for the absolute power and authority of the *Fatherhood*, as they call it, that the Mother should have any Share in it. And it would have but ill supported the *Monarchy* they contend for, when by the very Name it appeared, that that fundamental Authority, from whence they would derive their Government of a single Person only, was not plac'd in one, but two Persons jointly. But to let this of Names pass.

54. Though I have said above *Chap. 2. That all Men by Nature are equal*, I cannot be supposed to understand all sorts of *Equality*: *Age* or *Virtue* may give Men a just Precedency: *Excellency of Parts and Merit* may place others above the common Level: *Birth* may subject some, and *Alliance* or *Benefits* others to pay an Observance to those to whom Nature, Gratitude, or other Respects may have made it due; and yet all this consists with the *Equality*, which all Men are in, in respect of Jurisdiction or Dominion, one over another; which was the *Equality* I there spoke of, as proper to the Business in hand, being that *equal Right*, that every Man hath, *to his natural Freedom*, without being subjected to the Will or Authority of any other Man.

55. *Children*, I confess, are not born in this full state of *Equality*, though they are born to it. Their Parents have a sort of Rule and Jurisdiction over them, when they come into the World, and for some time after, but 'tis but a temporary one. The Bonds of this Subjection are like the swadling Cloths they are wrapt up in, and supported by in the weakness of their Infancy: Age and Reason as they grow up, loosen them, till at length they drop quite off, and leave a Man at his own free Disposal.

56. *Adam* was created a perfect Man, his Body and Mind in full possession of their Strength and Reason, and so was capable, from the first Instant of his Being to provide for his own Support and Preservation, and govern his Actions according to the Dictates of the Law of Reason which God had implanted in him. From him the World is peopled with his Descendants, who are all born Infants, weak and helpless, without Knowledge or Understanding: But to supply the defects of this imperfect State, till the improvement of Growth and Age hath removed them, *Adam* and *Eve*, and after them

all *Parents* were, by the Law of Nature, *under an Obligation to pre-serve, nourish, and educate the Children*, they had begotten; not as their own Workmanship, but the Workmanship of their own Maker, the Almighty, to whom they were to be accountable for them.

57. The Law, that was to govern *Adam*, was the same, that was to govern all his Posterity, the *Law of Reason*. But his Off-spring hav-ing another way of entrance into the World, different from him, by a natural Birth, that produced them ignorant and without the use of *Reason*, they were not presently* *under that Law*; for no body can be under a Law, which is not promulgated to him; and this Law being promulgated or made known by *Reason* only, he that is not come to the Use of his *Reason*, cannot be said to be *under this Law*; and *Adam's* Children, being not presently as soon as born *under this Law of Reason*, were not presently *free*. For *Law*, in its true Notion, *is* not so much the Limitation as *the direction of a free and intelligent Agent* to his proper Interest, and prescribes no farther than is for the general Good of those under that Law: Could they be happier without it, the *Law*, as an useless thing, would of itself vanish; and that ill deserves the Name of Confinement which hedges us in only from Bogs and Precipices. So that, however it may be mistaken, *the end of Law is* not to abolish or restrain, but *to preserve and enlarge Freedom*: For in all the states of created Beings capable of Laws, *where there is no Law, there is no Freedom*. For *Liberty* is to be free from Restraint and Violence from others; which cannot be, where there is no Law: But Freedom is not, as we are told, *A Liberty for every Man to do what he lists*: (For who could be Free, when every other Man's Humour might domineer over him?) But a *Liberty* to dispose, and order as he lists, his Person, Actions, Possessions, and his whole Property, within the Allowance of those Laws, under which he is, and therein not to be subject to the Arbitrary Will of another, but freely follow his own.

58. The *Power*, then, *that Parents have* over their Children, arises from that Duty which is incumbent on them, to take care of their Off-spring, during the imperfect state of Childhood. To inform the Mind, and govern the Actions of their yet ignorant Nonage,* till Reason shall take its Place, and ease them of that Trouble, is what the Children want,* and the Parents are bound to. For God having given Man an Understanding to direct his Actions, has allowed him a freedom of Will, and liberty of Acting, as properly belonging there-unto, within the bounds of that Law he is under. But whilst he is in

an Estate,* wherein he has not *Understanding* of his own to direct his *Will*, he is not to have any *Will* of his own to follow: He that *understands* for him, must *will* for him too; he must prescribe to his Will, and regulate his Actions; but when he comes to the Estate that made his *Father a Freeman*, the *Son is a Freeman* too.

59. This holds in all the Laws a Man is under, whether Natural or Civil. Is a Man under the Law of Nature? *What made him Free* of that Law? What gave him a free disposing of his Property, according to his own Will, within the compass of that Law? I answer; a State of Maturity wherein he might be suppos'd capable to know that Law, that so he might keep his Actions within the Bounds of it. When he has acquired that State, he is presumed to know how far that Law is to be his Guide, and how far he may make use of his *Freedom*, and so comes to have it; 'till then, some body else must guide him, who is presumed to know, how far the Law allows a Liberty. If such a State of Reason, such an Age of Discretion *made him Free*, the same shall make his Son Free too. Is a Man under the Law of *England*? *What made him Free* of that Law? That is, to have the Liberty to dispose of his Actions and Possessions according to his own Will, within the Permission of that Law? A Capacity of knowing that Law. Which is supposed by that Law, at the Age of one and twenty Years, and in some Cases sooner. If this *made* the Father *Free*, it shall *make* the Son *Free* too. Till then we see the Law allows the Son to have no Will, but he is to be guided by the Will of his Father or Guardian, who is to understand for him. And if the Father die, and fail to substitute a Deputy in his Trust; if he hath not provided a Tutor, to govern his Son, during his Minority, during his want of Understanding, the Law takes care to do it, some other must govern him, and be a Will to him, till he hath *attained to a State of Freedom*, and his Understanding be fit to take the Government of his Will. But after that, the Father and Son are equally *Free* as much as Tutor and Pupil after Nonage; equally Subjects of the same Law together, without any Dominion left in the Father over the Life, Liberty, or Estate of his Son, whether they be only in the State and under the Law of Nature, or under the positive Laws of an Establish'd Government.

60. But if, through defects that may happen out of the ordinary course of Nature, any one comes not to such a degree of Reason, wherein he might be supposed capable of knowing the Law, and so living within the Rules of it, he is *never capable of being a Free*

Man, he is never let loose to the disposure of his own Will (because
he knows no bounds to it, has not Understanding, its proper Guide)
but is continued under the Tuition and Government of others, all
the time his own Understanding is uncapable of that Charge. And so
Lunaticks and *Ideots* are never set free from the Government of their
Parents; *Children, who are not as yet come unto those Years whereat they
may have; and Innocents which are excluded by a natural defect from
ever having*; Thirdly, *Madmen, which for the present cannot possibly
have the use of right Reason to guide themselves, have for their Guide,
the Reason that guideth other Men which are Tutors over them, to seek
and procure their good for them*, says Hooker, Eccl. Pol. *lib.* 1. *Sect.* 7.
All which seems no more than that Duty, which God and Nature has
laid on Man, as well as other Creatures, to preserve their Off-spring,
till they can be able to shift for themselves, and will scarce amount to
an instance or proof of *Parents* Regal Authority.

61. Thus we are *born Free*, as we are born Rational; not that we
have actually the Exercise of either: Age that brings one, brings with
it the other too. And thus we see how *natural Freedom and Subjection
to Parents* may consist together, and are both founded on the same
Principle. A *Child* is *Free* by his Father's Title, by his Father's
Understanding, which is to govern him, till he hath it of his own. The
Freedom of a Man at years of Discretion, and the *Subjection* of a Child
to his *Parents*, whilst yet short of that Age, are so consistent, and so
distinguishable, that the most blinded Contenders for Monarchy, *by
Right of Fatherhood*, cannot miss this *Difference*; the most obstinate
cannot but allow their Consistency. For were their Doctrine all true,
were the right Heir of Adam now known, and by that Title settled
a Monarch in his Throne, invested with all the absolute unlimited
Power Sir *R. F.** talks of; if he should die as soon as his Heir were
Born, must not the *Child*, notwithstanding he were never so Free,
never so much Sovereign, be in Subjection to his Mother and Nurse,
to Tutors and Governors, till Age and Education brought him Reason
and Ability to govern himself, and others? The Necessities of his Life,
the Health of his Body, and the Information of his Mind would require
him to be directed by the Will of others and not his own; and yet will
any one think, that this Restraint and Subjection were inconsistent
with, or spoiled him of that Liberty or Sovereignty he had a Right
to, or gave away his Empire* to those who had the Government of his
Nonage? This Government over him only prepared him the better

and sooner for it. If any body should ask me, when my Son is *of Age to be Free*? I shall answer, Just when his Monarch is of Age to govern. *But at what time*, says the judicious *Hooker*, Eccl. Pol. l. 1. Sect. 6. *a Man may be said to have attain'd so far forth the use of Reason, as sufficeth to make him capable of those Laws whereby he is then bound to guide his Actions; this is a great deal more easie for sense to discern, than for any one by Skill and Learning to determine.*

62. Commonwealths themselves take notice of, and allow, that there is a *time when Men* are to *begin to act like free Men*, and therefore till that time require not Oaths of Fealty, or Allegiance, or other publick owning of, or Submission to the Government of their Countries.

63. The *Freedom* then of Man, and Liberty of acting according to his own Will, is *grounded on* his having *Reason*, which is able to instruct him in that Law he is to govern himself by, and make him know how far he is left to the Freedom of his own Will. To turn him loose to an unrestrain'd Liberty, before he has Reason to guide him, is not the allowing him the privilege of his Nature to be Free; but to thrust him out amongst Brutes, and abandon him to a State as wretched, and as much beneath that of a Man, as theirs. This is that which puts the *Authority* into the *Parents* hands to govern the *Minority* of their Children. God hath made it their business to imploy this Care on their Off-spring, and hath placed in them suitable Inclinations of Tenderness, and concern to temper this Power, to apply it, as his Wisdom designed it, to the Childrens good, as long as they should need to be under it.

64. But what reason can hence advance this care of the *Parents* due to their Off-spring into an *absolute Arbitrary Dominion* of the Father, whose Power reaches no farther, than by such a Discipline, as he finds most effectual, to give such Strength and Health to their Bodies, such vigour and rectitude to their Minds, as may best fit his Children to be most useful to themselves and others; and, if it be necessary to his Condition, to make them Work, when they are able, for their own Subsistence. But in this Power the *Mother* too has her share with the *Father*.

65. Nay this *Power* so little belongs to the *Father* by any peculiar right of Nature, but only as he is Guardian of his Children, that when he quits his care of them, he loses his Power over them, which goes along with their Nourishment and Education, to which it is inseparably annexed; and it belongs as much to the *Foster-Father* of an

exposed Child, as to the Natural Father of another. So little Power does the bare *act of begetting* give a Man over his Issue, if all his Care ends there, and this be all the Title he hath to the Name and Authority of a Father. And what will become of this *Paternal Power* in that part of the World, where one Woman hath more than one Husband at a Time? Or in those parts of *America*, where, when the Husband and Wife part, which happens frequently, the Children are all left to the Mother, follow her, and are wholly under her Care and Provision? If the Father die whilst the Children are young, do they not naturally every where owe the same Obedience to their *Mother*, during their Minority, as to their Father were he alive? And will any one say, that the Mother hath a Legislative Power over her Children? that she can make standing Rules, which shall be of perpetual Obligation, by which they ought to regulate all the concerns of their Property, and bound their Liberty all the course of their Lives? Or can she inforce the Observation of them with Capital Punishments? For this is the proper *Power of the Magistrate*, of which the Father hath not so much as the shadow. His Command over his Children is but Temporary, and reaches not their Life or Property: It is but a help to the weakness and imperfection of their Nonage, a Discipline necessary to their Education: And though a *Father* may dispose of his own Possessions as he pleases, when his Children are out of danger of perishing for Want, yet *his Power* extends not to the Lives or Goods, which either their own Industry, or anothers bounty has made theirs; nor to their Liberty neither, when they are once arrived to the infranchisement of the Years of Discretion. The *Father's Empire* then ceases, and he can from thence forwards no more dispose of the liberty of his Son, than that of any other Man: And it must be far from an absolute or perpetual Jurisdiction, from which a Man may withdraw himself, having Licence from Divine Authority to *leave Father and Mother and cleave to his Wife.**

66. But though there be a time when a *Child* comes to be as *Free* from Subjection to the Will and Command of his Father, as the Father himself is Free from Subjection to the Will of any body else, and they are each under no other restraint, but that which is common to them both, whether it be the Law of Nature, or municipal Law of their Country: Yet this Freedom exempts not a Son from that *Honour* which he ought, by the Law of God and Nature, *to* pay his *Parents*. God having made the Parents Instruments in his great design of

continuing the Race of Mankind, and the occasions of Life to their Children; as he hath laid on them an obligation to Nourish, preserve, and bring up their Off-spring; So he has laid on the Children a perpetual obligation of *honouring their Parents*, which containing in it an inward Esteem and Reverence to be shewn by all outward Expressions, ties up the Child from any thing, that may ever injure or affront, disturb, or endanger the Happiness or Life of those, from whom he received his; and engages him in all actions of Defence, Relief, Assistance and Comfort of those, by whose means he entred into being, and has been made capable of any Enjoyments of Life. From this Obligation no State, no Freedom can absolve Children. But this is very far from giving Parents a Power of Command over their Children, or an Authority to make Laws and dispose as they please, of their Lives or Liberties. 'Tis one thing to owe Honour, Respect, Gratitude and Assistance; another to require an absolute Obedience and Submission. The *Honour due to Parents*, a Monarch in his Throne owes his Mother, and yet this lessens not his Authority, nor subjects him to her Government.

67. The subjection of a Minor places in the Father a temporary Government, which terminates with the Minority of the Child: and the *Honour due from a Child*, places in the Parents a perpetual Right to Respect, Reverence, Support and Compliance too, more or less, as the Father's Care, Cost, and Kindness in his Education, has been more or less. This ends not with Minority; but holds in all Parts and Conditions of a Man's Life. The want of distinguishing these two Powers; *viz.* That which the Father hath in the Right of *Tuition*, during Minority; and the Right of *Honour* all his Life, may perhaps have caused a great part of the Mistakes about this Matter. For to speak properly of them, the first of these is rather the Privilege of Children, and Duty of Parents, than any Prerogative of paternal Power. The Nourishment and Education of their Children, is a Charge so incumbent on Parents for their Children's Good, that nothing can absolve them from taking Care of it. And tho' the *Power of commanding and chastising* them go along with it, yet God hath woven into the Principles of human Nature such a Tenderness for their Off-spring, that there is little Fear that Parents should use their Power with too much Rigour; the Excess is seldom on the severe side, the strong byass of Nature drawing the other way. And therefore God Almighty when he would express his gentle Dealing with the *Israelites*, he tells

them, that tho' he chasten'd them, *he chasten'd them as a Man chastens his Son*, Deut. viii. 5. *i.e.* with Tenderness and Affection, and kept them under no severer Discipline, than what was absolutely best for them, and had been less Kindness to have slacken'd. This is that Power to which *Children* are commanded *Obedience*, that the Pains and Care of their Parents may not be increased, or ill rewarded.

68. On the other side, *Honour* and *Support* all that which Gratitude requires to return for the Benefits received by and from them is the indispensible Duty of the Child, and the proper Privilege of the Parents. This is intended for the Parents Advantage, as the other is for the Child's; though Education, the Parents Duty, seems to have most Power, because the Ignorance and Infirmities of Childhood stand in need of Restraint and Correction; which is a visible Exercise of Rule, and a kind of Dominion. And that Duty which is comprehended in the Word *Honour*, requires less Obedience, though the Obligation be stronger on grown, than younger Children. For who can think the Command, *Children obey your Parents*,* requires in a Man, that has Children of his own, the same Submission to his Father, as it does in his yet young Children to him; and that by this Precept he were bound to obey all his Father's Commands, if, out of a Conceit of Authority, he should have the Indiscretion to treat him still as a Boy?

69. The first part then of *Paternal Power*, or rather Duty, which is *Education*, belongs so to the Father, that it terminates at a certain season; when the Business of Education is over it ceases of itself, and is also alienable before. For a Man may put the Tuition of his Son in other Hands; and he that has made his Son an *Apprentice* to another, has discharged him, during that time, of a great part of his Obedience both to himself and to his Mother. But all the *Duty of Honour*, the other part, remains never the less entire to them; nothing can cancel that: It is so inseparable from them both, that the Father's Authority cannot dispossess the Mother of this Right, nor can any Man discharge his Son from *honouring* her that bore him. But both these are very far from a Power to make Laws, and inforcing them with Penalties, that may reach Estate, Liberty, Limbs and Life. The Power of Commanding ends with Nonage; and though after that, *Honour* and Respect, Support and Defence, and whatsoever Gratitude can oblige a Man to, for the highest Benefits he is naturally capable of, be always due from a Son to his Parents; yet all this puts no Scepter into the Father's Hand, no sovereign Power of Commanding.

He has no Dominion over his Son's Property, or Actions; nor any Right, that his Will should prescribe to his Sons in all things; however it may become his Son in many things, not very inconvenient to him and his Family, to pay a Deference to it.

70. A Man may owe *Honour* and Respect to an ancient, or wise Man; Defence to his Child or Friend; Relief and Support to the Distressed; and Gratitude to a Benefactor, to such a degree, that all he has, all he can do, cannot sufficiently pay it: But all these give no Authority, no Right to any one, of making Laws over him from whom they are owing. And 'tis plain, all this is due not only to the bare Title of Father; not only because, as has been said, it is owing to the Mother too; but because these Obligations to Parents, and the Degrees of what is required of Children, may be varied by the different Care and Kindness, Trouble and Expence, which is often employed upon one Child more than another.

71. This shews the Reason how it comes to pass, that *Parents in Societies*, where they themselves are Subjects, retain a *Power over their Children*, and have as much Right to their Subjection, as those who are in the state of Nature. Which could not possibly be, if all Political Power were only Paternal, and that in truth they were one and the same thing: For then, all Paternal Power being in the Prince, the Subject could naturally have none of it. But these two *Powers*, *Political* and *Paternal*, are so perfectly distinct and separate; are built upon so different Foundations, and given to so different Ends, that every Subject that is a Father, has as much a Paternal Power over his Children, as the Prince has over his: And every Prince, that has Parents, owes them as much filial Duty and Obedience, as the meanest of his Subjects do to theirs; and can therefore contain not any part or Degree of that kind of Dominion, which a Prince or Magistrate has over his Subject.

72. Though the Obligation on the Parents to *bring up* their Children, and the Obligation on Children to *honour* their Parents, contain all the Power on the one Hand, and Submission on the other, which are proper to this Relation; yet there is *another Power* ordinarily *in the Father*, whereby he has a tie on the Obedience of his Children; which though it be common to him with other Men, yet the Occasions of shewing it, almost constantly happening to Fathers in their private Families, and the Instances of it elsewhere being rare, and less taken notice of, it passes in the World for a part of *Paternal Jurisdiction*. And this is the Power Men generally have to *bestow their*

Estates on those who please them best. The Possession of the Father being the Expectation and Inheritance of the Children, ordinarily in certain Proportions, according to the Law and Custom of each Country; yet it is commonly in the Father's Power to bestow it with a more sparing or liberal Hand, according as the Behaviour of this or that Child hath comported with his Will and Humour.

73. This is no small Tie on the Obedience of Children: And there being always annexed to the Enjoyment of Land, a Submission to the Government of the Country, of which that Land is a part; it has been commonly suppos'd, That a *Father* could *oblige his Posterity to that Government*, of which he himself was a Subject, and that his Compact held them; whereas, it being only a necessary Condition annexed to the Land, and the Inheritance of an Estate which is under that Government, reaches only those who will take it on that Condition, and so is no natural Tie or Engagement, but a voluntary Submission. For *every Man's Children* being by Nature as *free* as himself, or any of his Ancestors ever were, may, whilst they are in that Freedom, choose what Society they will join themselves to, what Common-wealth they will put themselves under. But if they will enjoy the *Inheritance* of their Ancestors, they must take it on the same Terms their Ancestors had it, and submit to all the Conditions annex'd to such a Possession. By this Power indeed Fathers oblige their Children to Obedience to themselves, even when they are past Minority, and most commonly too subject them to this or that Political Power. But neither of these by any peculiar Right of *Fatherhood*, but by the Reward they have in their Hands to inforce and recompence such a Compliance; and is no more Power than what a *French Man* has over an *English Man*, who by the Hopes of an Estate he will leave him, will certainly have a strong Tie on his Obedience: And if when it is left him, he will enjoy it, he must certainly take it upon the Conditions annex'd to the *Possession of Land* in that Country where it lies, whether it be *France* or *England*.

74. To conclude then, though the *Father's Power* of commanding extends no farther than the Minority of his Children, and to a Degree only fit for the Discipline and Government of that Age; and though that *Honour* and *Respect*, and all that which the *Latins* call *Piety*,* which they indispensibly owe to their Parents all their Life-time, and in all Estates, with all that Support and Defence [which] is due to them, gives the Father no Power of Governing, *i.e.* making Laws and enacting Penalties on his Children; though by all

this he has no Dominion over the Property or Actions of his Son: Yet 'tis obvious to conceive how easie it was, in the first Ages of the World, and in Places still, where the thinness of People gives Families leave to separate into unpossessed Quarters, and they have room to remove and plant themselves in yet vacant Habitations; for the *Father of the Family* to become the Prince of it;[1] he had been a Ruler from the beginning of the Infancy of his Children: and since without some Government it would be hard for them to live together, it was likeliest it should, by the express or tacit Consent of the Children when they were grown up, be in the Father, where it seemed without any Change barely to continue; when indeed nothing more was required to it, than the permitting the *Father* to exercise alone in his Family, that executive Power of the Law of Nature, which every free Man naturally hath, and by that Permission resigning up to him a Monarchical Power whilst they remained in it. But that this was not by any *paternal Right*, but only by the Consent of his Children, is evident from hence, That no Body doubts, but if a Stranger, whom Chance or Business had brought to his Family, had there kill'd any of his Children, or committed any other Fact,* he might condemn and put him to death, or otherwise have punish'd him, as well as any of his Children; which it was impossible he should do by virtue of any paternal Authority over one who was not his Child, but by vertue of that Executive Power of the Law of Nature, which, as a Man, he had a Right to: And he alone could punish him in his Family, where the Respect of his Children had laid by the Exercise of such a Power, to give way to the Dignity and Authority they were willing should remain in him, above the rest of his Family.

75. Thus 'twas easie, and almost natural for Children by a tacit, and scarce avoidable Consent, to make way for the *Father's Authority*

---

[1] *It is no improbable Opinion therefore, which the* Arch-Philosopher* *was of, That the chief Person in every Houshold was always, as it were, a King: So when Numbers of Housholds joyn'd themselves in civil Societies together, Kings were the first kind of Governours amongst them, which is also, as it seemeth, the reason why the Name of Fathers continued still in them, who, of Fathers, were made Rulers; as also the ancient Custom of Governours to do as* Melchizedec, *and being Kings, to exercise the Office of Priests, which Fathers did, at the first grew perhaps by the same Occasion. Howbeit, this is not the only kind of Regiment* *that has been received in the World. The Inconveniences of one kind have caused sundry others to be devised; so that in a word, all publick Regiment of what kind soever, seemeth evidently to have risen from the deliberate Advice, Consultation and Composition between Men, judging it convenient and behoveful; there being no Impossibility in Nature considered by itself, but that Man might have lived without any publick Regiment.* Hooker's Eccl. P. L. 1. Sect. 10.

and Government. They had been accustomed in their Childhood to follow his Direction, and to refer their little Differences to him; and when they were Men, who fitter to rule them? Their little Properties, and less Covetousness, seldom afforded greater Controversies; and when any should arise, where could they have a fitter Umpire than he, by whose Care they had every one been sustain'd and brought up, and who had a Tenderness for them all? 'Tis no wonder that they made no Distinction betwixt Minority and full Age; nor looked after one and twenty, or any other Age that might make them the free Disposers of themselves and Fortunes, when they could have no Desire to be out of their Pupillage: The Government they had been under, during it, continued still to be more their Protection than Restraint; And they could no where find a greater Security to their Peace, Liberties, and Fortunes, than in the *Rule of a Father*.

76. Thus the natural *Fathers of Families*, by an insensible Change, became the *politick Monarchs* of them too: And as they chanced to live long, and leave able and worthy Heirs, for several Successions, or otherwise; so they laid the Foundations of Hereditary, or Elective Kingdoms, under several Constitutions and Manners, according as Chance, Contrivance, or Occasions happen'd to mould them. But if Princes have their Titles in their Fathers Right, and it be a sufficient Proof of the natural *Right of Fathers* to political Authority, because they commonly were those in whose Hands we find, *de facto*, the Exercise of Government: I say, if this Argument be good, it will as strongly prove, that all Princes, nay Princes only, ought to be Priests, since 'tis as certain, that in the Beginning, *The Father of the Family was Priest, as that he was Ruler in his own Houshold.**

CHAP. VII.

Of Political or Civil Society.

77. God having made Man such a Creature, that, in his own Judgment, it was not good for him to be alone, put him under strong Obligations of Necessity, Convenience, and Inclination to drive him into *Society*, as well as fitted him with Understanding and Language to continue and enjoy it. The *first Society* was between Man and Wife, which gave beginning to that between Parents and Children; to which, in time, that between Master and Servant came to be added:

And though all these might, and commonly did meet together, and make up but one Family, wherein the Master or Mistress of it had some sort of Rule proper to a Family; each of these, or all together, came short of *political Society*, as we shall see, if we consider the different Ends, Ties, and Bounds of each of these.

78. *Conjugal Society* is made by a voluntary Compact between Man and Woman; and tho' it consist chiefly in such a Communion and Right in one anothers Bodies as is necessary to its chief End, Procreation; yet it draws with it mutual Support and Assistance, and a Communion of Interests too, as necessary not only to unite their Care and Affection, but also necessary to their common Off-spring, who have a Right to be nourished, and maintained by them, till they are able to provide for themselves.

79. For the end of *Conjunction, between Male and Female*, being not barely Procreation, but the Continuation of the Species; this Conjunction betwixt Male and Female ought to last, even after Procreation, so long as is necessary to the Nourishment and Support of the young Ones, who are to be sustained by those that got them, till they are able to shift and provide for themselves. This Rule, which the infinite wise Maker hath set to the Works of his Hands, we find the inferior Creatures steadily obey. In those viviparous Animals which feed on Grass, the *Conjunction between Male and Female* lasts no longer than the very Act of Copulation; because the Teat of the Dam being sufficient to nourish the Young, till it be able to feed on Grass, the Male only begets, but concerns not himself for the Female or Young, to whose Sustenance he can contribute nothing. But in Beasts of Prey the *Conjunction* lasts longer: because the Dam not being able well to subsist her self, and nourish her numerous Off-spring by her own Prey alone, a more laborious, as well as more dangerous way of living, than by feeding on Grass, the Assistance of the Male is necessary to the Maintenance of their common Family, which cannot subsist till they are able to prey for themselves, but by the joynt Care of Male and Female. The same is to be observed in all Birds (except some domestick Ones, where Plenty of Food excuses the Cock from feeding, and taking Care of the young Brood) whose Young needing Food in the Nest, the Cock and Hen continue Mates, till the Young are able to use their Wing, and provide for themselves.

80. And herein I think lies the chief, if not the only Reason, *why the Male and Female in Mankind are tyed to a longer Conjunction*

than other Creatures, *viz.* Because the Female is capable of conceiving, and *de facto* is commonly with Child again, and brings forth too a new Birth, long before the former is out of a Dependency for Support on his Parents Help, and able to shift for himself, and has all the Assistance [which] is due to him from his Parents; whereby the Father, who is bound to take Care for those he hath begot, is under an Obligation to continue in conjugal Society with the same Woman longer than other Creatures, whose Young being able to subsist of themselves, before the time of Procreation returns again, the conjugal Bond dissolves of it self, and they are at Liberty, till *Hymen** at his usual Anniversary Season summons them again to chuse new Mates. Wherein one cannot but admire the Wisdom of the great Creator, who having given to Man Foresight, and an Ability to lay up for the future, as well as to supply the present Necessity, hath made it necessary, that *Society of Man and Wife should be more lasting*, than of Male and Female amongst other Creatures; that so their Industry might be encouraged, and their Interest better united, to make Provision and lay up Goods for their common Issue, which uncertain Mixture, or easy and frequent Solutions* of conjugal Society would mightily disturb.

81. * But though these are Ties upon *Mankind*, which make the *Conjugal Bonds* more firm and lasting in Man, than the other Species of Animals; yet it would give one Reason to enquire, why this *Compact*, where Procreation and Education are secured, and Inheritance taken Care for, may not be made determinable, either by Consent, or at a certain time, or upon certain Conditions, as well as any other voluntary Compacts, there being no Necessity in the Nature of the thing, nor to the Ends of it, that it should always be for Life; I mean, to such as are under no Restraint of any positive Law, which ordains all such Contracts to be perpetual.

82. But the Husband and Wife, though they have but one common Concern, yet having different Understandings, will unavoidably sometimes have different Wills too; it therefore being necessary that the last Determination, *i.e.* the Rule, should be placed somewhere; it naturally falls to the Man's Share, as the abler and the stronger. But this reaching but to the things of their common Interest and Property, leaves the Wife in the full and free Possession of what by Contract is her peculiar Right, and gives the Husband no more Power over her Life than she has over his. The *Power of the Husband* being so

far from that of an absolute Monarch, that the *Wife* has in many Cases a Liberty to separate from him; where natural Right, or their Contract allows it, whether that Contract be made by themselves in the State of Nature, or by the Customs or Laws of the Country they live in; and the Children upon such Separation fall to the Father or Mother's Lot, as such Contract does determine.

83. For all the Ends of *Marriage* being to be obtained under politick Government, as well as in the State of Nature, the Civil Magistrate doth not abridge the Right or Power of either naturally necessary to those Ends, *viz.* Procreation and mutual Support and Assistance whilst they are together; but only decides any Controversy that may arise between Man and Wife about them. If it were otherwise, and that absolute *Sovereignty* and Power of Life and Death naturally belong'd to the Husband, and were *necessary to the Society between Man and Wife*, there could be no Matrimony in any of those Countries where the Husband is allow'd no such absolute Authority. But the Ends of Matrimony requiring no such Power in the Husband, the Condition of *Conjugal Society* put it not in him, it being not at all necessary to that State. *Conjugal Society* could subsist and obtain its Ends without it; nay, Community of Goods, and the Power over them, mutual Assistance and Maintenance, and other things belonging to *Conjugal Society*, might be varyd and regulated by that Contract which unites Man and Wife in that Society, as far as may consist with Procreation and the bringing up of Children till they could shift for themselves; nothing being necessary to any Society, that is not necessary to the Ends for which it is made.

84. The *Society betwixt Parents and Children*, and the distinct Rights and Powers belonging respectively to them, I have treated of so largely, in the foregoing Chapter, that I shall not here need to say any thing of it. And I think it is plain, that it is far different from a politick Society.

85. *Master* and *Servant* are Names as old as History, but given to those of far different Condition; for a Freeman makes himself a Servant to another, by selling him for a certain time, the Service he undertakes to do, in exchange for Wages he is to receive: And though this commonly puts him into the Family of his Master,* and under the ordinary Discipline thereof; yet it gives the Master but a temporary Power over him, and no greater, than what is contained in the *Contract* between 'em. But there is another sort of Servants, which

by a peculiar Name we call *Slaves*, who being Captives taken in a just War,* are by the Right of Nature subjected to the absolute Dominion and arbitrary Power of their Masters. These Men having, as I say, forfeited their Lives, and with it their Liberties, and lost their Estates; and being in the *State of Slavery*, not capable of any Property, cannot in that State be considered as any part of *Civil Society*; the chief End whereof is the Preservation of Property.

86. Let us therefore consider a *Master of a Family* with all these subordinate Relations of *Wife*, *Children*, *Servants*, and *Slaves*, united under the Domestick Rule of a Family; which, what Resemblance soever it may have in its Order, Offices, and Number too, with a little Commonwealth, yet is very far from it, both in its Constitution, Power and End: Or if it must be thought a Monarchy, and the *Paterfamilias* the absolute Monarch in it, absolute Monarchy will have but a very shattered and short Power, when 'tis plain, by what has been said before, That the *Master of the Family* has a very distinct and differently limited *Power*, both as to Time and Extent, over those several Persons that are in it; for excepting the Slave (and the Family is as much a Family, and his Power as *Paterfamilias* as great, whether there be any Slaves in his Family or no) he has no Legislative Power of Life and Death over any of them, and none too but what a *Mistress of a Family* may have as well as he. And he certainly can have no absolute Power over the whole *Family*, who has but a very limited one over every Individual in it. But how a *Family*, or any other Society of Men differ from that, which is properly *political Society*, we shall best see, by considering wherein *political Society* it self consists.

87. Man being born, as has been proved, with a Title to perfect Freedom, and an uncontrouled Enjoyment of all the Rights and Privileges of the Law of Nature, equally with any other Man, or Number of Men in the World, hath by Nature a Power, not only to preserve his Property, that is, his Life, Liberty and Estate, against the Injuries and Attempts of other Men; but to judge of, and punish the Breaches of that Law in others, as he is perswaded the Offence deserves, even with Death itself, in Crimes where the Heinousness of the Fact, in his Opinion, requires it. But because no *political Society* can be, nor subsist without having in itself the Power to preserve the Property, and in order thereunto, punish the Offences of all those of that Society; there, and there only is *political Society*, where every one of the Members hath quitted this natural Power, resign'd it

up into the Hands of the Community in all Cases that exclude him not from appealing for Protection to the Law established by it. And thus all private Judgment of every particular Member being excluded, the Community comes to be Umpire, by settled standing Rules, indifferent, and the same to all Parties; and by Men having Authority from the Community, for the Execution of those Rules, decides all the Differences that may happen between any Members of that Society concerning any Matter of Right; and punishes those Offences which any Member hath committed against the Society, with such Penalties as the Law has established; whereby it is easie to discern, who are, and who are not, in *political Society* together. Those who are united into one Body, and have a common establish'd Law and Judicature to appeal to, with Authority to decide Controversies between them, and punish Offenders, are in *Civil Society* one with another: But those who have no such common Appeal, I mean on Earth, are still in the state of Nature, each being, where there is no other, Judge for himself, and Executioner; which is, as I have before shew'd it, the perfect *state of Nature*.

88. And thus the Commonwealth comes by a Power to set down what Punishment shall belong to the several Transgressions which they think worthy of it, committed amongst the Members of that Society, (which is the *Power of making Laws*) as well as it has the Power to punish any Injury done unto any of its Members, by any one that is not of it, (which is the *power of War and Peace*;) and all this for the Preservation of the Property of all the Members of that Society, as far as is possible. But though every Man who has enter'd into civil Society, and is become a member of any Commonwealth has thereby quitted his Power to punish Offences, against the Law of *Nature*, in prosecution of his own private Judgment, yet with the Judgment of Offences, which he has given up to the Legislative in all Cases, where he can appeal to the Magistrate, he has given a Right to the Commonwealth to imploy his Force, for the execution of the Judgments of the Commonwealth, whenever he shall be called to it; which indeed are his own Judgments, they being made by himself, or his Representative. And herein we have the original of the *legislative* and *executive Power* of civil Society, which is to judge by standing Laws, how far Offences are to be punished, when committed within the Commonwealth; and also to determine, by occasional Judgments founded on the present Circumstances of the Fact, how far Injuries

from without are to be vindicated; and in both these to imploy all the force of all the Members, when there shall be need.

89. Wherever therefore any number of Men are so united into one Society, as to quit every one his executive power of the Law of Nature, and to resign it to the publick, there and there only is a *political, or civil Society*. And this is done, wherever any number of Men, in the state of Nature, enter into Society to make one People, one Body Politick, under one supream Government; or else when any one joyns himself to, and incorporates with any Government already made. For hereby he authorizes the Society, or which is all one, the Legislative thereof, to make Laws for him, as the publick good of the Society shall require; to the Execution whereof, his own Assistance (as to his own Decrees) is due. And this *puts Men* out of a state of Nature *into* that of a *Commonwealth*, by setting up a Judge on Earth, with Authority to determine all the Controversies, and redress the Injuries, that may happen to any Member of the Commonwealth; which Judge is the Legislative, or Magistrates appointed by it.* And wherever there are any number of Men, however associated, that have no such decisive Power to appeal to, there they are still in *the state of Nature*.

90. Hence it is evident, that *absolute Monarchy*, which by some Men* is counted the only Government in the World, is indeed *inconsistent with civil Society*, and so can be no form of Civil-Government at all. For the *end of civil Society*, being to avoid, and remedy those inconveniences of the state of Nature, which necessarily follow from every Man's being Judge in his own Case, by setting up a known Authority, to which every one of that Society may appeal upon any Injury received, or Controversie that may arise, and which every one of the Society ought to obey;[1] wherever any Persons are, who have not such an Authority to appeal to, for the decision of any Difference between them, there those Persons are still *in the state of Nature*. And so is every *absolute Prince* in respect of those who are under his *Dominion*.

91. For he being suppos'd to have all, both legislative and executive Power in himself alone, there is no Judge to be found, no appeal lies open to any one, who may fairly, and indifferently, and with

---

[1] *The publick Power of all Society is above every Soul contained in the same Society; and the principal Use of that power is, to give Laws unto all that are under it, which Laws in such Cases we must obey, unless there be reason shew'd which may necessarily inforce, that the Law of Reason, or of God, doth injoyn the contrary*, Hook. Eccl. Pol. L. 1. Sect. 16.

Authority decide, and from whose Decision Relief and Redress may be expected of any Injury or Inconveniency, that may be suffered from the Prince, or by his Order: So that such a Man, however intitled, *Czar*, or *Grand Signior*,* or how you please, is as much *in the state of Nature*, with all under his Dominion, as he is with the rest of Mankind. For wherever any two Men are, who have no standing Rule, and common Judge to appeal to on Earth, for the determination of Controversies of Right betwixt them, there they are still *in the state of Nature*,[1] and under all the inconveniences of it, with only this woful Difference to the Subject, or rather Slave of an absolute Prince: That whereas, in the ordinary state of Nature, he has a Liberty to judge of his Right, and according to the best of his Power, to maintain it; now whenever his Property is invaded by the will and order of his Monarch, he has not only no Appeal, as those in Society ought to have, but as if he were degraded from the common state of rational Creatures, is denied a Liberty to judge of, or to defend his Right; and so is exposed to all the Misery and Inconveniencies, that a Man can fear from one, who being in the unrestrained state of Nature, is yet corrupted with Flattery, and armed with Power.

92. For he that thinks *absolute Power purifies Mens Bloods*, and corrects the baseness of human Nature, need read but the History of this, or any other Age to be convinced of the contrary. He that would have been insolent and injurious in the Woods of *America*, would not probably be much better in a Throne; where perhaps Learning and Religion shall be found out to justifie all, that he shall do to his Subjects, and the Sword presently silence all those that dare question it. For what the *Protection of absolute Monarchy* is, what kind of Fathers of their Countries it makes Princes to be, and to what

---

[1] *To take away all such mutual Grievances, Injuries and Wrongs*, i.e. such as attend Men in the state of Nature, *There was no way but only by growing into Composition and Agreement amongst themselves, by ordaining some kind of Government publick, and by yielding themselves subject thereunto, that unto whom they granted Authority to rule and govern, by them the Peace, Tranquility and happy Estate of the rest might be procured. Men always knew that where Force and Injury was offered, they might be Defenders of themselves; they knew that however Men may seek their own Commodity;* yet if this were done with Injury unto others, it was not to be suffered, but by all Men, and all good Means to be withstood. Finally, they knew that no Man might in reason take upon him to determine his own Right, and according to his own Determination proceed in Maintenance thereof, in as much as every Man is towards himself, and them whom he greatly affects, partial; and therefore that Strifes and Troubles would be endless, except they gave their common Consent all to be ordered by some, whom they should agree upon, without which Consent there would be no reason that one Man should take upon him to be Lord or Judge over another.* Hooker's Eccl. Pol. L. 1. Sect. 10.

a degree of Happiness and Security it carries civil Society, where this sort of Government is grown to perfection, he that will look into the late Relation of *Ceylon*,* may easily see.

93. *In absolute Monarchies* indeed, as well as other Governments of the World, the Subjects have an Appeal to the Law, and Judges to decide any Controversies, and restrain any Violence that may happen betwixt the Subjects themselves, one amongst another. This every one thinks necessary, and believes he deserves to be thought a declared Enemy to Society and Mankind, who should go about to take it away. But whether this be from a true Love of Mankind and Society, and such a Charity as we owe all one to another, there is Reason to doubt. For this is no more, than what every Man, who loves his own Power, Profit, or Greatness, may and naturally must do, keep those Animals from hurting, or destroying one another, who labour and drudge only for his Pleasure and Advantage; and so are taken care of, not out of any Love the Master has for them, but Love of himself, and the Profit they bring him. For if it be asked, what Security, *what Fence* is there, in such a State, *against the Violence and Oppression of this absolute Ruler?* The very Question can scarce be born. They are ready to tell you, that it deserves Death only to ask after Safety. Betwixt Subject and Subject, they will grant, there must be Measures, Laws and Judges, for their mutual Peace and Security: But as for the *Ruler*, he ought to be *absolute*, and is above all such Circumstances; because he has Power to do more Hurt and Wrong, 'tis right when he does it. To ask how you may be guarded from Harm, or Injury, on that side where the strongest Hand is to do it, is presently the voice of Faction and Rebellion. As if when Men quitting the state of Nature entered into Society, they agreed that all of them but one, should be under the restraint of Laws, but that he should still retain all the Liberty of the state of Nature, increased with Power, and made licentious by Impunity. This is to think, that Men are so foolish, that they take care to avoid what Mischiefs may be done them by *Pole-Cats*, or *Foxes*; but are content, nay think it Safety, to be devoured by *Lions*.

94. But whatever Flatterers may talk to amuze* Peoples Understandings, it hinders not Men from feeling; and when they perceive, that any Man in what Station soever, is out of the Bounds of the civil Society which they are of, and that they have no Appeal on Earth against any Harm, they may receive from him, they are apt to think themselves in the state of Nature, in respect of him, whom

they find to be so; and to take Care as soon as they can, to have that *Safety and Security in civil Society*, for which it was first instituted, and for which only they entered into it. And therefore, though perhaps at first, (as shall be shewed more at large hereafter in the following part of this Discourse) some one good and excellent Man having got a Preheminency amongst the rest, had this Deference* paid to his Goodness and Vertue, as to a kind of natural Authority, that the chief Rule, with Arbitration of their Differences, by a tacit Consent devolved into his Hands, without any other Caution, but the Assurance they had of his Uprightness and Wisdom; yet when time, giving Authority, and (as some Men would perswade us) Sacredness to Customs, which the negligent, and unforeseeing Innocence of the first Ages began, had brought in Successors of another Stamp, the People finding their Properties not secure under the Government, as then it was, (whereas Government has no other end but the preservation of Property) could never be safe nor at rest, *nor think themselves in civil Society*, till the Legislature was placed in collective Bodies of Men, call them Senate, Parliament, or what you please.[1] By which Means every single Person became subject, equally with other the meanest Men, to those Laws, which he himself, as part of the Legislative, had established; nor could any one, by his own Authority avoid the force of the Law, when once made; nor by any pretence of Superiority plead Exemption, thereby to license his own, or the Miscarriages of any of his Dependents. *No Man in civil Society can be exempted from the Laws of it.*[2] For if any man may do, what he thinks fit, and there be no Appeal on Earth, for Redress or Security against any Harm he shall do: I ask, whether he be not perfectly still in the state of Nature, and so can be *no Part or Member of that civil Society*; unless any one will say, the state of Nature and civil Society are one and the same thing, which I have never yet found any one so great a patron of Anarchy as to affirm.

[1] *At the first, when some certain kind of Regiment was once appointed, it may be that nothing was then farther thought upon for the manner of governing, but all permitted unto their Wisdom and Discretion, which were to Rule, till by Experience they found this for all Parts very inconvenient, so as the thing which they had devised for a Remedy, did indeed but increase the Sore, which it should have cured. They saw, that to live by one Man's Will, became the cause of all Mens Misery. This constrained them to come unto Laws, wherein all Men might see their Duty beforehand, and know the Penalties of transgressing them.* Hooker's Eccl. Pol. L. 1. Sect. 10.

[2] *Civil Law being the Act of the whole Body politick, doth therefore over-rule each several part of the same Body.* Hooker ibid.

CHAP. VIII.

Of the Beginning of Political Societies.

95. Men being, as has been said, by Nature, all free, equal, and independent, no one can be put out of this Estate, and subjected to the political Power of another, without his own Consent. The only Way whereby any one devests himself of his natural Liberty, and puts on the *Bonds of civil Society* is by agreeing with other Men to joyn and unite into a Community, for their comfortable, safe, and peaceable Living one amongst another, in a secure Enjoyment of their Propertics, and a greater Security against any, that are not of it. This any number of Men may do, because it injures not the Freedom of the rest; they are left as they were in the Liberty of the state of Nature. When any number of Men have so *consented to make one Community or Government*, they are thereby presently incorporated, and make *one Body politick*, wherein the *Majority* have a Right to act and conclude the rest.

96. For when any number of Men have, by the consent of every individual, made a *Community*, they have thereby made that *Community* one Body, with a Power to act as one Body, which is only by the Will and Determination of the *Majority*. For that which acts any Community, being only the consent of the individuals of it, and it being necessary to that which is one Body to move one way; it is necessary the Body should move that way whither the greater force carries it, which is the *consent of the Majority*: Or else it is impossible it should act or continue one Body, *one Community*, which the consent of every individual that united into it, agreed that it should; and so every one is bound by that consent to be concluded by the *Majority*. And therefore we see, that in Assemblies, impowered to act by positive Laws, where no number is set by that positive Law which impowers them, the *Act of the Majority* passes for the Act of the whole, and of course determines, as having by the Law of Nature and Reason, the Power of the whole.

97. And thus every Man, by consenting with others to make one Body Politick under one Government, puts himself under an Obligation, to every one of that Society, to submit to the determination of the *Majority*, and to be concluded by it; or else this *original Compact*, whereby he with others incorporates into *one Society*, would signifie nothing, and be no Compact, if he be left Free, and under no other Ties, than he was in before in the State of Nature. For what

appearance would there be of any Compact? What new Engagement if he were no farther tied by any decrees of the Society, than he himself thought fit, and did actually consent to? This would be still as great a Liberty, as he himself had before his Compact, or any one else in the State of Nature hath, who may submit himself, and consent to any acts of it if he thinks fit.

98. For if *the consent of the Majority* shall not, in Reason, be received, as *the act of the whole*, and conclude every individual; nothing but the consent of every individual can make any thing to be the act of the whole: But such a consent is next impossible ever to be had, if we consider the Infirmities of Health, and Avocations of Business, which in a Number, though much less than that of a Commonwealth, will necessarily keep many away from the publick Assembly. To which if we add the variety of Opinions, and contrariety of Interests, which unavoidably happen in all Collections of Men, the coming into Society upon such terms would be only like *Cato's* coming into the Theatre, only to go out again.* Such a Constitution, as this, would make the mighty *Leviathan** of a shorter Duration, than the feeblest Creatures; and not let it outlast the day it was born in: Which cannot be suppos'd, till we can think, that Rational Creatures should desire and constitute Societies only to be dissolved. For where the *majority* cannot conclude the rest, there they cannot act as one Body, and consequently will be immediately dissolved again.

99. Whosoever therefore out of a state of Nature unite into a *Community*, must be understood to give up all the Power, necessary to the ends for which they unite into Society, to the *majority* of the Community, unless they expressly agreed in any number greater than the Majority.* And this is done by barely agreeing to *unite into one Political Society*, which is *all the Compact* that is, or needs be, between the Individuals, that enter into, or make up a *Commonwealth*. And thus that, which begins and actually *constitutes any Political Society*, is nothing but the consent of any number of Freemen capable of a majority to unite and incorporate into such a Society. And this is that, and that only, which did, or could give beginning to any *lawful Government* in the World.

100. To this I find two Objections made.

First, *That there are no Instances to be found in Story,* of a Company of Men Independent, and equal one amongst another, that met together, and in this way began and set up a Government.*

Secondly, '*Tis impossible of Right, that Men should do so, because all Men being born under Government, they are to submit to that, and are not at liberty to begin a new one.*

101. To the first there is this to answer, That it is not at all to be wonder'd, that *History* gives us but a very little account of *Men, that lived together in the State of Nature.* The Inconveniences of that Condition, and the Love, and want of Society no sooner brought any number of them together, but they presently united, and incorporated, if they designed to continue together. And if we may not suppose *Men* ever to have been *in the State of Nature,* because we hear not much of them in such a State, we may as well suppose the Armies of *Salmanasser,* or *Xerxes** were never Children, because we hear little of them, till they were Men, and imbodied in Armies. Government is every where antecedent to Records, and Letters* seldom come in amongst a People, till a long continuation of Civil Society has, by other more necessary Arts, provided for their Safety, Ease, and Plenty. And then they begin to look after the History of their Founders, and search into their *Original,* when they have outlived the memory of it. For 'tis with *Commonwealths* as with particular Persons, they are commonly *ignorant of their own Births and Infancies:* And if they know any thing of their *Original,* they are beholding, for it, to the accidental Records, that others have kept of it. And those that we have, of the beginning of any Polities in the World, excepting that of the *Jews,* where God himself immediately interpos'd, and which favours not at all paternal Dominion, are all either plain instances of such a beginning, as I have mentioned, or at least have manifest footsteps of it.

102. He must shew a strange inclination to deny evident matter of Fact, when it agrees not with his Hypothesis, who will not allow, that the *beginning of Rome* and *Venice* were by the uniting together of several Men free and independent one of another, amongst whom there was no natural Superiority or Subjection.* And if *Josephus Acosta's* word may be taken, he tells us, that in many parts of *America* there was no Government at all. *There are great and apparent Conjectures,* says he, *that these Men,* speaking of those of Peru, *for a long time had neither Kings nor Commonwealths, but lived in Troops, as they do this day in* Florida, *the* Cheriquanas, *those of* Brasil, *and many other Nations, which have no certain Kings, but as occasion is offered in Peace or War, they choose their Captains as they please,* l. 1. c. 25.* If it be said, that

every Man there was born subject to his Father, or the head of his Family. That the subjection due from a Child to a Father, took not away his Freedom of uniting into what Political Society he thought fit, has been already proved. But be that as it will, these Men, 'tis evident, were actually *Free*; and whatever Superiority some Politicians* now would place in any of them, they themselves claimed it not: but by consent were all *equal*, till by the same consent they set Rulers over themselves. So that their *Politick Societies* all *began* from a voluntary Union, and the mutual agreement of Men freely acting in the choice of their Governors, and forms of Government.

103. And I hope those who went away from *Sparta* with *Palantus*, mentioned by *Justin** l. 3. c. 4. will be allowed to have been *Freemen Independent* one of another, and to have set up a Government over themselves, by their own Consent. Thus I have given several Examples out of History, of *People Free and in the State of Nature*, that being met together incorporated and *began a Common-wealth*. And if the want of such instances be an Argument to prove that *Government* were not, nor could not be so *begun*, I suppose the Contenders for Paternal Empire were better [to] let it alone, than urge it against natural Liberty. For if they can give so many instances, out of History, of *Governments begun* upon paternal Right, I think (though at best an Argument from what has been, to what should of right be, has no great force) one might, without any great danger, yield them the cause. But if I might advise them in the Case, they would do well not to search too much into the *Original of Governments*, as they have begun *de facto*, lest they should find at the foundation of most of them, something very little favourable to the design they promote, and such a Power as they contend for.

104. But to conclude, Reason being plain on our side, that Men are naturally Free, and the Examples of History shewing, that the *Governments* of the World, that were begun in Peace, had their beginning laid on that Foundation, and were *made by the Consent of the People*; There can be little room for doubt, either where the Right is, or what has been the Opinion, or Practice of Mankind, about the *first erecting of Governments*.

105. I will not deny, that if we look back as far as History will direct us, towards the *Original of Commonwealths*, we shall generally find them under the Government and Administration of one Man. And I am also apt to believe, that where a Family was numerous

enough to subsist by itself, and continued entire together, without mixing with others, as it often happens, where there is much Land, and few People, the Government commonly began in the Father. For the Father having, by the Law of Nature, the same Power with every Man else to punish, as he thought fit, any Offences against that Law, might thereby punish his transgressing Children, even when they were Men, and out of their Pupilage; and they were very likely to submit to his Punishment, and all joyn with him against the Offender, in their turns, giving him thereby Power to Execute his Sentence against any transgression, and so in effect make him the Law-Maker, and Governor over all, that remained in Conjunction with his Family. He was fittest to be trusted; Paternal affection secured their Property, and Interest under his Care; and the Custom of obeying him, in their Childhood, made it easier to submit to him, rather than to any other. If therefore they must have one to rule them, as Government is hardly to be avoided amongst Men that live together; who [was] so likely to be the Man, as he that was their common Father; unless Negligence, Cruelty, or any other defect of Mind, or Body made him unfit for it? But when either the Father died, and left his next Heir, for want of Age, Wisdom, Courage, or any other Qualities, less fit for Rule; or where several Families met, and consented to continue together; There 'tis not to be doubted, but they used their natural Freedom, to set up him, whom they judged the ablest, and most likely, to Rule well over them. Conformable hereunto we find the People of *America*, who (living out of the reach of the Conquering Swords, and spreading domination of the two great Empires of *Peru* and *Mexico*)* enjoy'd their own natural Freedom, though, *ceteris paribus*,* they commonly prefer the Heir of their deceased King; yet if they find him any way weak, or uncapable, they pass him by, and set up the stoutest, and bravest Man for their Ruler.

106. Thus, though looking back as far as Records give us any account of peopling the World, and the History of Nations, we commonly find the *Government* to be in one Hand; yet it destroys not that which I affirm, *viz.* That the *Beginning of politick Society* depends upon the Consent of the Individuals, to joyn into, and make one Society; who, when they are thus incorporated, might set up what Form of Government they thought fit. But this having given Occasion to Men to mistake, and think, that by Nature Government was monarchical, and belong'd to the Father, it may not be amiss here

to consider, why People in the beginning generally pitch'd upon this Form, which though perhaps the Father's Preheminency might in the first Institution of some Commonwealths, give a rise to, and place in the beginning, the Power in one Hand; yet it is plain that the Reason, that continued the Form of *Government in a single Person*, was not any Regard, or Respect to paternal Authority; since all petty *Monarchies*, that is, almost all Monarchies, near their Original, have been commonly, at least upon occasion, *Elective*.

107. First then, in the beginning of things, the Father's Government of the Childhood of those sprung from him, having accustomed them to the *Rule of one Man*, and taught them that where it was exercised with Care and Skill, with Affection and Love to those under it, it was sufficient to procure and preserve to Men all the political Happiness they sought for in Society. It was no wonder that they should pitch upon, and naturally run into that Form of Government, which from their Infancy they had been all accustomed to; and which, by Experience, they had found both easie and safe. To which, if we add, that *Monarchy* being simple, and most obvious to Men, whom neither Experience had instructed in Forms of Government, nor the Ambition or Insolence of Empire had taught to beware of the Encroachments of Prerogative, or the Inconveniencies of absolute Power, which Monarchy in Succession was apt to lay claim to, and bring upon them; it was not at all strange, that they should not much trouble themselves, to think of Methods of restraining any Exorbitances of those to whom they had given the Authority over them, and of balancing the Power of Government, by placing several parts of it in different Hands. They had neither felt the Oppression of tyrannical Dominion, nor did the fashion of the Age, nor their Possessions, or way of living, (which afforded little Matter for Covetousness or Ambition) give them any Reason to apprehend or provide against it; and therefore 'tis no wonder they put themselves into such a *Frame of Government*, as was not only, as I said, most obvious and simple, but also best suited to their present State and Condition; which stood more in need of Defence against foreign Invasions and Injuries, than of Multiplicity of Laws. The Equality of a simple poor way of living, confining their Desires within the narrow Bounds of each Man's small Property, made few Controversies, and so no need of many Laws to decide them, or Variety of Officers to superintend the Process, or look after the Execution of Justice,*

where there were but few Trespasses, and few Offenders. Since then those, who liked one another so well as to joyn into Society, cannot but be supposed to have some Acquaintance and Friendship together, and some Trust one in another; they could not but have greater Apprehensions of others, than of one another: And therefore their first Care and Thought cannot but be supposed to be, how to secure themselves against foreign Force. 'Twas natural for them to put themselves under a *Frame of Government*, which might best scrve to that End; and chuse the wisest and bravest Man to conduct them in their Wars, and lead them out against their Enemies, and in this chiefly be their *Ruler*.

108. Thus we see, that the *Kings* of the *Indians* in *America*, which is still a Pattern of the first Ages in *Asia* and *Europe*, whilst the Inhabitants were too few for the Country, and want of People and Money gave Men no Temptation to enlarge their Possessions of Land, or contest for wider Extent of Ground, are little more than *Generals of their Armies*; and though they command absolutely in War, yet at home and in time of Peace they exercise very little Dominion, and have but a very moderate Sovereignty, the Resolutions of Peace and War being ordinarily either in the People, or in a Council. Though the War itself, which admits not of Plurality of Governours, naturally devolves the Command into the *King's sole Authority*.

109. And thus in *Israel* it self, *the chief Business of their Judges, and first Kings* seems to have been *to be Captains in War*, and Leaders of their Armies; which, (besides what is signifyed by *going out and in before the People,** which was, to march forth to War, and home again in* the Heads of their Forces) appears plainly in the Story of *Jephtha*. The *Ammonites* making War upon *Israel*, the *Gileadites* in fear send to *Jephtha*, a Bastard of their Family whom they had cast off, and article* with him, if he will assist them against the *Ammonites*, to make him their Ruler; which they do in these Words, *And the People made him Head and Captain over them*, Judg. xi. 11. which was, as it seems, all one as to be *Judge. And he judged Israel*, Judg. xii. 7. that is, was their *Captain-General six Years*. So when *Jotham* upbraids the *Shechemites* with the Obligation they had to *Gideon*, who had been their *Judge* and Ruler, he tells them, *He fought for you, and adventured his Life far, and delivered you out of the Hands of Midian*, Judg. ix. 17. Nothing mentioned of him, but what he did as a *General*: and indeed that is all is found in his History, or in any of the rest of the Judges.

And *Abimelech* particularly is called *King*, tho' at most he was but their *General*. And when, being weary of the ill Conduct of *Samuel's* Sons, the Children of *Israel* desired a *King, like all the Nations to judge them, and to go out before them, and to fight their Battels,* 1 Sam. viii. 20. God granting their Desire, says to *Samuel, I will send thee a Man, and thou shalt anoint him to be Captain over my People Israel, that he may save my People out of the Hands of the Philistines,* c. ix. v. 16. As if the only *Business of a King* had been to lead out their Armies, and fight in their Defence; and accordingly at his Inauguration pouring a Vial of Oyl upon him, declares to *Saul,* that *the Lord had anointed him to be Captain over his Inheritance,* c. x. v. 1. And therefore those, who after *Saul's* being solemnly chosen and saluted *King* by the *Tribes* at *Mispah,* were unwilling to have him their King, make no other Objection but this, *How shall this Man save us?* v. 27. as if they should have said, This Man is unfit to be our *King,* not having Skill and Conduct enough in War, to be able to defend us. And when God resolved to transfer the Government to *David,* it is in these Words, *But now thy Kingdom shall not continue: The Lord hath sought him a Man after his own Heart, and the Lord hath commanded him to be Captain over his People,* c. xiii. v. 14. As if the whole *Kingly Authority* were nothing else but to be their *General*: And therefore the *Tribes* who had stuck to *Saul's* Family, and opposed *David's* Reign, when they came to *Hebron* with Terms of Submission to him, they tell him, amongst other arguments they had to submit to him as to their King, That he was in effect their *King* in *Saul's* time, and therefore they had no reason but to receive him as their *King* now. *Also* (say they) *in time past, when Saul was King over us, thou wast he that leddest out and broughtest in Israel, and the Lord said unto thee, thou shalt feed my People Israel, and thou shalt be a Captain over Israel.**

110. Thus, whether a *Family* by degrees *grew up into a Commonwealth*, and the fatherly Authority being continued on to the elder Son, every one in his turn growing up under it, tacitly submitted to it, and the Easiness and Equality of it not offending any one, every one acquiesced, till time seemed to have confirmed it, and settled a right of Succession by Prescription; or whether several Families, or the Descendants of several Families, whom Chance, Neighbourhood, or Business brought together, uniting into Society, the need of a General, whose Conduct might defend them against their Enemies in War, and the great Confidence the Innocence and

Sincerity of that poor but vertuous Age, (such as are almost all those which begin Governments, that ever come to last in the World) gave Men one of another, made the first Beginners of Commonwealths generally put the Rule into one Man's Hand, without any other express Limitation or Restraint, but what the Nature of the thing, and the End of Government required: Which ever of those it was that at first put the Rule into the Hand of a single Person, certain it is that no body was ever intrusted with it but for the publick Good and Safety, and to those Ends in the Infancies of Commonwealths commonly used it. And unless those who had it had done so, young Societies could not have subsisted; without such nursing Fathers tender and careful of the Publick Weale, all Governments would have sunk under the Weakness and Infirmities of their Infancy, and the Prince and the People had soon perished together.

111. But though the *Golden Age* (before vain Ambition, and *amor sceleratus habendi*,* evil Concupiscence had corrupted Mens Minds into a Mistake of true Power and Honour) had more Virtue, and consequently better Governours, as well as less vicious Subjects; and there was then *no stretching Prerogative* on the one side, to oppress the People; *nor* consequently on the other, any *Dispute about Privilege*, to lessen or restrain the Power of the Magistrate; and so no Contest betwixt Rulers and People about Governours or Government:[1] Yet, when Ambition and Luxury in future Ages would retain and increase the Power, without doing the Business for which it was given; and aided by Flattery, taught Princes to have distinct and separate Interests from their People, Men found it necessary to examine more carefully *the Original* and Rights of *Government*; and to find out ways to *restrain the Exorbitances*, and *prevent the Abuses* of that Power, which they having intrusted in another's Hands only for their own Good they found was made use of to hurt them.

112. Thus we may see how probable it is, that People that were naturally free, and by their own Consent either submitted to the Government of their Father, or united together out of different Families to make a Government, should generally put the *Rule into one Man's Hands*, and chuse to be under the Conduct of a *single Person*, without so much as by express Conditions limiting or regulating his Power, which they thought safe enough in his Honesty

---

[1] . . .* Hooker's Eccl. Pol. L. 1. Sect. 10.

and Prudence. Though they never dream'd of Monarchy being *Jure Divino*,* which we never heard of among Mankind, till it was revealed to us by the Divinity of this last Age;* nor ever allowed paternal Power to have a Right to Dominion, or to be the Foundation of all Government. And thus much may suffice to shew, that as far as we have any Light from History, we have reason to conclude, that all peaceful beginnings of *Government* have been *laid in the Consent of the People.* I say *peaceful*, because I shall have occasion in another Place to speak of Conquest, which some esteem a way of beginning of Governments.

The other Objection I find urged against the beginning of Polities, in the way I have mentioned, is this, viz.

113. *That all Men being born under Government, some or other, it is impossible any of them should ever be free, and at liberty to unite together, and begin a new one, or ever be able to erect a lawful Government.*

If this Argument be good; I ask, how came so many lawful Monarchies into the World? For if any body, upon this Supposition, can shew me any one Man in any Age of the World free to begin a lawful Monarchy; I will be bound to shew him ten other *free Men* at liberty, at the same time to unite and begin a new Government under a regal, or any other Form. It being Demonstration,* that if any one, *born under the Dominion* of another, may be so *free* as to have a Right to command others in a new and distinct Empire; every one that is *born under the Dominion* of an other may be so free too, and may become a Ruler, or Subject, of a distinct separate Government. And so by this their own Principle, either all Men, however *born*, are *free*, or else there is but one lawful Prince, one lawful Government in the World. And then they have nothing to do but barely to shew us, which that is. Which when they have done, I doubt not but all Mankind will easily agree to pay Obedience to him.

114. Though it be a sufficient Answer to their Objection to shew, that it involves them in the same Difficulties that it doth those, they use it against; yet I shall endeavour to discover the weakness of this Argument a little farther.

All Men, say they, *are born under Government, and therefore they cannot be at Liberty to begin a new one. Every one is born a Subject to his Father, or his Prince, and is therefore under the perpetual tie of Subjection and Allegiance.* 'Tis plain Mankind never owned* nor considered any such natural *Subjection that they were born in*, to one or to the other that tied them, without their own Consents, to a Subjection to them and their Heirs.

115. For there are no Examples so frequent in History, both sacred and prophane, as those of Men withdrawing themselves, and their Obedience, from the Jurisdiction they were born under, and the Family or Community they were bred up in, and *setting up new Governments* in other Places; from whence sprang all that number of petty Commonwealths in the Beginning of Ages, and which always multiplied, as long as there was room enough, till the stronger, or more fortunate, swallowed the weaker; and those great ones again breaking to Pieces, dissolved into lesser Dominions. All which are so many Testimonies against paternal Sovereignty, and plainly prove, That it was not the natural right of the *Father* descending to his Heirs, that made Governments in the Beginning, since it was impossible, upon that Ground, there should have been so many little Kingdoms; all must have been but only one universal Monarchy, if Men had not been at *Liberty to separate* themselves from their Families, and the Government, be it what it will, that was set up in it, and go and make distinct Commonwealths and other Governments, as they thought fit.

116. This has been the practice of the World from its first beginning to this day; Nor is it now any more Hindrance to the freedom of Mankind, that they are *born under constituted and ancient Polities*, that have established Laws, and set Forms of Government, than if they were born in the Woods, amongst the unconfined Inhabitants, that ran loose in them. For those, who would persuade us, that *by being born under any Government, we are naturally Subjects to it*, and have no more any Title or Pretence to the freedom of the state of Nature, have no other reason (bating* that of paternal Power, which we have already answer'd) to produce for it, but only, because our Fathers or Progenitors passed away their natural Liberty, and thereby bound up themselves and their Posterity to a perpetual Subjection to the Government, which they themselves submitted to. 'Tis true, that whatever Engagements or Promises any one has made for himself, he is under the Obligation of them, but *cannot* by any *Compact* whatsoever, *bind his Children or Posterity*. For his Son, when a Man, being altogether as free as the Father, any *Act of the Father can no more give away the liberty of the Son*, than it can of any Body else: He may indeed annex such Conditions to the Land, he enjoyed as a Subject of any Commonwealth, as may oblige his Son to be of that Community,

if he will enjoy those Possessions which were his Father's; because that Estate being his Father's Property, he may dispose, or settle it, as he pleases.

117. And this has generally given the occasion to mistake in this Matter; because Commonwealths not permitting any part of their Dominions to be dismembred, nor to be enjoyed by any but those of their Community, the Son cannot ordinarily enjoy the Possession of his Father, but under the same Terms his Father did; by becoming a member of the Society; whereby he puts himself presently under the Government, he finds there established, as much as any other Subject of that Commonwealth. And thus *the Consent of Freemen, born under Government*, which only *makes them Members of it*, being given separately in their Turns, as each comes to be of Age, and not in a Multitude together; People take no Notice of it, and thinking it not done at all, or not necessary, conclude they are naturally Subjects as they are Men.

118. But, 'tis plain, *Governments* themselves understand it otherwise; they claim *no Power over the Son, because of that they had over the Father*; nor look on Children as being their Subjects, by their Fathers being so. If a Subject of *England* have a Child, by an *English* Woman in *France*, whose Subject is he? Not the King of *England's*; for he must have leave to be admitted to the Privileges of it. Nor the King of *France's*: For how then has his Father a Liberty to bring him away, and breed him as he pleases? And whoever was judged as a *Traytor* or *Deserter*, if he left, or warr'd against a Country, for being barely born in it of Parents that were Aliens there? 'Tis plain then, by the practice of Governments themselves, as well as by the Law of right Reason, that *a Child is born a Subject of no Country or Government*. He is under his Father's Tuition and Authority, till he comes to Age of Discretion; and then he is a Freeman, at Liberty what Government he will put himself under; what Body politick he will unite himself to. For if an *Englishman's* Son, born in *France*, be at Liberty, and may do so, 'tis evident there is no Tye upon him by his Father's being a Subject of this Kingdom; nor is he bound up, by any Compact of his Ancestors. And why then hath not his Son, by the same Reason, the same Liberty, though he be born any where else? Since the Power that a Father hath naturally over his Children, is the same, wherever they be born; and the Tyes of natural Obligations, are not bounded by the positive limits of Kingdoms and Commonwealths.

119. *Every Man* being, as has been shewed, *naturally free*, and nothing being able to put him into Subjection to any earthly Power, but only his own *Consent*, it is to be consider'd, what shall be understood to be a *sufficient Declaration* of a Man's *Consent*, *to make him subject* to the Laws of any Government. There is a common distinction of an express and a tacit Consent,* which will concern our present Case. No Body doubts but an express *Consent*, of any Man, entering into any Society, makes him a perfect member of that Society, a Subject of that Government. The Difficulty is, what ought to be look'd upon as a *tacit Consent*, and how far it binds, *i.e.* how far any one shall be looked on to have consented, and thereby submitted to any Government, where he has made no Expressions of it at all. And to this I say, that every Man, that hath any Possessions, or Enjoyment, of any part of the Dominions of any Government, doth thereby give his *tacit Consent*, and is as far forth obliged to Obedience to the Laws of that Government, during such Enjoyment, as any one under it; whether this his Possession be of Land, to him and his Heirs for ever, or a Lodging only for a Week; or whether it be barely travelling freely on the Highway; and in Effect, it reaches as far as the very being of any one within the Territories of that Government.

120. To understand this the better, it is fit to consider, that every Man, when he, at first, incorporates himself into any Commonwealth, he, by his uniting himself thereunto, annexed also, and submits to the Community those Possessions, which he has, or shall acquire, that do not already belong to any other Government. For it would be a direct Contradiction, for any one, to enter into Society with others for the securing and regulating of Property: And yet to suppose his Land, whose Property is to be regulated by the Laws of the Society, should be exempt from the Jurisdiction of that Government, to which he himself, the Proprietor of the Land, is a Subject. By the same Act therefore, whereby any one unites his Person, which was before free, to any Commonwealth; by the same he unites his Possessions, which were before free, to it also; and they become, both of them, Person and Possession, subject to the Government and Dominion of that Commonwealth, as long as it hath a Being. Whoever therefore, from thenceforth, by Inheritance, Purchase, Permission, or otherways, *enjoys any part of the Land*, so annext to, and under the Government *of that Commonwealth, must take it with the Condition* it is under; that

is, *of submitting to the Government of the Commonwealth*, under whose Jurisdiction it is, as far forth as any Subject of it.

121. But since the Government has a direct Jurisdiction only over the Land, and reaches the Possessor of it, (before he has actually incorporated himself in the Society) only as he dwells upon, and enjoys that: The Obligation any one is under, by Virtue of such Enjoyment, to *submit to the Government, begins and ends with the Enjoyment*; so that whenever the Owner, who has given nothing but such a *tacit Consent* to the Government, will, by Donation, Sale, or otherwise, quit the said Possession, he is at Liberty to go and incorporate himself into any other Commonwealth; or to agree with others to begin a new one, *in vacuis locis*,* in any part of the World, they can find free and unpossessed: Whereas he, that has once, by actual Agreement, and any *express* Declaration, given his *Consent* to be of any Commonweal, is perpetually and indispensably obliged to be, and remain unalterably a Subject to it, and can never be again in the Liberty of the state of Nature; unless, by any Calamity, the Government, he was under, comes to be dissolved; or else by some publick Act cuts him off from being any longer a Member of it.

122. But submitting to the Laws of any Country, living quietly, and enjoying Privileges and Protection under them, *makes not a Man a Member of that Society*: This is only a local Protection and Homage due to, and from all those, who, not being in a state of War, come within the Territories belonging to any Government, to all Parts whereof the force of its Law extends. But this no more *makes a Man a Member of that Society*, a perpetual Subject of that Commonwealth, than it would make a Man a Subject to another, in whose Family he found it convenient to abide for some time; though, whilst he continued in it, he were obliged to comply with the Laws, and submit to the Government, he found there. And thus we see, that *Foreigners*, by living all their Lives under another Government, and enjoying the Privileges and Protection of it, though they are bound, even in Conscience, to submit to its Administration, as far forth as any Denison; yet do not thereby come to be *Subjects or Members of that Commonwealth*. Nothing can make any Man so, but his actually entering into it by positive Engagement, and express Promise and Compact. This is that, which I think, concerning the beginning of political Societies, and that *Consent which makes any one a Member* of any Commonwealth.

CHAP. IX.

Of the Ends of Political Society and Government.

123. If Man in the state of Nature be so free, as has been said; if he be absolute Lord of his own Person and Possessions, equal to the greatest and subject to no Body, why will he part with his Freedom? Why will he give up this Empire, and subject himself to the Dominion and Controul of any other Power? To which 'tis obvious to answer, that though in the state of Nature he hath such a Right, yet the Enjoyment of it is very uncertain, and constantly exposed to the Invasion of others. For all being Kings as much as he, every Man his Equal and the greater Part no strict Observers of Equity and Justice, the enjoyment of the Property he has in this State, is very unsafe, very unsecure. This makes him willing to quit this Condition, which however free, is full of Fears and continual Dangers: And 'tis not without Reason, that he seeks out, and is willing to joyn in Society with others, who are already united, or have a Mind to unite, for the mutual *Preservation* of their Lives, Liberties and Estates,* which I call by the general Name, *Property*.

124. The great and *chief End* therefore, of Mens uniting into Commonwealths, and putting themselves under Government, *is the Preservation of their Property*. To which in the state of Nature there are many things wanting.

First, There wants an *establish'd*, settled, known *Law*, received and allowed by common Consent to be the Standard of right and wrong, and the common Measure to decide all Controversies between them. For though the Law of Nature be plain and intelligible to all rational Creatures; yet Men being biassed by their Interest, as well as ignorant for want of Study of it, are not apt to allow of it as a Law binding to them in the application of it to their particular Cases.

125. *Secondly*, In the state of Nature there wants *a known and indifferent Judge*, with Authority to determine all Differences according to the established Law. For every one in that State being both Judge and Executioner of the Law of Nature, Men being partial to themselves, Passion and Revenge is very apt to carry them too far, and with too much Heat, in their own Cases; as well as Negligence, and unconcernedness, to make them too remiss in other Mens.

126. *Thirdly*, In the state of Nature there often wants *Power* to back and support the Sentence when right, and to *give* it due *Execution*.

They who by any Injustice offended, will seldom fail, where they are able, by Force to make good their Injustice; such Resistance many times makes the Punishment dangerous, and frequently destructive, to those who attempt it.

127. Thus Mankind, notwithstanding all the Privileges of the state of Nature, being but in an ill Condition, while they remain in it, are quickly driven into Society. Hence it comes to pass, that we seldom find any number of Men live any time together in this State. The Inconveniences that they are therein exposed to, by the irregular, and uncertain exercise of the Power every Man has of punishing the transgressions of others, make them take Sanctuary under the establish'd Laws of Government, and therein seek *the preservation of their Property*. 'Tis this makes them so willingly give up every one his single Power of punishing, to be exercised by such alone, as shall be appointed to it, amongst them; and by such Rules as the Community, or those authorized by them to that purpose, shall agree on. And in this we have the original *right and rise of both the Legislative and Executive Power*, as well as of the Governments, and Societies themselves.

128. For in the State of Nature, to omit the liberty he has of innocent Delights, a Man has two Powers.

The first is to do whatsoever he thinks fit for the preservation of himself, and others within the permission of the *Law of Nature*, by which Law common to them all, he and all the rest of *Mankind are one Community*, make up one Society, distinct from all other Creatures. And were it not for the Corruption and Vitiousness of degenerate Men, there would be no need of any other; no Necessity that Men should separate from this great and natural Community, and by positive agreements combine into smaller and divided Associations.

The other Power a Man has in the state of Nature, is the *power to punish the Crimes* committed against that Law. Both these he gives up, when he joyns in a private, if I may so call it, or particular Political Society, and incorporates into any Commonwealth, separate from the rest of Mankind.

129. The first *Power, viz. of doing whatsoever he thought fit for the preservation of himself*, and the rest of Mankind, *he gives up* to be regulated by Laws made by the Society, so far forth as the preservation of himself, and the rest of that Society shall require; which Laws of the Society in many things confine the liberty he had by the Law of Nature.

130. *Secondly*, The *Power of punishing he wholly gives up*, and engages his natural Force, (which he might before imploy in the Execution of the Law of Nature, by his own single Authority, as he thought fit) to assist the Executive Power of the Society, as the Law thereof shall require. For being now in a new State, wherein he is to enjoy many Conveniencies, from the Labour, Assistance, and Society of others in the same Community, as well as Protection from its whole Strength; he is to part also with as much of his natural Liberty, in providing for himself, as the Good, Prosperity, and Safety of the Society shall require; which is not only necessary, but just; since the other Members of the Society do the like.

131. But though Men when they enter into Society, give up the Equality, Liberty, and Executive Power they had in the State of Nature, into the hands of the Society, to be so far disposed of by the Legislative, as the good of the Society shall require; yet it being only with an intention in every one the better to preserve himself his Liberty and Property; (For no rational Creature can be supposed to change his condition with an intention to be worse) the Power of the Society, or *Legislative* constituted by them, can *never be suppos'd to extend farther than the common good*; but is obliged to secure every ones Property, by providing against those three defects above-mentioned, that made the State of Nature so unsafe and uneasie. And so whoever has the Legislative or supream Power of any Commonwealth, is bound to govern by establish'd *standing Laws*, promulgated and known to the People, and not by Extemporary Decrees, by *indifferent* and upright *Judges*, who are to decide Controversies by those Laws; And to imploy the force of the Community at home, *only in the Execution of such Laws*, or abroad to prevent or redress Foreign Injuries, and secure the Community from Inroads and Invasion. And all this to be directed to no other *End*, but the *Peace*, *Safety*, and *publick good* of the People.

CHAP. X.
Of the Forms of a Commonwealth.

132. The Majority having, as has been shew'd, upon Mens first uniting into Society, the whole Power of the Community, naturally in them, may imploy all that Power in making Laws for the Community from time to time, and executing those Laws by Officers of their

own appointing; and then the *Form* of the Government is a perfect *Democracy*: Or else may put the Power of making Laws into the hands of a few select Men, and their Heirs or Successors; and then it is an *Oligarchy*: Or else into the hands of one Man, and then it is a *Monarchy*: If to him and his Heirs, it is a *Hereditary Monarchy*: If to him only for Life, but upon his Death the Power only of nominating a Successor to return to them; an *Elective Monarchy*. And so accordingly of these the Community may make compounded and mixed Forms of Government,* as they think good. And if the Legislative Power be at first given by the Majority to one or more Persons only for their Lives, or any limited time, and then the supream Power to revert to them again; when it is so reverted, the Community may dispose of it again anew into what hands they please, and so constitute a new Form of Government. For the *Form of Government depending upon the placing* the supream Power, which is *the Legislative*, it being impossible to conceive that an inferior Power should prescribe to a superior, or any but the supream make Laws, according as the Power of making Laws is placed, such is the *Form of the Common-wealth*.

133. By *Commonwealth*, I must be understood all along to mean, not a Democracy, or any Form of Government, but *any Independent Community* which the *Latines* signified by the word *Civitas*, to which the word which best answers in our Language, is *Commonwealth*, and most properly expresses such a Society of Men, which Community or City in *English* does not, for there may be subordinate Communities in a Government; and City amongst us has a quite different Notion from Commonwealth; And therefore to avoid Ambiguity, I crave leave to use the word *Commonwealth* in that Sense, in which I find it used by King *James the first*,* and I take it to be its genuine signification; which if any Body dislike, I consent with him to change it for a better.

CHAP. XI.
Of the Extent of the Legislative Power.

134. The great end of Mens entring into Society, being the Enjoyment of their Properties in Peace and Safety, and the great instrument and means of that being the Laws establish'd in that Society; the *first and fundamental positive Law** of all Commonwealths, *is the establishing of the Legislative* Power; as the *first and fundamental*

natural Law, which is to govern even the Legislative it self, *is the preservation of the Society*, and (as far as will consist with the publick good) of every person in it. This *Legislative* is not only *the supream Power* of the Commonwealth, but sacred and unalterable in the hands where the Community have once placed it; nor can any Edict of any Body else, in which form soever conceived, or by what Power soever backed, have the force and obligation of a *Law*, which has not its *Sanction from* that *Legislative*, which the publick has chosen and appointed. For without this the Law could not have that, which is absolutely necessary to its being a *Law, the consent of the Society*, over whom no Body can have a Power to make Laws, but by their own Consent,[1] and by Authority received from them; and therefore all the *Obedience*, which by the most solemn Ties any one can be obliged *to* Pay, ultimately terminates in this *Supream Power*, and is directed by those Laws which it enacts: Nor can any Oaths to any foreign Power whatsoever, or any Domestick Subordinate Power, discharge any Member of the Society from his *Obedience to the Legislative*, acting pursuant to their Trust; nor oblige him to any Obedience contrary to the Laws so enacted, or farther than they do allow; it being ridiculous to imagine one can be tied ultimately to *obey* any *Power* in the Society, which is not the *Supream*.

135. Though the *Legislative*, whether placed in one or more, whether it be always in being, or only by intervals, tho' it be the *supream* Power in every Commonwealth; yet,

First, It is *not*, nor can possibly be absolutely *Arbitrary* over the Lives and Fortunes of the People. For it being but the joint Power of every Member of the Society given up to that Person, or Assembly, which is Legislator; it can be no more than those Persons had in a state of Nature before they enter'd into Society, and gave up to the

---

[1] *The lawful Power of making Laws to Command whole Politick Societies of Men, belonging so properly unto the same intire Societies, that for any Prince or Potentate of what kind soever upon Earth, to exercise the same of himself, and not by express Commission immediately and personally received from God, or else by authority derived at the first from their Consent, upon whose persons they impose Laws, it is no better than mere Tyranny. Laws they are not therefore which publick approbation hath not made so.* Hooker's Eccl Pol. L. 1. Sect. 10. *Of this point therefore we are to Note, that sith Men naturally have no full and perfect Power to Command whole Politick Multitudes of Men, therefore utterly without our Consent, we could in such sort be at no Man's Commandment living. And to be commanded we do consent when that Society, whereof we be a part, hath at any time before consented, without revoking the same after by the like universal agreement. Laws therefore human, of what kind so ever, are available by consent.* Ibid.

Community. For no Body can transfer to another more Power, than he has in himself; and no Body has an absolute Arbitrary Power over himself, or over any other, to destroy his own Life, or take away the Life or Property of another. A Man, as has been proved, cannot subject himself to the Arbitrary Power of another; and having in the State of Nature no Arbitrary Power over the Life, Liberty, or Possession of another, but only so much as the Law of Nature gave him for the preservation of himself, and the rest of Mankind; this is all he doth, or can give up to the Commonwealth, and by it to the *Legislative Power*, so that the Legislative can have no more than this. Their Power in the utmost bounds of it, is *limited to the publick good* of the Society. It is a Power, that hath no other end but Preservation, and therefore can never have a right to destroy, enslave, or designedly to impoverish the Subjects.[1] The Obligations of the Law of Nature, cease not in Society, but only in many Cases are drawn closer, and have by human Laws known Penalties annexed to them, to inforce their Observation. Thus the Law of Nature stands as an Eternal Rule to all Men, *Legislators* as well as others. The *Rules* that they make for other Men's Actions, must, as well as their own, and other Men's Actions, be conformable to the Law of Nature, *i.e.* to the Will of God, of which that is a Declaration, and the *fundamental Law of Nature being the preservation of Mankind*, no Human Sanction can be good, or valid against it.

136. *Secondly*, The *Legislative*, or supream Authority, cannot assume to its self a Power to Rule by Extemporary Arbitrary Decrees,[2] but *is bound to dispense Justice*, and decide the Rights of the

---

[1] *Two Foundations there are which bear up publick Societies, the one a natural inclination, whereby all Men desire sociable Life and Fellowship; the other an Order, expressly or secretly agreed upon, touching the manner of their union in living together; the latter is that which we call the Law of a Commonweal, the very Soul of a Politick Body, the parts whereof are by Law animated, held together, and set on work in such Actions as the common good requireth. Laws Politick, ordain'd for external order and regiment amongst Men, are never framed as they should be, unless presuming the will of Man to be inwardly Obstinate, Rebellious, and Averse from all Obedience to the sacred Laws of his Nature; in a word, unless presuming Man to be in regard of his depraved Mind, little better than a wild Beast, they do accordingly provide notwithstanding, so to frame his outward Actions, that they be no hindrance unto the common good, for which Societies are instituted. Unless they do this they are not perfect.* Hooker's Eccl. Pol. L. 1. Sect. 10.

[2] *Human Laws are measures in respect of Men whose Actions they must direct, howbeit such measures they are as have also their higher Rules to be measured by, which Rules are two, the Law of God, and the Law of Nature; so that Laws Human must be made according to the general Laws of Nature, and without contradiction to any positive Law of Scripture, otherwise they are ill made.* Ibid. L. 3. Sect. 9. *To constrain Men to any thing inconvenient doth seem unreasonable.* Ibid. L. 1. Sect. 10.

Subject *by promulgated standing Laws, and known Authoris'd Judges.* For the Law of Nature being unwritten, and so no where to be found but in the minds of Men, they who through Passion or Interest shall miscite, or misapply it, cannot so easily be convinced of their mistake where there is no establish'd Judge: And so it serves not, as it ought[,] to determine the Rights, and fence the Properties of those that live under it, especially where every one is Judge, Interpreter, and Executioner of it too, and that in his own Case: And he that has right on his side, having ordinarily but his own single Strength, hath not force enough to defend himself from Injuries, or to punish Delinquents. To avoid these Inconveniencies, which disorder Mens Properties in the state of Nature, Men unite into Societies, that they may have the united strength of the whole Society to secure and defend their Properties, and may have *standing Rules* to bound it, by which every one may know, what is his. To this end it is that Men give up all their natural Power to the Society, which they enter into, and the Community put the Legislative Power into such hands as they think fit, with this Trust, that they shall be govern'd by *declared Laws*, or else their Peace, Quiet, and Property will still be at the same uncertainty, as it was in the state of Nature.

137. Absolute Arbitrary Power, or governing without *settled standing Laws*, can neither of them consist with the ends of Society and Government, which Men would not quit the freedom of the state of Nature for, and tie themselves up under, were it not to preserve their Lives, Liberties and Fortunes; and by *stated Rules* of Right and Property to secure their Peace and Quiet. It cannot be suppos'd that they should intend, had they a Power so to do, to give to any one, or more, an *absolute Arbitrary Power* over their Persons and Estates, and put a force into the Magistrates hand to execute his unlimited Will arbitrarily upon them. This were to put themselves into a worse condition than the state of Nature, wherein they had a Liberty to defend their Right against the Injuries of others, and were upon equal terms of force to maintain it, whether invaded by a single Man, or many in Combination.* Whereas by supposing they have given up themselves to the *absolute Arbitrary Power* and Will of a Legislator, they have disarmed themselves, and armed him, to make a prey of them when he pleases. He being in a much worse condition, who is exposed to the Arbitrary Power of one Man, who has the Command of 100000, than he that is expos'd to the Arbitrary Power of 100000 single

Men; no Body being secure, that his Will, who has such a Command, is better, than that of other Men, though his force be 100000 times stronger. And therefore whatever form the Commonwealth is under, the ruling Power ought to govern by *declared* and *received Laws*, and not by extemporary Dictates and undetermin'd Resolutions. For then Mankind will be in a far worse condition, than in the state of Nature, if they shall have armed one, or a few Men with the joint Power of a Multitude, to force them to obey at pleasure the exorbitant and unlimited decrees of their sudden Thoughts, or unrestrain'd, and till that moment unknown Wills, without having any measures set down which may guide and justify their Actions. For all the Power the Government has, being only for the good of the Society, as it ought not to be *Arbitrary* and at Pleasure, so it ought to be exercised by *established and promulgated Laws*; that both the People may know their Duty, and be safe and secure within the limits of the Law; and the Rulers too kept within their due Bounds, and not to be tempted, by the Power they have in their hands, to imploy it to such Purposes, and by such Measures, as they would not have known, and own not willingly.

138. *Thirdly*, The *supream Power cannot take* from any Man any part of his *Property* without his own Consent.* For the preservation of Property being the end of Government, and that for which Men enter into Society, it necessarily supposes and requires, that the People should *have Property*, without which they must be suppos'd to lose that, by entering into Society, which was the end for which they entered into it, too gross an absurdity for any Man to own. *Men* therefore *in Society having Property*, they have such a right to the Goods, which by the Law of the Community are theirs, that no Body hath a right to take their Substance or any part of it from them, without their own Consent; without this they have no *Property* at all. For I have truly no *Property* in that, which another can by right take from me, when he pleases, against my Consent. Hence it is a mistake to think, that the *Supream or Legislative Power* of any Commonwealth, can do what it will, and dispose of the Estates of the Subject *Arbitrarily*, or take any part of them at Pleasure. This is not much to be fear'd in Governments where the *Legislative* consists, wholly or in part, in Assemblies which are variable, whose Members upon the dissolution of the Assembly, are Subjects under the common Laws of their Country, equally with the rest. But in Governments, where the

Legislative is in one lasting Assembly always in Being, or in one Man, as in absolute Monarchies, there is danger still, that they will think themselves to have a distinct interest, from the rest of the Community; and so will be apt to increase their own Riches and Power, by taking what they think fit from the People. For a Man's *Property* is not at all secure, though there be good and equitable Laws to set the bounds of it, between him and his fellow Subjects, if he who Commands those Subjects, have Power to take from any private Man, what part he pleases of his *Property*, and use and dispose of it as he thinks good.

139. But *Government* into whatsoever hands it is put, being as I have before shew'd, intrusted with this Condition, and *for this End*, that Men might have and secure their *Properties*, the Prince, or Senate, however it may have Power to make Laws, for the regulating of *Property*, between the Subjects one amongst another, yet can never have a Power to take to themselves the whole, or any part of the Subjects *Property*, without their own Consent. For this would be in effect to leave them no *Property* at all. And to let us see, that even *absolute Power*, where it is necessary, is *not Arbitrary* by being absolute, but is still limited by that Reason, and confined to those Ends, which required it in some Cases to be absolute, we need look no farther than the common practice of Martial Discipline. For the preservation of the Army, and in it of the whole Commonwealth, requires an *absolute Obedience* to the Command of every superior Officer, and it is justly Death to disobey or dispute the most dangerous or unreasonable of them; but yet we see, that neither the Serjeant, that could Command a Soldier to march up to the mouth of a Cannon, or stand in a Breach, where he is almost sure to perish, can command that Soldier to give him one Penny of his Money; nor the *General*, that can condemn him to Death for deserting his Post, or for not obeying the most desperate Orders, can yet with all his *absolute Power* of Life and Death, dispose of one Farthing of that Soldier's Estate, or seize one jot of his Goods; whom yet he can command any Thing, and hang for the least Disobedience. Because such a blind Obedience is necessary to that end, for which the Commander has his Power, *viz.* the preservation of the rest; but the disposing of his Goods has nothing to do with it.

140. 'Tis true, Governments cannot be supported without great Charge, and 'tis fit every one who enjoys his share of the Protection, should pay out of his Estate his proportion for the maintenance of

it. But still it must be with his own Consent, *i.e.* the Consent of the Majority, giving it either by themselves, or their Representatives chosen by them. For if any one shall claim a *Power to lay* and levy *Taxes* on the People, by his own Authority, and without such consent of the People, he thereby invades the *Fundamental Law of Property*, and subverts the end of Government. For what Property have I in that, which another may by right take, when he pleases to himself?

141. *Fourthly*, The *Legislative cannot transfer the Power of making Laws* to any other hands. For it being but a delegated Power from the People, they who have it, cannot pass it over to others. The People alone can appoint the Form of the Commonwealth, which is by Constituting the Legislative, and appointing in whose hands that shall be. And when the People have said, we will submit to Rules, and be govern'd by *Laws* made by such Men, and in such Forms, no Body else can say other Men shall make *Laws* for them; nor can the People be bound by any *Laws*, but such as are Enacted by those whom they have Chosen, and Authorized to make *Laws* for them. The Power of the *Legislative* being derived from the People by a positive voluntary Grant and Institution, can be no other, than what that positive Grant conveyed, which being only to make *Laws*, and not to make *Legislators*, the *Legislative* can have no Power to transfer their Authority of making Laws, and place it in other hands.*

142. These are the *Bounds* which the trust, that is put in them by the Society, and the Law of God and Nature, have *set to the Legislative* Power of every Commonwealth, in all Forms of Government.

First, They are to govern by *promulgated establish'd Laws*, not to be varied in particular Cases, but to have one Rule for Rich and Poor, for the Favourite at Court, and the Country Man at Plough.

Secondly, These *Laws* also ought to be designed *for* no other end ultimately, but *the good of the People*.

Thirdly, They must *not raise Taxes* on the *Property of the People*, *without the Consent of the People*, given by themselves, or their Deputies. And this properly concerns only such Governments where the *Legislative* is always in Being, or at least where the People have not reserv'd any part of the *Legislative* to Deputies, to be from time to time chosen by themselves.

Fourthly, The *Legislative* neither must *nor can transfer the Power of making Laws* to any Body else, or place it any where, but where the People have.

CHAP. XII.

Of the Legislative, Executive, and Federative Power of the Commonwealth.

143.* The *Legislative* Power is that, which has a right *to direct how the Force of the Commonwealth* shall be imploy'd for preserving the Community and the Members of it. But because those Laws which are constantly to be Executed, and whose force is always to continue, may be made in a little time; therefore there is no need, that the *Legislative* should be always in Being, not having always business to do. And because it may be too great a temptation to human frailty apt to grasp at Power, for the same Persons, who have the Power of making Laws, to have also in their hands the Power to execute them, whereby they may exempt themselves from Obedience to the Laws they make, and suit the Law, both in its making, and execution, to their own private advantage, and thereby come to have a distinct interest from the rest of the Community, contrary to the end of Society and Government: Therefore in well order'd Commonwealths, where the good of the whole is so considered, as it ought, the *Legislative* Power is put into the hands of divers Persons, who duly Assembled, have by themselves, or jointly with others, a Power to make Laws, which when they have done, being separated again, they are themselves subject to the Laws, they have made; which is a new and near tie upon them, to take Care, that they make them for the publick good.

144. But because the Laws, that are at once, and in a short time made, have a constant and lasting Force, and need a *perpetual Execution*, or an attendance thereunto: Therefore 'tis necessary there should be a *Power always in Being*, which should see to the *Execution* of the Laws that are made, and remain in Force. And thus the *Legislative* and *Executive Power* come often to be separated.

145. There is another *Power* in every Commonwealth, which one may call *natural*, because it is that which answers to the Power every Man naturally had before he entered into Society. For though in a Commonwealth the Members of it are distinct Persons still in reference to one another, and as such are governed by the Laws of the Society; yet in reference to the rest of Mankind, they make one Body, which is, as every Member of it before was, still in the state of Nature with the rest of Mankind. Hence it is, that the Controversies that

happen between any Man of the Society with those that are out of it, are managed by the Publick; and an injury done to a Member of their Body, engages the whole in the reparation of it. So that under this Consideration, the whole Community is one Body in the state of Nature, in respect of all other States or Persons out of its Community.

146. This therefore contains the Power of War and Peace, Leagues and Alliances, and all the Transactions, with all Persons and Communities without the Commonwealth, and may be called *Federative*, if any one pleases. So the thing be understood, I am indifferent as to the Name.

147. These two Powers, *Executive* and *Federative*, though they be really distinct in themselves, yet one comprehending the *Execution* of the Municipal Laws of the Society *within* its self, upon all that are parts of it; the other the management of the *security and interest of the publick without*, with all those that it may receive benefit or damage from, yet they are always almost united. And though this *Federative Power* in the well or ill management of it be of great moment to the Commonwealth, yet it is much less capable to be directed by antecedent, standing, positive Laws, than the *Executive*; and so must necessarily be left to the Prudence and Wisdom of those, whose hands it is in, to be managed for the publick good. For the *Laws* that concern Subjects one amongst another, being to direct their Actions, may well enough *precede* them. But what is to be done in reference to *Foreigners*, depending much upon their Actions, and the variation of designs and interests, must be *left* in great part to the *Prudence* of those, who have this Power committed to them, to be managed by the best of their Skill, for the advantage of the Commonwealth.

148. Though, as I said, the *Executive* and *Federative Power* of every Community be really distinct in themselves, yet they are hardly to be separated, and placed at the same time, in the hands of distinct Persons. For both of them requiring the force of the Society for their Exercise, it is almost impracticable to place the Force of the Commonwealth in distinct, and not subordinate hands; or that the *Executive* and *Federative Power* should be *placed* in Persons, that might act separately, whereby the Force of the Publick would be under different Commands, which would be apt sometime or other to cause Disorder and Ruine.

CHAP. XIII.

Of the Subordination of the Powers of the Commonwealth.

149. Though in a constituted Commonwealth, standing upon its own Basis, and acting according to its own Nature, that is, acting for the preservation of the Community, there can be but *one supream Power*, which is *the Legislative*, to which all the rest are and must be Subordinate, yet the Legislative being only a Fiduciary Power* to act for certain ends, there remains still *in the People a supream Power to remove or alter the Legislative*, when they find the *Legislative* act contrary to the trust reposed in them. For all *Power given with trust* for the attaining an *end*, being limited by that end, whenever that *end* is manifestly neglected, or opposed, the *trust* must necessarily be *forfeited*, and the Power devolve into the Hands of those that gave it, who may place it anew where they shall think best for their safety and security. And thus the *Community* perpetually *retains a supream Power* of saving themselves from the attempts and designs of any body, even of their Legislators, whenever they shall be so foolish, or so wicked, as to lay and carry on designs against the Liberties and Properties of the Subject. For no Man or Society of Men, having a Power to deliver up their *Preservation*, or consequently the means of it, to the absolute Will and arbitrary Dominion of another; when ever any one shall go about to bring them into such a slavish Condition, they will always have a right to preserve, what they have not a Power to part with; and to rid themselves of those, who invade this Fundamental, Sacred, and unalterable Law of *Self-preservation*, for which they enter'd into Society. And thus the *Community* may be said in this respect to be *always the supream Power*, but not as considered under any Form of Government, because this Power of the People can never take place till the Government be dissolved.

150. In all Cases, whilst the Government subsists, the *Legislative is the supream Power*. For what can give Laws to another, must needs be superior to him; and since the Legislative is no otherwise Legislative of the Society, but by the right it has to make Laws for all the parts, and for every Member of the Society, prescribing Rules to their Actions, and giving power of Execution, where they are transgressed, the *Legislative* must needs be the *Supream*, and all other Powers in any Members or parts of the Society, derived from and subordinate to it.

151. In some Commonwealths where the *Legislative* is not always in Being, and the *Executive* is vested in a single Person, who has also a share in the Legislative; there that single Person in a very tolerable Sense may also be called *Supream*, not that he has in himself all the supream Power, which is that of Law-making: But because he has in him the *supream Execution*, from whom all inferiour Magistrates derive all their several subordinate Powers, or at least the greatest part of them; having also no Legislative superiour to him, there being no Law to be made without his Consent, which cannot be expected should ever subject him to the other part of the Legislative, *he* is properly enough in this Sense *Supream*. But yet it is to be observed, that though *Oaths of Allegiance* and Fealty are taken to him, 'tis not to him as supream Legislator, but as *supream Executor* of the Law, made by a joint Power of him with others; *Allegiance* being nothing but an *Obedience according to Law*, which when he violates, he has no right to Obedience, nor can claim it otherwise than as the publick Person vested with the Power of the Law, and so is to be consider'd as the Image, Phantom, or Representative of the Commonwealth, acted by the will of the Society, declared in its Laws; and thus he has no Will, no Power, but that of the Law. But when he quits this Representation, this publick Will, and acts by his own private Will, he degrades himself, and is but a single private Person without Power, and without Will, that has any Right to *Obedience*; the Members owing no *Obedience* but to the publick Will of the Society.

152. The *executive Power* placed any where but in a Person, that has also a Share in the Legislative, is visibly subordinate and accountable to it, and may be at pleasure changed and displaced; so that it is not the *supream Executive Power*, that is exempt from *Subordination*, but the *supream Executive Power* vested in one, who having a Share in the Legislative, has no distinct superior Legislative to be subordinate and accountable to, farther than he himself shall joyn and consent; so that he is no more subordinate than he himself shall think fit, which one may certainly conclude will be but very little. Of other *ministerial and subordinate Powers* in a Commonwealth, we need not speak, they being so multiply'd with infinite Variety, in the different Customs and Constitutions of distinct Commonwealths, that it is impossible to give a particular Account of them all. Only thus much, which is necessary to our present Purpose, we may take Notice of concerning them, that they have no manner of Authority any of them, beyond what is by

positive Grant and Commission, delegated to them, and are all of them accountable to some other Power in the Commonwealth.

153. It is not necessary, no nor so much as convenient, that the *Legislative* should be *always in Being*. But absolutely necessary that the Executive Power should, because there is not always need of new Laws to be made, but always need of Execution of the Laws that are made. When the *Legislative* hath put the *Execution* of the Laws, they make, into other Hands, they have a Power still to resume it out of those Hands, when they find Cause, and to punish for any mal-administration against the Laws. The same holds also in regard of the *federative* Power, that and the *Executive* being both *ministerial* and *subordinate to the Legislative*, which as has been shew'd in a constituted Commonwealth, is the supream. The *Legislative* also in this Case being suppos'd to consist of several Persons; (for if it be a single Person, it cannot but be always in Being, and so will as Supream, naturally have the Supream Executive Power, together with the Legislative) may *assemble and exercise their Legislature*, at the Times, that either their original Constitution, or their own Adjournment appoints, or when they please; if neither of these hath appointed any time, or there be no other Way prescribed to convoke them. For the supream Power being placed in them by the People, 'tis always in them, and they may exercise it when they please, unless by their original Constitution they are limited to certain Seasons, or by an Act of their supream Power, they have adjourned to a certain time; and when that time comes, they have a Right to *assemble* and act again.

154. If the *Legislative*, or any part of it be made up of *Representatives* chosen for that time by the People, which afterwards return into the ordinary state of Subjects, and have no Share in the Legislature but upon a new Choice, this Power of chusing must also be exercised by the People, either at certain appointed Seasons, or else when they are summon'd to it; and in this latter Case, the Power of convoking the Legislative, is ordinarily placed in the Executive, and has one of these two Limitations in respect of time: That either the original Constitution requires their *assembling* and *acting* at certain Intervals, and then the executive Power does nothing but ministerially issue Directions for their electing and assembling, according to due Forms: Or else it is left to his Prudence to call them by new Elections, when the Occasions or Exigencies of the Publick require

the Amendment of old, or making of new Laws, or the redress or pre-
vention of any Inconveniencies, that lie on, or threaten the People.*

155. It may be demanded here, What if the Executive Power being
possessed of the Force of the Commonwealth, shall make use of that
Force to hinder the *meeting* and *acting of the Legislative*, when the original Constitution, or the publick Exigencies require it? I say using
Force upon the People without Authority, and contrary to the Trust
put in him, that does so, is a state of War with the People, who have
a Right to *reinstate* their *Legislative in the Exercise* of their Power.
For having erected a Legislative, with an Intent they should exercise
the Power of making Laws, either at certain set times, or when there
is need of it, when they are hinder'd by any Force from, what is so
necessary to the Society, and wherein the safety and Preservation of
the People consists, the People have a Right to remove it by Force. In
all States and Conditions the true remedy of *Force* without Authority,
is to oppose *Force* to it. The use of *Force* without Authority, always
puts him that uses it into a *state of War*, as the Aggressor, and renders
him liable to be treated accordingly.

156. The *Power of assembling and dismissing the Legislative*, placed
in the Executive, gives not the Executive a superiority over it, but is
a fiduciary Trust placed in him, for the safety of the People, in a Case
where the uncertainty, and variableness of human Affairs could not
bear a steady fixed Rule. For it not being possible, that the first fram-
ers of the Government should, by any foresight, be so much Masters of
future Events, as to be able to prefix so just periods of Return and
Duration to the *Assemblies of the Legislative*, in all times to come, that
might exactly answer all the Exigencies of the Commonwealth; the
best Remedy could be found for this Defect, was to trust this to the
Prudence of one who was always to be present, and whose Business it
was to watch over the publick Good. Constant *frequent Meetings of the
Legislative*, and long Continuations of their Assemblies, without necessary Occasion, could not but be burthensome to the People,* and
must necessarily in time produce more dangerous Inconveniencies,
and yet the quick turn of Affairs might be sometimes such as to need
their present Help: Any Delay of their *convening* might endanger the
publick; and sometimes too their Business might be so great, that
the limited time of their sitting might be too short for their Work,
and rob the publick of that Benefit which could be had only from
their mature Deliberation. What then could be done in this Case

to prevent the Community from being exposed some time or other to eminent Hazard, on one side or the other, by fixed Intervals and Periods, set to the *meeting and acting of the Legislative*, but to intrust it to the Prudence of some, who being present, and acquainted with the state of publick Affairs, might make use of this Prerogative for the publick Good? And where else could this be so well placed as in his Hands, who was intrusted with the Execution of the Laws for the same End? Thus supposing the Regulation of Times for the *assembling and sitting of the Legislative*, not settled by the original Constitution, it naturally fell into the Hands of the Executive, not as an arbitrary Power depending on his good Pleasure, but with this trust always to have it exercised only for the publick Weal, as the Occurrences of Times and change of Affairs might require. Whether *settled Periods of their convening*, or *a Liberty* left to the Prince for *convoking the Legislative*, or perhaps a Mixture of both, hath the least Inconvenience attending it, 'tis not my Business here to inquire, but only to shew, that though the Executive Power may have the Prerogative of *convoking* and *dissolving* such *Conventions of the Legislative*, yet it is not thereby superior to it.

157. Things of this World are in so constant a Flux, that nothing remains long in the same State. Thus People, Riches, Trade, Power, change their Stations, flourishing mighty Cities come to ruine, and prove in time neglected desolate Corners, whilst other unfrequented Places grow into populous Countries, fill'd with Wealth and Inhabitants. But things not always changing equally, and private Interest often keeping up Customs and Privileges, when the Reasons of them are ceased, it often comes to pass, that in Governments, where part of the Legislative consists of *Representatives* chosen by the People, that in tract of time this *Representation* becomes very *unequal* and disproportionate* to the Reasons it was at first establish'd upon. To what gross Absurdities the following of Custom, when Reason has left it, may lead, we may be satisfied, when we see the bare Name of a Town, of which there remains not so much as the Ruines, where scarce so much Housing as a Sheepcoat, or more Inhabitants than a Shepherd is to be found, sends *as many Representatives* to the grand Assembly of Law-makers, as a whole County numerous in People, and powerful in Riches.* This Strangers stand amazed at, and every one must confess needs a Remedy. Though most think it hard to find one, because the Constitution of the Legislative being the original and supream Act of the Society, antecedent to all positive Laws in it, and

depending wholly on the People, no inferior Power can alter it. And therefore the *People*, when the *Legislative* is once constituted, *having* in such a Government as we have been speaking of, *no Power* to act as long as the Government stands; this Inconvenience is thought incapable of a Remedy.

158. *Salus Populi Suprema Lex*,* is certainly so just and fundamental a Rule, that he, who sincerely follows it, cannot dangerously err. If therefore the Executive, who has the Power of convoking the Legislative, observing rather the true Proportion, than Fashion of *Representation*, regulates, not by old Custom, but true Reason, the *Number of Members*, in all Places, that have a Right to be distinctly represented, which no part of the People however incorporated can pretend to, but in Proportion to the Assistance which it affords to the Publick,* it cannot be judg'd to have set up a new Legislative, but to have restored the old and true one, and to have rectified the Disorders, which Succession of time had insensibly, as well as inevitably introduced. For it being the Interest, as well as Intention of the People, to have a fair and *equal Representative*; whoever brings it nearest to that, is an undoubted Friend to, and Establisher of the Government, and cannot miss the Consent and Approbation of the Community. *Prerogative* being nothing but a Power in the Hands of the Prince, to provide for the publick Good, in such Cases, which depending upon unforeseen and uncertain Occurrences, certain and unalterable Laws could not safely direct; whatsoever shall be done manifestly for the good of the People, and the establishing the Government upon its true Foundations, is and always will be just *Prerogative*. The Power of erecting new Corporations, and therewith *new Representatives*, carries with it a Supposition, that in time the *Measures of Representation* might vary, and those Places have a just Right to be represented which before had none; and by the same Reason, those cease to have a Right, and be too inconsiderable for such a Privilege, which before had it.* 'Tis not a Change from the present State, which perhaps Corruption or Decay has introduced, that makes an Inroad upon the Government, but the Tendency of it to injure or oppress the People, and to set up one Part, or Party, with a Distinction from, and an unequal Subjection of the rest. Whatsoever cannot but be acknowledged to be of Advantage to the Society, and People in general, upon just and lasting Measures, will always, when done, justifie itself; and whenever the People shall chuse their *Representatives upon*

just and undeniably *equal Measures*, suitable to the original Frame of the Government, it cannot be doubted to be the Will and Act of the Society, whoever permitted or caused them so to do.

CHAP. XIV.
Of Prerogative.

159.* Where the Legislative and Executive Power are in distinct Hands, (as they are in all moderated Monarchies, and well-framed Governments) there the Good of the Society requires, that several things should be left to the Discretion of him, that has the Executive Power. For the Legislators not being able to foresee and provide by Laws, for all that may be useful to the Community, the Executor of the Laws having the Power in his Hands, has by the common Law of Nature a Right to make use of it for the good of the Society, in many Cases, where the municipal Law has given no Direction, till the Legislative can conveniently be assembled to provide for it. Many things there are, which the Law can by no means provide for, and those must necessarily be left to the Discretion of him that has the executive Power in his Hands, to be ordered by him as the publick Good and Advantage shall require: Nay, 'tis fit that the Laws themselves should in some Cases give way to the executive Power, or rather to this fundamental Law of Nature and Government, *viz.* That as much as may be, *all* the Members of the Society are to be preserved. For since many Accidents may happen, wherein a strict and rigid Observation of the Laws may do harm; (as not to pull down an innocent Man's House to stop the Fire, when the next to it is burning) and a Man may come sometimes within the reach of the Law, which makes no Distinction of Persons, by an Action that may deserve Reward and Pardon; 'tis fit the Ruler should have a Power, in many Cases, to mitigate the Severity of the Law, and pardon some Offenders: For the *End of Government* being *the Preservation of all*, as much as may be, even the Guilty are to be spared, where it can prove no Prejudice to the Innocent.

160. This Power to act according to Discretion, for the Publick Good, without the Prescription of the Law, and sometimes even against it, *is* that which is called *Prerogative*. For since in some Governments the Law-making Power is not always in Being, and is usually too numerous, and so too slow, for the Dispatch requisite to Execution: and

because also it is impossible to foresee, and so by Laws to provide for all Accidents and Necessities that may concern the Publick; or to make such Laws as will do no harm, if they are executed with an inflexible Rigour, on all Occasions, and upon all Persons that may come in their way, therefore there is a Latitude left to the Executive Power, to do many things of Choice which the Laws do not prescribe.

161. This Power, whilst employed for the Benefit of the Community, and suitably to the Trust and Ends of the Government, *is undoubted Prerogative*, and never is questioned. For the People are very seldom or never scrupulous or nice in the Point; they are far from examining *Prerogative*, whilst it is in any tolerable Degree employ'd for the use it was meant, that is, for the Good of the People, and not manifestly against it. But if there comes to be a *Question* between the Executive Power and the People, about a thing claimed as a *Prerogative*; the Tendency of the Exercise of such *Prerogative* to the Good or Hurt of the People will easily decide that Question.

162. It is easie to conceive, that in the Infancy of Governments, when Commonwealths differed little from Families in Number of People, they differ'd from them too but little in Number of Laws: And the Governours, being as the Fathers of them, watching over them for their Good, the Government was almost all *Prerogative*. A few establish'd Laws serv'd the Turn, and the Discretion and Care of the Ruler supply'd the rest. But when Mistake or Flattery prevailed with weak Princes to make use of this Power for private Ends of their own, and not for the publick Good, the People were fain by express Laws to get Prerogative determin'd in those Points wherein they found Disadvantage from it: And thus declared *Limitations of Prerogative* were by the People found necessary in Cases which they and their Ancestors had left, in the utmost Latitude, to the Wisdom of those Princes, who made no other but a right use of it, that is, for the Good of their People.

163. And therefore they have a very wrong Notion of Government, who say, that the People have *incroach'd upon the Prerogative*, when they have got any part of it to be defined by positive Laws. For in so doing they have not pulled from the Prince any thing that of right belong'd to him, but only declared, that that Power which they indefinitely left in his or his Ancestors Hands, to be exercised for their Good, was not a thing which they intended him when he used it otherwise. For the End of Government being the good of the Community,

whatsoever Alterations are made in it, tending to that End, cannot be an *Incroachment* upon any body, since no body in Government can have a right tending to any other end. And those only are *Incroachments* which prejudice or hinder the publick good. Those who say otherwise, speak as if the Prince had a distinct and separate Interest from the Good of the Community, and was not made for it, the Root and Source from which spring almost all those Evils and Disorders which happen in Kingly Governments. And indeed if that be so, the People under his Government are not a Society of rational Creatures, entred into a Community for their mutual Good; they are not such as have set Rulers over themselves, to guard, and promote that good; but are to be looked on as an Herd of inferior Creatures under the Dominion of a Master, who keeps them and works them for his own Pleasure or Profit. If Men were so void of Reason, and brutish, as to enter into Society upon such Terms, *Prerogative* might indeed be, what some Men would have it, an arbitrary Power to do things hurtful to the People.

164. But since a rational Creature cannot be supposed when free, to put himself into Subjection to another, for his own Harm: (Though where he finds a good and wise Ruler, he may not perhaps think it either necessary or useful, to set precise Bounds to his Power in all things) *Prerogative* can be nothing but the Peoples permitting their Rulers to do several things of their own free Choice, where the Law was silent, and sometimes too against the direct Letter of the Law, for the publick good; and their acquiescing in it when so done. For as a good Prince, who is mindful of the Trust put into his Hands, and careful of the Good of his People, cannot have too much *Prerogative*, that is, Power to do good: So a weak and ill Prince, who would claim that Power which his Predecessors excrcised without the Direction of the Law, as a Prerogative belonging to him by Right of his Office, which he may exercise at his pleasure, to make or promote an Interest distinct from that of the publick, gives the People an Occasion to claim their Right, and limit that Power, which, whilst it was exercised for their Good, they were content should be tacitly allowed.

165. And therefore he that will look into the *History of England*, will find, that *Prerogative* was always *largest* in the Hands of our wisest and best Princes; because the People observing the whole Tendency of their Actions to be the publick good, contested not what was done without Law to that end; or if any human Frailty or Mistake (for Princes are but Men, made as others) appear'd in some

small Declinations from that end; yet 'twas visible, the main of their Conduct tended to nothing but the Care of the publick. The People therefore finding reason to be satisfyed with these Princes, whenever they acted without or contrary to the Letter of the Law, acquiesced in what they did, and, without the least Complaint, let them inlarge their *Prerogative* as they pleased, judging rightly, that they did nothing herein to the prejudice of their Laws, since they acted conformable to the Foundation and End of all Laws, the publick good.

166. Such God-like Princes indeed had some Title to arbitrary Power, by that Argument, that would prove absolute Monarchy the best Government, as that which God himself governs the Universe by; because such Kings partake of his Wisdom and Goodness. Upon this is founded that saying,* That the Reigns of good Princes have been always most dangerous to the Liberties of their People. For when their Successors, managing the Government with different Thoughts, would draw the Actions of those good Rulers into Precedent, and make them the Standard of their *Prerogative*, as if what had been done only for the good of the People, was a Right in them to do, for the Harm of the People, if they so pleased; it has often occasioned Contest, and sometimes publick Disorders, before the People could recover their original Right, and get that to be declared not to be *Prerogative*, which truly was never so:* Since it is impossible that any body in the Society should ever have a Right to do the People Harm; though it be very possible, and reasonable, that the People should not go about to set any Bounds to the *Prerogative* of those Kings or Rulers, who themselves transgressed not the Bounds of the publick Good. For *Prerogative is nothing but the Power of doing publick Good without a Rule*.

167. The Power of *calling Parliaments* in *England*, as to precise Time, Place, and Duration, is certainly a *Prerogative* of the King, but still with this trust, that it shall be made use of for the good of the Nation, as the Exigencies of the Times, and Variety of Occasions shall require. For it being impossible to foresee which should always be the fittest place for them to assemble in, and what the best Season; the Choice of these was left with the Executive Power, as might be most subservient to the publick Good, and best suit the Ends of Parliaments.

168. The old Question will be asked in this Matter of *Prerogative*. But *who shall be Judge* when this Power is made a right use of? I answer: Between an Executive Power in Being, with such a Prerogative, and

a Legislative that depends upon his Will for their convening, there can be no *Judge on Earth*: As there can be none between the Legislative and the People, should either the Executive, or the Legislative, when they have got the Power in their Hands, design, or go about to enslave or destroy them. The People have no other Remedy in this, as in all other Cases where they have no Judge on Earth, but to *appeal to Heaven*. For the Rulers, in such Attempts, exercising a Power the People never put into their Hands, (who can never be supposed to consent that any body should rule over them for their harm) do that which they have not a Right to do. And where the Body of the People, or any single Man is deprived of their Right, or is under the Exercise of a Power without Right, and have no Appeal on Earth, then they have a Liberty to appeal to Heaven, whenever they judge the Cause of sufficient Moment. And therefore tho' the *People cannot* be *Judge*, so as to have by the Constitution of that Society any superior Power, to determine and give effective Sentence in the Case; yet they have, by a Law antecedent and paramount to all positive Laws of Men, reserv'd that ultimate Determination to themselves which belongs to all Mankind, where there lies no Appeal on Earth, *viz.* to judge, whether they have just Cause to make their Appeal to Heaven. And this Judgment they cannot part with, it being out of a Man's Power so to submit himself to another, as to give him a Liberty to destroy him; God and Nature never allowing a Man so to abandon himself, as to neglect his own Preservation: And since he cannot take away his own Life, neither can he give Another power to take it. Nor let any one think, this lays a perpetual Foundation for Disorder; for this operates not, till the Inconveniency is so great that the Majority feel it, and are weary of it, and find a Necessity to have it amended. But this the Executive Power, or wise Princes never need come in the Danger of: And 'tis the thing of all others, they have most need to avoid, as of all others the most perilous.

CHAP. XV.

Of Paternal, Political, and Despotical Power Consider'd Together.

169. Though I have had occasion to speak of these separately before, yet the great Mistakes of late about Government, having, as I suppose, arisen from confounding these distinct Powers one with another, it may not, perhaps, be amiss to consider them here together.

170. *First* then, *paternal* or *parental Power* is nothing but that which Parents have over their Children, to govern them for the Childrens good, till they come to the use of Reason, or a State of Knowledge, wherein they may be supposed capable to understand that Rule, whether it be the Law of Nature, or the municipal Law of their Country, they are to govern themselves by: Capable, I say, to know it, as well as several others, who live as Freemen under that Law. The Affection and Tenderness which God hath planted in the Breasts of Parents towards their Children, makes it evident, that this is not intended to be a severe arbitrary Government, but only for the Help, Instruction, and Preservation of their Offspring. But happen it as it will, there is, as I have proved, no reason why it should be thought to extend to Life and Death, at any time over their Children, more than over any body else; neither can there be any pretence why this *parental Power* should keep the Child when grown to a Man, in subjection to the Will of his Parents, any farther than the having received Life and Education from his Parents, obliges him to Respect, Honour, Gratitude, Assistance, and Support all his Life to both Father and Mother. And thus, 'tis true, the *Paternal* is a natural *Government*, but not at all extending it self to the Ends and Jurisdictions of that, which is Political. The *Power of the Father doth not reach* at all to the *Property* of the Child, which is only in his own disposing.

171. *Secondly*, *Political Power* is that Power, which every Man having in the state of Nature, has given up into the hands of the Society, and therein to the Governours, whom the Society hath set over itself, with this express or tacit Trust, That it shall be imployed for their good, and the preservation of their Property: Now this *Power*, which every Man has *in the State of Nature*, and which he parts with to the Society, in all such Cases, where the Society can secure him, is to use such means, for the preserving of his own Property, as he thinks good, and Nature allows him; and to punish the Breach of the Law of Nature in others so, as (according to the best of his Reason) may most conduce to the preservation of himself, and the rest of Mankind. So that the *end and measure of this Power*, when in every Man's hands in the state of Nature, being the preservation of all of his Society, that is, all Mankind in general, it can have no other *end or measure*, when in the hands of the Magistrate, but to preserve the Members of that Society in their Lives, Liberties, and Possessions; and so cannot be an Absolute, Arbitrary Power over their Lives and Fortunes, which

are as much as possible to be preserved; but a *Power to make Laws*, and annex such *Penalties* to them, as may tend to the preservation of the whole, by cutting off those Parts, and those only, which are so corrupt, that they threaten the sound and healthy, without which no severity is lawful. And this *Power has its Original only from Compact* and Agreement, and the mutual Consent of those who make up the Community.

172. *Thirdly, Despotical Power* is an Absolute, Arbitrary Power one Man has over another, to take away his Life, whenever he pleases. This is a Power, which neither Nature gives, for it has made no such distinction between one Man and another; nor Compact can convey, for Man not having such an Arbitrary Power over his own Life, cannot give another Man such a Power over it; but it is the *effect only of Forfeiture*, which the Aggressor makes of his own Life, when he puts himself into the state of War with another. For having quitted Reason, which God hath given to be the Rule betwixt Man and Man, and the common bond whereby human kind is united into one Fellowship and Society; and having renounced the way of Peace which that teaches, and made use of the Force of War, to compass his unjust ends upon another; where he has no right, and so revolting from his own Kind to that of Beasts, by making Force, which is theirs, to be his Rule of Right, he renders himself liable to be destroyed by the injur'd Person, and the rest of Mankind, that will join with him in the execution of Justice, as any other wild Beast, or noxious Brute with whom Mankind can have neither Society nor Security.* And thus *Captives*, taken in a just and lawful War, and such only, are *subject to a Despotical Power*, which as it arises not from Compact, so neither is it capable of any, but is the state of War continued. For what Compact can be made with a Man that is not Master of his own Life? What Condition can he perform? And if he be once allowed to be Master of his own Life, the *Despotical, Arbitrary Power* of his Master ceases. He that is Master of himself, and his own Life, has a right too to the means of preserving it; so that *as soon as Compact enters, Slavery ceases*, and he so far quits his absolute Power, and puts an end to the state of War, who enters into Conditions with his Captive.

173. *Nature gives* the first of these, *viz. Paternal Power to Parents* for the Benefit of their Children during their Minority, to supply their want of Ability, and understanding how to manage their Property. (By *Property* I must be understood here, as in other places,

to mean that Property which Men have in their Persons as well as Goods.) *Voluntary Agreement gives* the second, *viz. Political Power to Governours* for the Benefit of their Subjects, to secure them in the Possession and Use of their Properties. And *Forfeiture gives* the third, *Despotical Power to Lords* for their own Benefit, over those who are stripp'd of all Property.

174. He, that shall consider the distinct rise and extent, and the different ends of these several Powers, will plainly see, that *paternal Power* comes as far short of that of the *Magistrate*, as *Despotical* exceeds it; and that *absolute Dominion*, however placed, is so far from being one kind of civil Society, that it is as inconsistent with it, as Slavery is with Property. *Paternal Power* is only where Minority makes the Child incapable to manage his property; *Political* where Men have Property in their own Disposal; and *Despotical* over such as have no Property at all.

CHAP. XVI.
Of Conquest.

175.* Though Governments can originally have no other Rise than that before mentioned, nor *Polities* be *founded on* any thing but *the Consent of the People*; yet such has been the Disorders Ambition has fill'd the World with, that in the noise of War, which makes so great a part of the History of Mankind, *this Consent* is little taken notice of: And therefore many have mistaken the Force of Arms, for the Consent of the People; and reckon Conquest as one of the Originals of Government. But *Conquest* is as far from setting up any Government, as demolishing an House is from building a new one in the Place. Indeed it often makes way for a new Frame of a Commonwealth, by destroying the former; but, without the Consent of the People, can never erect a new one.

176. * That the *Aggressor*, who puts himself into the state of War with another, and *unjustly invades* another Man's Right, *can*, by such an unjust War, *never* come to *have a right over the Conquered*, will be easily agreed by all Men, who will not think, that Robbers and Pyrates have a Right of Empire* over whomsoever they have Force enough to master, or that Men are bound by Promises, which unlawful Force extorts from them. Should a Robber break into my House, and with

a Dagger at my Throat, make me seal Deeds to convey my Estate to him, would this give him any title? Just such a Title by his Sword, has an *unjust Conqueror*, who forces me into Submission.* The Injury and the Crime is equal, whether committed by the wearer of a Crown, or some petty Villain. The Title of the Offender, and the Number of his Followers make no difference in the Offence, unless it be to aggravate it. The only difference is, Great Robbers punish little ones, to keep them in their Obedience, but the great ones are rewarded with Laurels and Triumphs, because they are too big for the weak hands of Justice in this World, and have the Power in their own Possession, which should punish Offenders. What is my Remedy against a Robber, that so broke into my House? *Appeal* to the Law for Justice. But perhaps Justice is deny'd, or I am crippled and cannot stir, Robbed and have not the means to do it. If God has taken away all means of seeking Remedy, there is nothing left but patience. But my Son, when able, may seek the Relief of the Law, which I am denied: He or his Son may renew his *Appeal*, till he recover his Right. But the Conquered, or their Children have no Court, no Arbitrator on Earth to appeal to. Then they may *Appeal*, as *Jephtha* did to *Heaven*, and repeat their *Appeal*, till they have recovered the native Right of their Ancestors, which was, to have such a Legislative over them, as the Majority should approve, and freely acquiesce in. If it be objected, this would cause endless trouble; I answer, No more than Justice does, where she lies open to all that appeal to her. He that troubles his Neighbour without a Cause, is punished for it by the Justice of the Court he appeals to. And he that *appeals to Heaven*, must be sure he has Right on his side; and a Right too that is worth the Trouble and Cost of the Appeal, as he will answer at a Tribunal, that cannot be deceived, and will be sure to retribute to every one according to the Mischiefs he hath created to his Fellow Subjects; that is, any part of Mankind. From whence 'tis plain, that he that *Conquers in an unjust War can thereby have no Title to the Subjection and Obedience of the Conquered.*

177. But supposing Victory favours the right side, let us consider a *Conqueror in a lawful War*, and see what Power he gets, and over whom.

First, 'Tis plain he *gets no Power by his Conquest over those that Conquered with him*. They that fought on his side cannot suffer by the Conquest, but must at least be as much Freemen as they were before.

And most commonly they serve upon Terms, and on Condition to share with their Leader, and enjoy a part of the Spoil, and other Advantages that attend the Conquering Sword: Or at least have a part of the sub- dued Country bestowed upon them. And *the conquering People are not I hope to be Slaves by Conquest*, and wear their Laurels only to shew they are Sacrifices to their Leaders Triumph. They that found abso- lute Monarchy upon the Title of the Sword make their Heroes, who are the Founders of such Monarchies, arrant *Draw-can-Sirs*,* and forget they had any Officers and Soldiers that fought on their Side in the Battles they won; or assisted them in the subduing, or shared in possessing the Countries they master'd. We are told by some, that the *English* Monarchy is founded in the *Norman* Conquest, and that our Princes have thereby a Title to absolute Dominion: Which if it were true, (as by the History it appears otherwise) and that *William** had a Right to make War on this Island; yet his Dominion by Conquest could reach no farther than to the *Saxons* and *Britains*, that were then Inhabitants of this Country. The *Normans* that came with him, and helped to conquer, and all descended from them, are Freemen and no Subjects by Conquest; let that give what Dominion it will. And if I, or any Body else shall claim Freedom, as derived from them, it will be very hard to prove the contrary: And 'tis plain, the Law that has made no distinction between the one and the other, intends not there should be any Difference in their Freedom or Privileges.

178. But supposing, which seldom happens, that the Conquerors and conquered never incorporate into one People, under the same Laws and Freedom. Let us see next *what Power a lawful Conqueror has over the Subdued*: And that I say is purely despotical. He has an absolute Power over the Lives of those, who by an unjust War have forfeited them; but not over the Lives or Fortunes of those, who ingaged not in the War, nor over the Possessions even of those, who were actually engaged in it.

179. *Secondly*, I say then the *Conqueror* gets no Power but only over those, who have actually assisted, concurr'd, or consented to that unjust Force, that is used against him. For the People having given to their Governours no Power to do an unjust thing, such as is to make an unjust War, (for they never had such a Power in them- selves:) They ought not to be charged, as guilty of the Violence and Unjustice, that is committed in an Unjust War, any farther, than they actually abet it; no more, than they are to be thought guilty of

any Violence or Oppression their Governours should use upon the People themselves, or any part of their Fellow Subjects, they have impowered them no more to the one, than to the other. Conquerors, 'tis true, seldom trouble themselves to make the distinction, but they willingly permit the Confusion of War to sweep all together; but yet this alters not the Right: For the Conqueror's Power over the Lives of the Conquered, being only because they have used Force to do, or maintain an Injustice, he can have that Power only over those, who have concurred in that Force, all the rest are innocent; and he has no more Title over the People of that Country, who have done him no Injury, and so have made no forfeiture of their Lives, than he has over any other, who without any Injuries or Provocations, have lived upon fair Terms with him.

180. *Thirdly*, The *Power a Conqueror gets* over those he overcomes *in a just War, is perfectly despotical*; he has an absolute Power over the Lives of those, who by putting themselves in a state of War, have forfeited them; but he has not thereby a Right and Title to their Possessions. This I doubt not, but at first Sight will seem a strange Doctrine, it being so quite contrary to the practice of the World; there being nothing more familiar in speaking of the Dominion of Countries, than to say such an one conquer'd it. As if Conquest, without any more ado, convey'd a Right of Possession. But when we consider, that the Practice of the strong and powerful, how universal soever it may be, is seldom the rule of Right, however it be one part of the Subjection of the Conquered, not to argue against the Conditions, cut out to them by the Conquering Sword.

181. Though in all War there be usually a complication of Force and Damage, and the Aggressor seldom fails to harm the Estate, when he uses Force against the Persons of those he makes War upon; yet 'tis the use of Force only that puts a Man into the state of War. For whether by Force he begins the Injury, or else having quietly, and by fraud, done the Injury, he refuses to make Reparation and by Force maintains it, (which is the same thing, as at first to have done it by Force) 'tis the unjust use of Force, that makes the War. For he that breaks open my House, and violently turns me out of Doors; or having peaceably got in, by Force keeps me out, does in Effect the same thing; supposing we are in such a state, that we have no common Judge on Earth, whom I may appeal to, and to whom we are both obliged to submit: For of such I am now speaking. 'Tis the *unjust*

use of Force then, that *puts a Man into the state of War* with another, and thereby he, that is guilty of it, makes a forfeiture of his Life. For quitting Reason, which is the Rule given between Man and Man, and using Force the way of Beasts, he becomes liable to be destroyed by him he uses Force against, as any savage ravenous Beast, that is dangerous to his Being.

182. But because the miscarriages of the Father are no faults of the Children, and they may be rational and peaceable, notwithstanding the brutishness and injustice of the Father; the Father, by his Miscarriages and Violence, can forfeit but his own Life, but involves not his Children in his Guilt or Destruction. His Goods, which Nature that willeth the preservation of all Mankind as much as is possible, hath made to belong to the Children to keep them from perishing, do still continue to belong to his Children. For supposing them not to have joyn'd in the War, either through Infancy, Absence, or Choice, they have done nothing to forfeit them: *nor has the Conqueror any Right* to take them away, by the bare Title of having subdued him, that by Force attempted his Destruction; though perhaps he may have some Right to them, to repair the Damages, he has sustained by the War, and the Defence of his own Right; which how far it reaches to the possessions of the Conquered, we shall see by and by. So that he that *by Conquest has a Right over a Man's Person* to destroy him if he pleases, has *not* thereby a Right over *his Estate* to possess and enjoy it. For it is the brutal Force the Aggressor has used, that gives his Adversary a Right to take away his Life, and destroy him if he pleases, as a noxious Creature, but 'tis Damage sustain'd that alone gives him Title to another Man's Goods: For though I may kill a Thief that sets on me in the Highway, yet I may not (which seems less) take away his Money, and let him go; this would be Robbery on my side. His Force, and the state of War he put himself in, made him forfeit his Life, but gave me no Title to his Goods. The *Right* then of *Conquest extends only to the Lives* of those who joyn'd in the War, *not to their Estates*, but only in order to make Reparation for the Damages received, and the Charges of the War, and that too with Reservation of the right of the innocent Wife and Children.

183. Let the *Conqueror* have as much Justice on his Side, as could be supposed, he *has* no *Right* to seize more than the vanquished could forfeit; his Life is at the Victor's Mercy, and his Service, and Goods he may appropriate, to make himself Reparation; but he cannot

take the Goods of his Wife and Children; they too had a Title to the Goods he enjoy'd, and their Shares in the Estate he possessed. For Example, I in the state of Nature (and all Commonwealths are in the state of Nature one with another) have injured another Man, and refusing to give Satisfaction, it comes to a state of War, wherein my defending by Force, what I had gotten unjustly, makes me the Aggressor. I am conquered: My Life, 'tis true, as forfeit, is at mercy, but not my Wives and Childrens. They made not the War, nor assisted in it. I could not forfeit their Lives, they were not mine to forfeit. My Wife had a Share in my Estate, that neither could I forfeit. And my Children also, being born of me, had a Right to be maintained out of my Labour or Substance. Here then is the Case; The Conqueror has a Title to Reparation for Damages received, and the Children have a Title to their Father's Estate for their Subsistence. For as to the Wife's share, whether her own Labour, or Compact gave her a Title to it, 'tis plain, her Husband could not forfeit what was hers. What must be done in the Case? I answer; The fundamental Law of Nature being, that all, as much as may be, should be preserved, it follows, that if there be not enough fully to *satisfie* both, *viz.* for the *Conqueror's Losses*, and Childrens Maintenance, he that hath, and to spare, must remit something of his full Satisfaction, and give way to the pressing and preferable Title of those, who are in Danger to perish without it.

184. But supposing the *Charge* and *Damages of the War* are to be made up to the Conqueror, to the utmost Farthing; and that the Children of the Vanquished, spoiled of all their Father's Goods, are to be left to starve and perish; yet the satisfying of what shall, on this Score, be due to the Conqueror, will scarce give him a *Title to any Countrey he shall conquer*. For the Damages of War can scarce amount to the value of any considerable Tract of Land, in any part of the World, where all the Land is possessed, and none lies waste. And if I have not taken away the Conqueror's Land, which, being vanquished, it is impossible I should; scarce any other Spoil I have done him, can amount to the Value of mine, supposing it equally cultivated, and of an Extent any way coming near, what I had over run of his. The destruction of a Years Product or two, (for it seldom reaches four or five) is the utmost Spoil, that usually can be done. For as to Money, and such Riches, and Treasure taken away, these are none of Natures Goods, they have but a phantastical imaginary Value: Nature has put no such upon them: They are of no more account by her

Standard, than the Wampompeke* of the *Americans* to an *European* Prince, or the Silver Money of *Europe* would have been formerly to an *American*. And five Years product is not worth the perpetual Inheritance of Land, where all is possessed, and none remains waste, to be taken up by him, that is disseiz'd:* Which will be easily granted, if one do but take away the imaginary value of Money, the disproportion being more, than between five and five hundred.* Though, at the same time, half a Years product is more worth, than the Inheritance, where there being more Land, than the Inhabitants possess, and make use of, any one has Liberty to make use of the Waste: But there Conquerors take little Care to possess themselves of the *Lands of the Vanquished*. No Damage therefore, that Men in the state of Nature (as all Princes and Governments are in reference to one another) suffer from one another, can give a Conqueror Power to dispossess the Posterity of the Vanquished, and turn them out of their Inheritance, which ought to be the Possession of them and their Descendants to all Generations. The Conqueror indeed will be apt to think himself Master: And 'tis the very Condition of the Subdued not to be able to dispute their Right. But if that be all, it gives no other Title than what bare Force gives to the stronger over the weaker: And, by this reason, he that is strongest will have a Right to whatever he pleases to seize on.

185. Over those then that joyned with him in the War, and over those of the subdued Country that opposed him not, and the Posterity even of those that did, the Conqueror, even in a just War, hath, by his Conquest no *Right of Dominion*: They are free from any Subjection to him, and if their former Government be dissolved, they are at Liberty to begin and erect another to themselves.

186. The Conqueror, 'tis true, usually, by the Force he has over them, compels them, with a Sword at their Breasts, to stoop to his Conditions, and submit to such a Government as he pleases to afford them; but the Enquiry is, What Right he has to do so? If it be said, they submit by their own Consent, then this allows their own *Consent* to be *necessary to give the Conqueror a Title to rule* over them. It remains only to be considered, whether *Promises extorted by Force*, without Right, can be thought Consent, and *how far they bind*. To which I shall say, they *bind not at all*; because whatsoever another gets from me by Force, I still retain the Right of, and he is obliged presently to restore. He that forces my Horse from me, ought presently

to restore him, and I have still a Right to retake him. By the same Reason, he that *forced a Promise* from me, ought presently to restore it, *i.e.* quit me of the Obligation of it; or I may resume it my self, *i.e.* chuse whether I will perform it. For the Law of Nature laying an Obligation on me only by the Rules she prescribes, cannot oblige me by the Violation of her Rules: Such is the extorting any thing from me by Force. Nor does it at all alter the Case to say, *I gave my Promise*, no more than it excuses the Force, and passes the Right, when I put my Hand in my Pocket, and deliver my Purse my self to a Thief, who demands it with a Pistol at my Breast.

187. From all which it follows, that the *Government of a Conqueror*, imposed by Force on the Subdued, against whom he had no Right of War, or who joyned not in the War against him, where he had Right, *has no Obligation* upon them.

188. But let us suppose, that all the Men of that Community being all Members of the same Body politick, may be taken to have joyn'd in that unjust War wherein they are subdued, and so their Lives are at the Mercy of the Conqueror.

189. I say, this concerns not their Children who are in their Minority. For since a Father hath not, in himself, a Power over the Life or Liberty of his Child, no act of his can possibly forfeit it. So that the Children, whatever may have happened to the Fathers, are Freemen, and the absolute Power of the *Conqueror* reaches no farther than the Persons of the Men that were subdued by him, and dies with them; and should he govern them as Slaves, subjected to his absolute arbitrary Power, he *has* no *such Right of Dominion over their Children*. He can have no Power over them but by their own Consent, whatever he may drive them to say or do; and he has no lawful Authority, whilst Force, and not Choice, compels them to Submission.

190. Every Man is born with a double Right: *First*, A *Right of Freedom to his Person*, which no other Man has a Power over, but the free Disposal of it lies in himself. *Secondly*, A *Right* before any other Man, *to inherit* with his Brethren his *Father's Goods*.

191. By the first of these, a Man is *naturally free* from Subjection to any Government, tho' he be born in a place under its Jurisdiction. But if he disclaim the lawful Government of the Country he was born in, he must also quit the Right that belong'd to him by the Laws of it, and the Possessions there descending to him from his Ancestors, if it were a Government made by their Consent.

192. By the second, the *Inhabitants* of any Country, who are descended, and derive a Title to their Estates from those who are subdued,
and had a Government forced upon them against their free Consents,
retain a Right to the Possession of their Ancestors, though they consent
not freely to the Government, whose hard Conditions were by Force
imposed on the Possessors of that Country. For the first *Conqueror
never having had a Title to the Land* of that Country, the People who
are the Descendants of, or claim under those who were forced to submit to the Yoke of a Government by Constraint, have always a Right
to shake it off, and free themselves from the Usurpation or Tyranny
which the Sword hath brought in upon them, till their Rulers put them
under such a Frame of Government as they willingly and of choice
consent to. Who doubts but the *Grecian* Christians, Descendants of
the ancient Possessors of that Country, may justly cast off the *Turkish*
Yoke which they have so long groaned under, whenever they have
an Opportunity to do it?* For no Government can have a Right to
Obedience from a People who have not freely consented to it; which
they can never be supposed to do, till either they are put in a full state of
Liberty, to chuse their Government and Governors, or at least till
they have such standing Laws, to which they have by themselves or
their Representatives given their free Consent, and also till they are
allow'd their due Property, which is so to be Proprietors of what they
have, that no body can take away any part of it without their own
Consent, without which, Men under any Government are not in the
state of Freemen, but are direct Slaves under the Force of War.

193. But granting that the *Conqueror* in a just War has a Right
to the Estates, as well as Power over the Persons, of the Conquered;
which, 'tis plain, he *hath* not: Nothing of *absolute Power* will follow
from hence, in the Continuance of the Government: Because the
Descendants of these being all Freemen, if he grants them Estates
and Possessions to inhabit his Country, (without which it would be
worth nothing) whatsoever he grants them, they have, so far as it is
granted, *Property* in. The Nature whereof is, that *without a Man's own
Consent* it *cannot be taken from him.*

194. Their *Persons* are *free* by a native Right, and their *Properties*,
be they more or less, are *their own, and at their own dispose*, and not at
his; or else it is no *Property.* Supposing the Conqueror gives to one
Man a thousand Acres, to him and his Heirs for ever, to another he
lets a thousand Acres for his Life, under the Rent of £50 or £500 *per*

Ann. Has not the one of these a Right to his thousand Acres for ever, and the other, during his Life, paying the said Rent? And hath not the Tenant for Life a *Property* in all that he gets over and above his Rent, by his Labour and Industry during the said Term, supposing it be double the Rent? Can any one say, the King, or Conqueror, after his Grant, may by his Power of Conqueror take away all, or part of the Land from the Heirs of one, or from the other during his Life, he paying the Rent? Or can he take away from either, the Goods or Money they have got upon the said Land, at his pleasure? If he can, then all free and voluntary *Contracts* cease, and are void in the World; there needs nothing to dissolve them at any time, but Power enough: And all the *Grants* and *Promises* of *Men in Power*, are but Mockery and Collusion. For can there be any thing more ridiculous than to say, I give you and yours this for ever; and that in the surest and most solemn way of conveyance [which] can be devised: And yet it is to be understood, that I have Right, if I please, to take it away from you again to Morrow?

195. I will not dispute now whether Princes are exempt from the Laws of their Country; but this I am sure, they owe Subjection to the Laws of God and Nature. No Body, no Power, can exempt them from the Obligations of that eternal Law. Those are so great, and so strong, in the Case of *Promises*, that Omnipotency itself can be tyed by them. *Grants*, *Promises*, and *Oaths*, are *Bonds* that *hold the Almighty*: Whatever some Flatterers say to Princes of the World, who all together, with all their People joyned to them, are, in Comparison of the Great God, but as a Drop of the Bucket, or a Dust on the Balance, inconsiderable, nothing!

196. The short of the *Case in Conquest* is this, The Conqueror, if he have a just Cause, has a despotical Right over the Persons of all, that actually aided, and concurred in the War against him, and a Right to make up his Damage and Cost out of their Labour and Estates, so he injure not the Right of any other. Over the rest of the People, if there were any that consented not to the War, and over the Children of the Captives themselves, or the Possessions of either, he has no Power; and so can have, *by virtue of Conquest, no lawful Title* himself *to Dominion* over them, or derive it to his Posterity; but is an Aggressor, if he attempts upon their Properties, and thereby puts himself in a state of War against them, and has no better a Right of Principality, he, nor any of his Successors, than *Hingar*, or *Hubba*,* the *Danes* had

here in *England*; or *Spartacus*,* had he conquered *Italy*, would have had; which is to have their Yoke cast off, as soon as God shall give those under their Subjection Courage and Opportunity to do it. Thus, notwithstanding whatever Title the Kings of *Assyria* had over *Judah*, by the Sword, God assisted *Hezekiah* to throw off the Dominion of that conquering Empire. *And the Lord was with Hezekiah, and he prospered; wherefore he went forth, and he rebelled against the King of Assyria, and served him not*, 2 Kings xviii. 7. Whence it is plain, that shaking off a Power, which Force, and not Right hath set over any one, though it hath the Name of *Rebellion*, yet is no Offence before God, but is that which he allows and countenances, though even Promises and Covenants, when obtain'd by Force, have intervened. For 'tis very probable, to any one that reads the Story of *Ahaz* and *Hezekiah* attentively, that the *Assyrians* subdued *Ahaz*, and deposed him, and made *Hezekiah* King in his Father's Lifetime; and that *Hezekiah* by Agreement had done him Homage, and paid him Tribute all this time.

CHAP. XVII.
Of Usurpation.

197. As Conquest may be called a foreign Usurpation, so Usurpation is a kind of domestick Conquest, with this Difference, that an Usurper can never have Right on his side, it being no *Usurpation*, but where one is got into the *Possession of what another has Right to*. This, so far as it is *Usurpation*, is a Change only of Persons, but not of the Forms and Rules of the Government: For if the Usurper extend his Power beyond what of Right belonged to the lawful Princes, or Governors of the Commonwealth, 'tis *Tyranny* added to *Usurpation*.

198. In all lawful Governments, the Designation of the Persons, who are to bear Rule, is as natural and necessary a part as the Form of the Government itself, and is that which had its Establishment originally from the People. Hence all Commonwealths, with the Form of Government established, have Rules also of appointing those, who are to have any share in the publick Authority, and settled Methods of conveying the Right to them. For the Anarchy is much alike to have no Form of Government at all; or to agree that it shall be monarchical, but to appoint no way to know or design the Person that shall have the Power, and be the Monarch.* Whoever gets into the

Exercise of any part of the Power, by other ways than what the Laws of the Community have prescribed, hath no Right to be obeyed, though the Form of the Commonwealth be still preserved; since he is not the Person the Laws have appointed, and consequently not the Person the People have consented to. Nor can such an *Usurper*, or any deriving from him, ever have a Title, till the People are both at liberty to consent, and have actually consented to allow, and confirm in him the Power he hath till then usurped.

CHAP. XVIII.
Of Tyranny.

199. As Usurpation is the Exercise of Power, which another hath a Right to; so *Tyranny is the Exercise of Power beyond Right*, which no body can have a Right to. And this is making use of the Power any one has in his Hands; not for the Good of those who are under it, but for his own private separate Advantage. When the Governor, however intituled, makes not the Law, but his Will, the Rule; and his Commands and Actions are not directed to the Preservation of the Properties of his People, but the Satisfaction of his own Ambition, Revenge, Covetousness, or any other irregular Passion.

200. If one can doubt this to be Truth, or Reason, because it comes from the obscure Hand of a Subject, I hope the Authority of a King will make it pass with him. King *James* the First, in his Speech to the Parliament 1603, tells them thus, *I will ever prefer the Weal of the Publick, and of the whole Commonwealth, in making of good Laws and Constitutions, to any particular and private Ends of mine. Thinking ever the Wealth and Weal of the Commonwealth to be my greatest Weal and worldly Felicity; a Point wherein a lawful King doth directly differ from a Tyrant. For I do acknowledge, that the special and greatest point of Difference that is between a rightful King, and an usurping Tyrant, is this, That whereas the proud and ambitious Tyrant doth think, his Kingdom and People are only ordained for Satisfaction of his Desires and unreasonable Appetites; the righteous and just King doth by the contrary acknowledge himself to be ordained for the procuring of the Wealth and Property of his People.* And again, in his Speech to the Parliament 1609, he hath these Words, *The King binds himself by a double Oath, to the Observation of the fundamental Laws of his Kingdom. Tacitly, as by being a King, and so bound to protect as well*

the People, as the Laws of his Kingdom, and expressly by his Oath at his Coronation; so as every just King, in a settled Kingdom, is bound to observe that Paction made to his People, by his Laws in framing his Government agreeable thereunto, according to that Paction which God made with Noah after the Deluge. Hereafter, Seed-time and Harvest, and Cold and Heat, and Summer and Winter, and Day and Night, shall not cease while the Earth remaineth.* And therefore a King governing in a settled Kingdom, leaves to be a King, and degenerates into a Tyrant, as soon as he leaves off to rule according to his Laws. And a little after, *Therefore all Kings that are not Tyrants, or perjured, will be glad to bound themselves within the Limits of their Laws. And they that perswade them the contrary, are Vipers, and Pests both against them and the Commonwealth.** Thus that learned King, who well understood the Notions of things, makes the Difference betwixt a *King* and a *Tyrant* to consist only in this, That one makes the Laws the Bounds of his Power, and the Good of the Publick, the End of his Government; the other makes all give way to his own Will and Appetite.

201. 'Tis a Mistake to think this Fault is proper only to Monarchies; other Forms of Government are lyable to it, as well as that. For wherever the Power, that is put in any Hands for the Government of the People, and the Preservation of their Properties is applied to other Ends, and made use of to impoverish, harass, or subdue them to the arbitrary and irregular Commands of those that have it: There it presently becomes *Tyranny* whether those that thus use it are one or many. Thus we read of the Thirty Tyrants at *Athens*, as well as One at *Syracuse*; and the intolerable Dominion of the *Decemviri* at *Rome** was nothing better.

202. *Wher-ever Law ends, Tyranny begins*, if the Law be transgressed to another's harm. And whosoever in Authority exceeds the Power given him by the Law, and makes use of the Force, he has under his Command, to compass that upon the Subject, which the Law, allows not, ceases in that to be a Magistrate, and acting without Authority, may be opposed, as any other Man, who by force invades the Right of another. This is acknowledged in subordinate Magistrates. He that hath Authority to seize my Person in the Street, may be opposed as a Thief and a Robber, if he indeavours to break into my House to execute a Writ, notwithstanding that I know, he has such a Warrant, and such a Legal Authority as will impower him to Arrest me abroad. And why this should not hold in the highest, as well as in the most Inferiour Magistrate, I would gladly be informed.

Is it reasonable, that the Eldest Brother, because he has the greatest part of his Father's Estate, should thereby have a Right to take away any of his younger Brother's Portions? Or that a Rich Man, who possessed a whole Country,* should from thence have a Right to seize, when he pleased, the Cottage and Garden of his poor Neighbour? The being rightfully possessed of great Power and Riches exceedingly beyond the greatest part of the Sons of *Adam*, is so far from being an Excuse, much less a Reason, for Rapine and Oppression, which the endamaging another without Authority is, that it is a great Aggravation of it. For the exceeding the Bounds of Authority, is no more a Right in a great, than a petty Officer; no more justifiable in a King than a Constable: But is so much the worse in him, in that he has more trust put in him, has already a much greater share than the rest of his Brethren, and is supposed, from the advantages of his Education, Imployment, and Counsellors, to be more knowing in the measures of Right and Wrong.

203. May the *Commands* then *of a Prince be Opposed*? May he be resisted as often as any one shall find himself aggrieved, and but imagine he has not Right done him? This will unhinge and overturn all Polities, and instead of Government and Order, leave nothing but Anarchy and Confusion.

204. To this I answer: That *Force* is to be *opposed* to nothing, but to unjust and unlawful *Force*; whoever makes any opposition in any other Case, draws on himself a just Condemnation both from God and Man; and so no such Danger or Confusion will follow, as is often suggested. For,

205. *First*, As in some Countries, the Person of the Prince by the Law is Sacred; and so whatever he commands or does, his Person is still free from all Question or Violence, not liable to Force, or any Judicial Censure or Condemnation. But yet opposition may be made to the illegal Acts of any inferiour Officer, or other commissioned by him; unless he will by actually putting himself into a state of War with his People, dissolve the Government, and leave them to that Defence, which belongs to every one in the state of Nature. For of such things who can tell what the end will be? And a Neighbour Kingdom has shewed the World an odd Example.* In all other Cases the *Sacredness* of the *Person exempts him from all Inconveniencies*, whereby he is secure, whilst the Government stands, from all violence and harm whatsoever; Than which there cannot be a wiser Constitution.

For the harm he can do in his own Person not being likely to happen often, nor to extend it self far; nor being able by his single strength to subvert the Laws, nor oppress the Body of the People, should any Prince have so much Weakness, and ill Nature as to be willing to do it, the Inconveniency of some particular mischiefs, that may happen sometimes, when a heady Prince comes to the Throne, are well recompensed, by the peace of the Publick, and security of the Government, in the Person of the Chief Magistrate, thus set out of the reach of danger: It being safer for the Body, that some few private Men should be sometimes in danger to suffer, than that the Head of the Republick* should be easily, and upon slight occasions exposed.

206. *Secondly*, But this Privilege belonging only to the King's Person, hinders not, but they may be questioned, opposed, and resisted, who use unjust Force, though they pretend a Commission from him, which the Law authorizes not. As is plain in the Case of him, that has the King's Writ to Arrest a Man, which is a full Commission from the King; and yet he that has it cannot break open a Man's House to do it, nor execute this Command of the King upon certain Days, nor in certain Places, though this Commission have no such exception in it, but they are the Limitations of the Law, which if any one transgress, the King's Commission excuses him not.* For the King's Authority being given him only by the Law, he cannot impower any one to act against the Law, or justifie him, by his Commission in so doing. The *Commission*, or *Command of any Magistrate, where he has no Authority*, being as *void* and insignificant, as that of any private Man. The difference between the one and the other, being that the Magistrate has some Authority so far, and to such ends, and the private Man has none at all. For 'tis not the *Commission*, but the *Authority*, that gives the Right of acting; and *against the Laws there can be no Authority*. But, notwithstanding such Resistance, the King's Person and Authority are still both secured, and so *no danger to Governor or Government*.

207. *Thirdly*, Supposing a Government wherein the Person of the Chief Magistrate is not thus Sacred; yet this *Doctrine* of the lawfulness of *resisting* all unlawful exercises of his Power, *will not* upon every slight occasion indanger him, or *imbroil the Government*. For where the injured Party may be relieved, and his Damages repaired by Appeal to the Law, there can be no pretence for Force, which is only to be used where a Man is intercepted from appealing to the Law. For nothing is

to be accounted Hostile Force, but where it leaves not the remedy of such an Appeal. And 'tis such *Force* alone, that *puts* him that uses it *into a state of War*, and makes it lawful to resist him. A Man with a Sword in his Hand demands my Purse in the High-way, when perhaps I have not 12*d.* in my Pocket; This Man I may lawfully kill. To another I deliver £100 to hold only whilst I alight, which he refuses to restore me, when I am got up again, but draws his Sword to defend the possession of it by Force, if I endeavour to retake it. The mischief this Man does me, is a hundred, or possibly a thousand times more, than the other perhaps intended me, (whom I killed before he really did me any) and yet I might lawfully kill the one, and cannot so much as hurt the other lawfully. The Reason whereof is plain; because the one using *Force*, which threatned my Life, I could not have *time to appeal* to the Law to secure it: And when it was gone, 'twas too late to appeal. The Law could not restore Life to my dead Carcass: The Loss was irreparable; which to prevent, the Law of Nature gave me a Right to *destroy* him, who had put himself into a state of War with me, and threatened my Destruction. But in the other Case, my Life not being in danger, I may have the *benefit of appealing* to the Law, and have Reparation for my £100 that way.

208. *Fourthly*, But if the unlawful acts done by the Magistrate, be maintained (by the Power he has got) and the remedy which is due by Law, be by the same Power obstructed; yet the *Right of Resisting*, even in such manifest Acts of Tyranny, *will not* suddenly, or on slight occasions, *disturb the Government*. For if it reach no farther than some private Mens Cases, though they have a right to defend themselves and to recover by force, what by unlawful Force is taken from them; yet the Right to do so, will not easily ingage them in a Contest, wherein they are sure to perish; it being as impossible for one, or a few oppressed Men to *disturb the Government*, where the Body of the People do not think themselves concerned in it, as for a raving mad Man, or heady Malecontent to overturn a well-setled State; the People being as little apt to follow the one, as the other.

209. But if either these illegal Acts have extended to the Majority of the People; or if the Mischief and Oppression has light only on some few, but in such Cases, as the Precedent, and Consequences seem to threaten all, and they are perswaded in their Consciences, that their Laws, and with them their Estates, Liberties, and Lives are in danger, and perhaps their Religion too, how they will be hindered

from resisting illegal force, used against them, I cannot tell. This is an *Inconvenience*, I confess, *that attends all Governments* whatsoever, when the Governours have brought it to this pass, to be generally suspected of their People; the most dangerous state which they can possibly put themselves in; wherein they are the less to be pitied, because it is so easie to be avoided; It being as impossible for a Governor, if he really means the good of his People, and the preservation of them, and their Laws together, not to make them see and feel it; as it is for the Father of a Family, not to let his Children see he loves, and takes care of them.

210. But if all the World shall observe Pretences of one kind, and Actions of another; Arts used to elude the Law, and the trust of Prerogative (which is an Arbitrary Power in some things left in the Prince's hand to do good, not harm to the People) employed, contrary to the end, for which it was given: If the People shall find the Ministers and subordinate Magistrates chosen suitable to such ends, and favoured, or laid by proportionably, as they promote, or oppose them: If they see several Experiments made of arbitrary Power, and that Religion underhand favoured,* (though publickly proclaimed against) which is readiest to introduce it; and the Operators in it supported, as much as may be; and when that cannot be done, yet approved still, and liked the better: If a *long Train of Actings shew the Councils* all tending that way, how can a Man any more hinder himself from being perswaded in his own Mind, which way things are going; or from casting about how to save himself, than he could from believing the Captain of a Ship he was in, was carrying him, and the rest of the Company to *Algiers*,* when he found him always steering that Course, though cross Winds, Leaks in his Ship, and want of Men and Provisions did often force him to turn his Course another way for some time, which he steadily returned to again, as soon as the Wind, Weather, and other Circumstances would let him?

CHAP. XIX.

Of the Dissolution of Government.

211.* He that will with any clearness speak of the *Dissolution of Government*, ought in the first place to distinguish between the *Dissolution of the Society*, and the *Dissolution of the Government*. That which makes the Community, and brings Men out of the loose state of Nature, into *one Politick Society*, is the Agreement which every one has with the rest to incorporate, and act as one Body, and so be one distinct Commonwealth. The usual, and almost only way whereby *this Union is dissolved*, is the Inroad of Foreign Force making a Conquest upon them. For in that Case, (not being able to maintain and support themselves, as *one intire* and *independent Body*) the Union belonging to that Body which consisted therein, must necessarily cease, and so every one return to the state he was in before, with a liberty to shift for himself, and provide for his own Safety as he thinks fit in some other Society. Whenever the *Society is dissolved*, 'tis certain the Government of that Society cannot remain. Thus Conquerours Swords often cut up Governments by the Roots, and mangle Societies to pieces, separating the subdued or scattered Multitude from the Protection of, and Dependence on that Society which ought to have preserved them from violence. The World is too well instructed in, and too forward to allow of this way of dissolving of Governments to need any more to be said of it; and there wants not much Argument to prove that where the *Society is dissolved*, the Government cannot remain; that being as impossible, as for the Frame of an House to subsist, when the Materials of it are scattered, and dissipated by a Whirlwind; or jumbled into a confused heap by an Earth-quake.

212. Besides this over-turning from without, *Governments are dissolved from within*,

First, When the *Legislative* is *altered*. Civil Society being a state of Peace, amongst those who are of it, from whom the state of War is excluded by the Umpirage, which they have provided in their Legislative, for the ending all Differences, that may arise amongst any of them, 'tis in their *Legislative*, that the Members of a Commonwealth are united, and combined together into one coherent living Body. This *is the Soul that gives Form, Life, and Unity* to the Commonwealth: From hence the several Members have their mutual Influence, Sympathy, and Connexion: And therefore when the *Legislative* is broken, or *dissolved*, Dissolution and Death follows. For the *Essence and Union of the Society* consisting in having one Will, the Legislative, when once established by the Majority, has the declaring, and as it were keeping of that Will. The *Constitution of the Legislative* is the first and fundamental Act of Society, whereby provision is made for the *Continuation of their Union*, under the Direction of Persons, and Bonds of Laws, made by Persons authorized thereunto, by the Consent and Appointment of the People, without which no one Man, or number of Men, amongst them, can have Authority of making Laws, that shall be binding to the rest. When any one or more, shall take upon them to make Laws, whom the People have not appointed so to do, they make Laws without Authority, which the People are not therefore bound to Obey; by which means they come again to be out of Subjection, and may constitute to themselves a *new Legislative*, as they think best, being in full liberty to resist the force of those, who without Authority would impose any thing upon them. Every one is at the disposure of his own Will, when those who had by the delegation of the Society, the declaring of the publick Will, are excluded from it, and others usurp the Place, who have no such Authority or Delegation.

213. This being usually brought about by such in the Commonwealth, who misuse the Power they have; it is hard to consider it aright, and know at whose door to lay it, without knowing the Form of Government in which it happens. Let us suppose then the Legislative placed in the Concurrence of three distinct Persons.*

(1) A single hereditary Person having the constant, supream, executive Power, and with it the Power of Convoking and Dissolving the other two within certain Periods of Time.

(2) An Assembly of Hereditary Nobility.

(3) An Assembly of Representatives chosen *pro tempore*,* by the People: Such a Form of Government supposed, it is evident,

214. *First*,* That when such a single Person, or Prince sets up his own arbitrary Will in place of the Laws, which are the will of the Society, declared by the Legislative, then the *Legislative is changed*. For that being in effect the Legislative, whose Rules and Laws are put in execution, and required to be obeyed; when other Laws are set up, and other Rules pretended, and inforced, than what the Legislative, constituted by the Society, have enacted, 'tis plain, that the *Legislative is changed*. Whoever introduces new Laws, not being thereunto authorized by the fundamental appointment of the Society, or subverts the old, disowns and overturns the Power by which they were made, and so sets up a *new Legislative*.

215. *Secondly*, When the Prince hinders the Legislative from assembling in its due time, or from acting freely, pursuant to those

ends, for which it was constituted, the *Legislative is altered*. For 'tis not a certain number of Men, no, nor their meeting, unless they have also Freedom of debating, and Leisure of perfecting, what is for the good of the Society, wherein the Legislative consists; when these are taken away or altered, so as to deprive the Society of the due exercise of their Power, the *Legislative* is truly altered. For it is not Names, that constitute Governments, but the Use and Exercise of those Powers, that were intended to accompany them, so that he, who takes away the Freedom, or hinders the acting of the Legislative in its due Seasons, in effect takes *away the Legislative*, and *puts an end to the Government*.

216. *Thirdly*, When by the arbitrary Power of the Prince, the Electors, or ways of Election are altered, without the Consent, and contrary to the common Interest of the People, there also the *Legislative is altered*. For if others, than those whom the Society has authorized thereunto, do chuse, or in another Way, than what the Society hath prescribed, those chosen are not the Legislative appointed by the People.

217. *Fourthly*, the Delivery also of the People into the Subjection of a foreign Power,* either by the Prince, or by the Legislative, is certainly a *Change of the Legislative*, and so a *Dissolution of the Government*. For the end why People entered into Society being to be preserved one intire, free, independent Society, to be governed by its own Laws; this is lost, whenever they are given up into the Power of another.

218. Why in such a Constitution as this, the *Dissolution of the Government* in these Cases is to be imputed to the Prince, is evident; because he having the Force, Treasure and Offices of the State to imploy, and often perswading himself, or being flattered by others, that as supream Magistrate he is uncapable of controul; he alone is in a Condition to make great Advances toward such Changes, under pretence of lawful Authority, and has it in his Hands to terrifie and suppress Opposers, as factious, seditious, and Enemies to the Government: Whereas no other part of the Legislative, or People is capable by themselves to attempt any alteration of the Legislative, without open and visible Rebellion, apt enough to be taken notice of, which when it prevails, produces Effects very little different from foreign Conquest. Besides the Prince in such a form of Government, having the Power of dissolving the other parts of the Legislative, and thereby rendering them private Persons, they can never in Opposition

to him, or without his Concurrence, alter the Legislative by a Law, his Consent being necessary to give any of their Decrees that Sanction. But yet so far as the other parts of the Legislative any Way contribute to any Attempt upon the Government, and do either promote, or not, what lies in them, hinder such Designs, they are guilty, and partake in this, which is certainly the greatest Crime Men can be guilty of one towards another.

219. There is one Way more whereby such a Government may be dissolved, and that is, when he who has the supream executive Power, neglects and abandons that Charge, so that the Laws already made can no longer be put in Execution. This is demonstratively to reduce all to Anarchy, and so effectually *to dissolve the Government*. For Laws not being made for themselves, but to be by their execution, the Bonds of the Society, to keep every part of the Body politick in its due Place and Function, when that totally ceases, the *Government* visibly *ceases*, and the People become a confused Multitude, without Order or Connexion. Where there is no longer the administration of Justice, for the securing of Mens Rights, nor any remaining Power within the Community to direct the Force, or provide for the Necessities of the Publick, there certainly is *no Government left*. Where the Laws cannot be executed, it is all one, as if there were no Laws, and a Government without Laws, is, I suppose, a Mystery in Politicks, unconceivable to human Capacity, and inconsistent with human Society.

220. In these and the like Cases, *when the Government is dissolved*, the People are at Liberty to provide for themselves, by erecting a new Legislative, differing from the other, by the change of Persons, or Form, or both, as they shall find it most for their Safety and Good. For the *Society* can never, by the Fault of another, lose the Native and Original Right it has to preserve it self, which can only be done by a settled Legislative, and a fair and impartial execution of the Laws made by it. But the state of Mankind is not so miserable that they are not capable of using this Remedy, till it be too late to look for any. To tell *People* they *may provide for themselves*, by erecting a new Legislative, when by Oppression, Artifice, or being delivered over to a foreign Power, their old one is gone, is only to tell them, they may expect Relief, when it is too late, and the evil is past Cure. This is in effect no more, than to bid them first be Slaves, and then to take care of their Liberty; and when their Chains are on, tell them, they may act like Freemen. This, if barely so, is rather Mockery, than

Relief; and Men can never be secure from Tyranny, if there be no means to escape it, till they are perfectly under it: And therefore it is, that they have not only a Right to get out of it, but to prevent it.

221. There is therefore Secondly another Way whereby *Governments are dissolved*, and that is, when the Legislative, or the Prince either of them act contrary to their Trust.

First, The *Legislative acts against the Trust* reposed in them, when they endeavour to invade the Property of the Subject, and to make themselves, or any part of the Community, Masters, or arbitrary Disposers of the Lives, Liberties, or Fortunes of the People.

222. The Reason why Men enter into Society, is the preservation of their Property; and the End why they chuse and authorize a Legislative, is, that there may be Laws made, and Rules set, as Guards and Fences to the Properties of all the Members of the Society, to limit the Power, and moderate the Dominion of every part and member of the Society. For since it can never be supposed to be the will of the Society, that the Legislative should have a Power to destroy that, which every one designs to secure, by entering into Society, and for which the People submitted themselves to Legislators of their own making, whenever the *Legislators endeavour to take away, and destroy the property of the People*, or to reduce them to Slavery under arbitrary Power, they put themselves into a state of War with the People, who are thereupon absolved from any farther Obedience, and are left to the common Refuge, which God hath provided for all Men, against Force and Violence. Whensoever therefore the *Legislative* shall transgress this fundamental Rule of Society; and either by Ambition, Fear, Folly or Corruption, *endeavour to grasp* themselves, *or put into the Hands of any other an absolute Power* over the Lives, Liberties, and Estates of the People; By this breach of Trust they *forfeit the Power*, the People had put into their Hands, for quite contrary ends, and it devolves to the People, who have a Right to resume their original Liberty, and, by the establishment of a new Legislative, (such as they shall think fit) provide for their own Safety and Security, which is the end for which they are in Society. What I have said here, concerning the Legislative in general, holds true also concerning the supreme Executor, who having a double Trust put in him, both to have a part in the Legislative, and the supreme Execution of the Law, acts against both, when he goes about to set up his own arbitrary Will, as the Law of the Society. He *acts* also *contrary to his Trust*, when he either

imploys the Force, Treasure, and Offices of the Society, to corrupt the *Representatives*, and gain them to his Purposes; or openly pre-ingages the *Electors*, and prescribes to their Choice, such, whom he has by Sollicitations, Threats, Promises, or otherwise won to his Designs; and imploys them to bring in such, who have promised before-hand, what to Vote, and what to Enact. Thus to regulate Candidates and Electors, and new model the ways of Election, what is it but to cut up the Government by the Roots, and poison the very Fountain of publick Security? For the People having reserved to themselves the Choice of their *Representatives*, as the Fence to their Properties, could do it for no other end, but that they might always be freely chosen, and so chosen, freely act and advise, as the necessity of the Commonwealth, and the publick Good should, upon examination, and mature Debate, be judged to require. This, those who give their Votes before they hear the Debate, and have weighed the Reasons on all sides, are not capable of doing. To prepare such an Assembly as this, and endeavour to set up the declared Abettors of his own Will, for the true *Representatives* of the People, and the Law-makers of the Society, is certainly as great a *breach of Trust*, and as perfect a Declaration of a Design to subvert the Government, as is possible to be met with. To which, if one shall add Rewards and Punishments visibly imploy'd to the same end, and all the Arts of perverted Law made use of, to take off and destroy all, that stand in the way of such a Design, and will not comply and consent to betray the Liberties of their Country, 'twill be past doubt what is doing. What Power they ought to have in the Society, who thus imploy it contrary to the Trust that went along with it in its first Institution, is easie to determine; and one cannot but see, that he, who has once attempted any such thing as this, cannot any longer be trusted.

223. To this perhaps it will be said, that the People being ignorant, and always discontented, to lay the foundation of Government in the unsteady Opinion and uncertain Humour of the People, is to expose it to certain Ruin; And *no Government will be able long to subsist*, if the People may set up a new Legislative, whenever they take offence at the old one. To this I answer, quite the contrary. People are not so easily got out of their old Forms, as some are apt to suggest. They are hardly to be prevailed with to amend the acknowledg'd Faults, in the Frame they have been accustom'd to. And if there be any original Defects, or adventitious ones introduced by time, or Corruption; 'tis

not an easie thing to get them changed, even when all the World sees there is an Opportunity for it. This Slowness and Aversion in the People to quit their old Constitutions, has, in the many Revolutions which have been seen in this Kingdom, in this and former Ages still kept us to, or, after some interval of fruitless Attempts, still brought us back again to our old Legislative of King, Lords and Commons: And whatever Provocations have made the Crown be taken from some of our Princes Heads, they never carried the People so far, as to place it in another Line.

224. But 'twill be said, this *Hypothesis* lays a *ferment for* frequent *Rebellion.* To which I Answer,

First, No more than any other *Hypothesis.* For when the People are made miserable, and find themselves *exposed to the ill Usage of arbitrary Power*, cry up their Governors, as much as you will, for Sons of *Jupiter*, let them be Sacred and Divine, descended, or authoriz'd from Heaven; give them out for whom or what you please, the same will happen. *The People generally ill treated*, and contrary to right, will be ready upon any Occasion to ease themselves of a Burden, that sits heavy upon them. They will wish, and seek for the Opportunity, which in the change, weakness and accidents of human Affairs, seldom delays long to offer it self. He must have lived but a little while in the World, who has not seen Examples of this in his time; and he must have read very little, who cannot produce Examples of it in all sorts of Governments in the World.

225. *Secondly*, I answer, such *Revolutions happen* not upon every little Mismanagement in publick Affairs. *Great Mistakes* in the ruling Part, many wrong and inconvenient Laws, and all the *Slips* of human Frailty will be *born by the People* without Mutiny or Murmur. But if a long train of Abuses,* Prevarications and Artifices, all tending the same Way, make the Design visible to the People, and they cannot but feel, what they lie under, and see, whither they are going; 'tis not to be wonder'd, that they should then rouze themselves, and endeavour to put the rule into such Hands, which may secure to them the ends for which Government was at first erected; and without which, ancient Names, and specious Forms, are so far from being better, that they are much worse, than the state of Nature, or pure Anarchy; the Inconveniences being all as great and as near, but the Remedy farther off and more difficult.

226. *Thirdly*, I answer, That *this Doctrine* of a Power in the People

of providing for their Safety a-new, by a new Legislative, when their Legislators have acted contrary to their Trust, by invading their Property, is *the best Fence against Rebellion*, and the probablest Means to hinder it. For *Rebellion* being an Opposition, not to Persons, but Authority, which is founded only in the Constitutions and Laws of the Government; those whoever they be, who by Force break through, and by Force justifie their Violation of them, are truly and properly *Rebels*. For when Men by entering into Society and Civil-Government, have excluded Force, and introduced Laws for the preservation of Property, Peace, and Unity amongst themselves, those who set up Force again in Opposition to the Laws, do *rebellare*, that is, bring back again the state of War, and are properly Rebels: Which they who are in Power, (by the Pretence they have to Authority, the temptation of Force they have in their Hands, and the Flattery of those about them) being likeliest to do; the properest Way to prevent the Evil, is to shew them the Danger and Injustice of it, who are under the greatest Temptation to run into it.

227. In both the forementioned Cases, when either the Legislative is changed, or the Legislators act contrary to the End for which they were constituted; those who are guilty are *guilty of Rebellion*. For if any one by Force takes away the establish'd Legislative of any Society, and the Laws by them made, pursuant to their Trust, he thereby takes away the Umpirage, which every one had consented to, for a peaceable decision of all their Controversies, and a Bar to the state of War amongst them. They, who remove, or change the Legislative, take away this decisive Power, which no Body can have, but by the appointment and consent of the People; and so destroying the Authority, which People did, and no Body else can set up, and introducing a Power, which the People hath not authoriz'd, they actually *introduce a state of War*, which is that of Force without Authority: And thus by removing the Legislative establish'd by the Society, (in whose Decisions the People acquiesced and united, as to that of their own Will) they unty the Knot, and *expose the People anew to the state of War*. And if those, who by Force take away the Legislative, are *Rebels*, the *Legislators* themselves, as has been shewn, can be no less esteemed so; when they, who were set up for the protection, and preservation of the People, their Liberties and Properties, shall by Force invade and endeavour to take them away; and so they putting themselves into a state of War with those, who made them the Protectors and Guardians of their

Peace, are properly, and with the greatest Aggravation, *Rebellantes*, Rebels.

228. But if they, who say *it lays a Foundation for Rebellion*, mean that it may occasion civil Wars, or intestine Broils, to tell the People they are absolved from Obedience, when illegal Attempts are made upon their Liberties or Properties, and may oppose the unlawful Violence of those, who were their Magistrates, when they invade their Properties contrary to the Trust put in them; and that therefore this Doctrine is not to be allow'd, being so destructive to the Peace of the World. They may as well say upon the same Ground, that honest Men may not oppose Robbers or Pirats, because this may occasion disorder or bloodshed. If any *Mischief* come in such Cases, it is not to be charged upon him who defends his own Right, but *on him, that invades* his Neighbours. If the innocent honest Man must quietly quit all he has for Peace sake, to him, who will lay violent Hands upon it, I desire it may be consider'd, what a kind of Peace there will be in the World, which consists only in Violence and Rapine; and which is to be maintain'd only for the benefit of Robbers and Oppressors. Who would not think it an admirable Peace betwixt the Mighty and the Mean, when the Lamb, without Resistance, yielded his Throat to be torn by the imperious Wolf? *Polyphemus's* Den* gives us a perfect Pattern of such a Peace, and such a Government, wherein *Ulysses* and his Companions had nothing to do, but quietly to suffer themselves to be devour'd. And no doubt *Ulysses*, who was a prudent Man, preach'd up *passive Obedience*,* and exhorted them to a quiet Submission, by representing to them of what concernment Peace was to Mankind; and by shewing the Inconveniencies [that] might happen, if they should offer to resist *Polyphemus*, who had now the Power over them.

229. The end of Government is the good of Mankind; and which is *best for Mankind*, that the People should be always expos'd to the boundless will of Tyranny, or that the Rulers should be sometimes liable to be oppos'd, when they grow exorbitant in the use of their Power, and imploy it for the destruction, and not the preservation of the Properties of their People?

230. Nor let any one say, that mischief can arise from hence, as often as it shall please a busie head, or turbulent spirit, to desire the alteration of the Government. 'Tis true, such Men may stir, whenever they please, but it will be only to their own just Ruine and Perdition. For till the mischief be grown general, and the ill

designs of the Rulers become visible, or their attempts sensible to the greater part, the People, who are more disposed to suffer, than right themselves by Resistance,* are not apt to stir. The examples of particular Injustice, or Oppression of here and there an unfortunate Man, moves them not. But if they universally have a perswasion, grounded upon manifest Evidence, that designs are carrying on against their Liberties, and the general course and tendency of things cannot but give them strong suspicions of the evil intention of their Governors, who is to be blamed for it? Who can help it, if they, who might avoid it, bring themselves, into this suspicion? Are the People to be blamed, if they have the sence of rational Creatures, and can think of things no otherwise, than as they find and feel them? And is it not rather *their Fault*, who puts things into such a posture, that they would not have them thought to be as they are? I grant, that the Pride, Ambition, and Turbulency of private Men have sometimes caused great Disorders in Commonwealths, and Factions have been fatal to States and Kingdoms. But whether *the mischief* hath *oftener* begun *in the Peoples Wantonness*, and a desire to cast off the lawful Authority of their Rulers; or *in the Rulers Insolence*, and Endeavours to get, and exercise an Arbitrary Power over their People; whether Oppression, or Disobedience gave the first rise to the Disorder, I leave it to impartial History to determine. This I am sure, whoever, either Ruler or Subject, by force goes about to invade the Rights of either Prince or People, and lays the foundation for *overturning* the Constitution and Frame of *any Just Government*, is guilty of the greatest Crime, I think, a Man is capable of, being to answer for all those mischiefs of Blood, Rapine, and Desolation, which the breaking to pieces of Governments bring on a Country. And he who does it, is justly to be esteemed the common Enemy and Pest of Mankind; and is to be treated accordingly.

231. That *Subjects* or *Foreigners* attempting by force on the Properties of any People, may be *resisted* with force, is agreed on all hands. But that *Magistrates*, doing the same thing, may be *resisted*, hath of late been denied: As if those who had the greatest Privileges and Advantages by the Law, had thereby a Power to break those Laws, by which alone they were set in a better place than their Brethren: Whereas their Offence is thereby the greater, both as being ungrateful for the greater share they have by the Law, and breaking also that Trust, which is put into their hands by their Brethren.

232. Whosoever uses *force without Right*, as every one does in

Society, who does it without Law, puts himself into a *state of War*
with those, against whom he so uses it, and in that state all former
Ties are cancelled, all other Rights cease, and every one has a right
to defend himself, and *to resist the Aggressor*. This is so evident, that
Barclay* himself, that great Assertor of the Power and Sacredness of
Kings, is forced to confess, That it is lawful for the People, in some
Cases, to *resist* their King; and that too in a Chapter, wherein he pretends to shew, that the Divine Law shuts up the People from all manner of Rebellion. Whereby it is evident, even by his own Doctrine,
that, since they may in some Cases *resist*, all resisting of *Princes* is
not Rebellion. His words are these.* . . . Barclay *contra Monarchom.*
L. 3. c. 8.

In *English* thus.

233. *But if any one should ask, must the People then always lay them-*
selves open to the Cruelty and Rage of Tyranny? Must they see their
Cities pillaged, and laid in Ashes, their Wives and Children exposed to
the Tyrant's Lust and Fury, and themselves and Families reduced by their
King to Ruine, and all the Miseries of Want and Oppression, and yet sit
still? Must Men alone be debarred the common Privilege of opposing Force
with Force, which Nature allows so freely to all other Creatures for their
preservation from Injury? I answer: Self-defence is a part of the Law of
Nature; nor can it be denied the Community, even against the King him-
self: But to revenge themselves upon him, must by no means be allowed
them; it being not agreeable to that Law Wherefore if the King shall shew
an hatred, not only to some particular Persons, but sets himself against
the Body of the Commonwealth, whereof he is the Head, and shall, with
intolerable ill Usage, cruelly tyrannize over the whole, or a considerable
part of the People, in this case the People have a right to resist and defend
themselves from Injury: But it must be with this Caution, that they only
defend themselves, but do not attack their Prince: They may repair the
Damages received, but must not for any provocation exceed the bounds of
due Reverence and Respect. They may repulse the present Attempt, but
must not revenge past Violences. For it is natural for us to defend Life
and Limb, but that an Inferiour should punish a Superiour, is against
Nature. The mischief which is designed them, the People may prevent
before it be done, but when it is done, they must not revenge it on the King,
though Author of the Villany. This therefore is the Privilege of the People
in general, above what any private Person hath; that particular Men

are allowed by our Adversaries themselves, (Buchanan* *only excepted*) *to have no other Remedy but Patience; but the Body of the People may with Respect resist intolerable Tyranny; for when it is but moderate, they ought to endure it.*

234. Thus far that great Advocate of Monarchical Power allows of *Resistance*.

235. 'Tis true, he has annexed two Limitations to it, to no purpose: *First*, He says, it must be with Reverence.

Secondly, It must be without Retribution, or Punishment; and the Reason he gives is, *Because an Inferiour cannot punish a Superiour.*

First, How to *resist Force without striking again*, or how to *strike with Reverence*, will need some Skill to make intelligible. He that shall oppose an Assault only with a Shield to receive the Blows, or in any more respectful Posture, without a Sword in his hand, to abate the Confidence and Force of the Assailant, will quickly be at an end of his *Resistance*, and will find such a defence serve only to draw on himself the worse Usage. This is as ridiculous a way of *resisting*, as *Juvenal** thought it of fighting; *ubi tu pulsas, ego vapulo tantum.** And the Success of the Combat will be unavoidably the same he there describes it: *Libertas pauperis haec est:* | *Pulsatus rogat, & pugnis concisus, adorat,* | *Ut liceat paucis cum dentibus inde reverti.** This will always be the event of such an imaginary *Resistance*, where Men may not strike again. He therefore *who may resist, must be allowed to strike*. And then let our Author, or any Body else join a knock on the Head, or a cut on the Face, with as much *Reverence* and *Respect* as he thinks fit. He that can reconcile blows and Reverence, may, for ought I know, deserve for his Pains, a Civil, Respectful, Cudgeling wherever he can meet with it.

Secondly, As to his Second, *An Inferiour cannot punish a Superiour*; that's true, generally speaking, whilst he is his Superiour. But to resist Force with Force, being *the state of War* that *levels the Parties*, cancels all former relation of Reverence, Respect, and *Superiority*: And then the odds that remains, is, That he, who opposes the unjust Aggressor, has this *Superiority* over him, that he has a Right, when he prevails, to punish the Offender, both for the Breach of the Peace, and all the Evils that followed upon it. *Barclay* therefore, in another place, more coherently to himself, denies it to be lawful to *resist* a King in any Case. But he there assigns two Cases, whereby a King may Un-king himself. His Words are,* . . . Barclay contra Monarchom. L. 3. c. 16.

Which in *English* runs thus.

237. *What then, Can there no Case happen wherein the People may of Right, and by their own Authority help themselves, take Arms, and set upon their King, imperiously domineering over them? None at all, whilst he remains a King.* Honour the King, *and* he that resists the Power, resists the Ordinance of God;* *are Divine Oracles that will never permit it. The People therefore can never come by a Power over him, unless he does something that makes him cease to be a King. For then he divests himself of his Crown and Dignity, and returns to the state of a private Man, and the People become Free and Superiour, the Power which they had in the* Interregnum,* *before they Crown'd him King, devolving to them again. But there are but few miscarriages which bring the matter to this State. After considering it well on all sides, I can find but two. Two Cases there are, I say, whereby a King,* ipso facto, *becomes no King; and loses all Power and Regal Authority over his People; which are also taken notice of by* Winzerus.*

The first is, If he endeavour to overturn the Government, that is, if he have a purpose and design to ruine the Kingdom and Commonwealth, as it is recorded of Nero, *that he resolved to cut off the Senate and People of* Rome, *lay the City waste with Fire and Sword, and then remove to some other Place. And of* Caligula,* *that he openly declar'd, that he would be no longer a Head to the People or Senate, and that he had it in his thoughts to cut off the worthiest Men of both Ranks, and then retire to* Alexandria: *And he wisht that the People had but one Neck, that he might dispatch them all at a blow.* *Such designs as these, when any King harbours in his thoughts, and seriously promotes, he immediately gives up all care and thought of the Commonwealth; and consequently forfeits the Power of Governing his Subjects, as a Master does the Dominion over his Slaves whom he hath abandon'd.*

238. *The other Case is, When a King makes himself the dependent of another, and subjects his Kingdom which his Ancestors left him, and the People put free into his hands, to the Dominion of another. For however perhaps it may not be in his intention to prejudice the People; yet because he has hereby lost the principal part of Regal Dignity, viz. to be next and immediately under God, Supream in his Kingdom; and also because he betray'd or forced his People, whose liberty he ought to have carefully preserved into the Power and Dominion of a Foreign Nation. By this as it were alienation of his Kingdom, he himself loses the Power he had in it*

before, without transferring any the least right to those on whom he would
have bestowed it; and so by this act sets the People free, and leaves them
at their own disposal. One Example of this is to be found in the Scotch
*Annals.**

239. In these Cases *Barclay* the great Champion of Absolute
Monarchy, is forced to allow, That a King may be *resisted*, and *ceases*
to be a King. That is, in short, not to multiply Cases, In whatsoever he
has *no Authority*, there he is *no King*, and may be *resisted*: For where-
soever the *Authority ceases, the King ceases too*, and becomes like other
Men who have no Authority. And these two Cases he instances
in, differ little from those above-mention'd, to be destructive to
Governments, only that he has omitted the Principle from which his
Doctrine flows; and that is, The Breach of Trust, in not preserving
the Form of Government agreed on, and in not intending the end of
Government itself, which is the publick Good and preservation of
Property. When a King has dethron'd himself, and put himself in
a State of War with his People, what shall hinder them from prosecuting him who is no King, as they would any other Man, who has
put himself into a state of War with them? *Barclay*, and those of his
Opinion, would do well to tell us. This farther I desire may be taken
notice of out of *Barclay*, that he says, *The Mischief that is designed them,*
the People may prevent before it be done, whereby he allows *Resistance*
when Tyranny is but in design. *Such Designs as these* (says he) *when*
any King harbours in his thoughts and seriously promotes, he immediately
gives up all Care and Thought of the Commonwealth; so that according
to him the neglect of the publick Good is to be taken as an Evidence of
such *Design*, or at least for a sufficient Cause of *Resistance*. And the
reason of all, he gives in these words, *Because he betray'd or forced*
his People whose Liberty he ought carefully to have preserved. What he
adds *into the Power and Dominion of a Foreign Nation*, signifies nothing, the Fault and Forfeiture lying in the Loss of their *Liberty*, which
he *ought to have preserved*, and not in any Distinction of the Persons to
whose Dominion they were subjected. The Peoples Right is equally
invaded, and their Liberty lost, whether they are made Slaves to any of
their own, or a *Foreign Nation*; and in this lies the Injury, and against
this only have they the Right of Defence. And there are Instances to be
found in all Countries, which shew, that 'tis not the change of Nations
in the Persons of their Governours, but the change of Government,
that gives the Offence.* *Bilson*,* a Bishop of our Church, and a great

Stickler for the Power and Prerogative of Princes, does, if I mistake not, in his Treatise of *Christian Subjection*, acknowledge, That *Princes may forfeit their Power*, and their Title to the Obedience of their Subjects; and if there needed Authority in a Case where reason is so plain, I could send my Reader to *Bracton, Fortescue*, and the Author of *the Mirrour*,* and others, Writers that cannot be suspected to be ignorant of our Government, or Enemies to it. But I thought *Hooker* alone might be enough to satisfy those Men, who relying on him for their Ecclesiastical Polity, are by a strange Fate carryd to deny those Principles upon which he builds it. Whether they arc herein made the Tools of cunninger Workmen, to pull down their own Fabrick, they were best look. This I am sure, their Civil Policy is so new, so dangerous, and so destructive to both Rulers and People, that as former Ages never could bear the broaching of it; so it may be hoped, those to come, redeem'd from the Impositions of these *Egyptian* Under-Taskmasters,* will abhor the Memory of such servile Flatterers, who whilst it seem'd to serve their turn, resolv'd all Government into absolute Tyranny, and would have all Men born to, what their mean Souls fitted them for, Slavery.

240. Here, 'tis like[ly], the common Question will be made, *Who shall be Judge,* whether the Prince or Legislative act contrary to their Trust? This, perhaps, ill affected and factious Men may spread amongst the People, when the Prince only makes use of his due Prerogative. To this I reply; *The People shall be Judge*; for who shall be *Judge* whether his Trustee or Deputy acts well, and according to the Trust reposed in him, but he who deputes him, and must, by having deputed him, have still a Power to discard him, when he fails in his Trust? If this be reasonable in particular Cases of private Men, why should it be otherwise in that of the greatest moment, where the Welfare of Millions is concerned, and also where the Evil, if not prevented, is greater, and the Redress very difficult, dear, and dangerous?

241. But farther, this Question, (*Who shall be Judge?*) cannot mean, that there is no Judge at all. For where there is no Judicature on Earth, to decide Controversies amongst Men, *God* in Heaven is *Judge.* He alone, 'tis true, is Judge of the Right. But *every Man* is *Judge* for himself, as in all other Cases, so in this, whether another hath put himself into a state of War with him, and whether he should appeal to the Supreme Judge, as *Jephtha* did.

242. If a Controversie arise betwixt a Prince and some of the People,

in a matter, where the Law is silent, or doubtful, and the thing be of great Consequence, I should think the proper *Umpire*, in such a Case, should be the Body of the *People*. For in Cases where the Prince hath a Trust reposed in him, and is dispensed from the common ordinary Rules of the Law; there, if any Men find themselves aggrieved, and think the Prince acts contrary to, or beyond that Trust, who so proper to *judge* as the Body of the *People*, (who, at first, lodg'd that Trust in him) how far they meant it should extend? But if the Prince, or who-ever they be in the Administration, decline that way of Determination, the Appeal then lies no where but to Heaven. Force between either Persons, who have no known Superior on Earth, or which permits no Appeal to a Judge on Earth, being properly a state of War, wherein the Appeal lies only to Heaven, and in that State the *injured Party must judge* for himself, when he will think fit to make use of that Appeal, and put himself upon it.

243. To conclude, The *Power that every Individual gave the Society*, when he entered into it, can never revert to the Individuals again, as long as the Society lasts, but will always remain in the Community; because without this, there can be no Community, no Commonwealth, which is contrary to the original Agreement: So also when the Society hath placed the Legislative in any Assembly of Men, to continue in them and their Successors, with Direction and Authority for pro-viding such Successors, *the Legislative can never revert to the People* whilst that Government lasts: Because having provided a Legislative with Power to continue for ever, they have given up their Political Power to the Legislative, and cannot resume it. But if they have set Limits to the Duration of their Legislative, and made this supreme Power in any Person, or Assembly, only temporary: Or else, when by the Miscarriages of those in Authority, it is forfeited; upon the Forfeiture, or at the Determination of the Time set, *it reverts to the Society*, and the People have a Right to act as Supreme, and continue the Legislative in themselves; or erect a new Form, or under the old Form place it in new Hands,* as they think good.

A

LETTER

Concerning

TOLERATION.

LICENSED, *Octob.* 3. 1689.

The Second Edition Corrected,

LONDON

Printed for *Awnsham Churchill*
at the *Black Swan in Ave-Mary Lane.*
MDCXC.

[*Quasi-facsimile title-page of the second edition of Locke's*
Letter Concerning Toleration]

A LETTER CONCERNING TOLERATION

TO THE READER.*

The Ensuing Letter concerning Toleration, *first Printed* in Latin *this very Year, in* Holland, *has already been Translated both into* Dutch *and* French.* *So general and speedy an Approbation may therefore bespeak its favourable Reception in* England. *I think indeed there is no Nation under Heaven, in which so much has already been said upon that Subject, as Ours.* *But yet certainly there is no People that stand in more need of having something further both said and done amongst them, in this Point, than We do.*

Our Government has not only been partial in Matters of Religion; but those also who have suffered under that Partiality, and have therefore endeavoured by their Writings to vindicate their own Rights and Liberties, have for the most part done it upon narrow Principles, suited only to the Interests of their own Sects. *

This narrowness of Spirit on all sides has undoubtedly been the principal Occasion of our Miseries and Confusions. But whatever have been the Occasion, it is now high time to seek for a thorow Cure. We have need of more generous Remedies than what have yet been made use of in our Distemper. It is neither Declarations of Indulgence,* *nor* Acts of Comprehension,* *such as have yet been practised or projected amongst us, that can do the Work. The first will but palliate, the second encrease our Evil.*

Absolute Liberty, Just and True Liberty, Equal and Impartial Liberty, *is the thing that we stand in need of. Now tho this has indeed been much talked of, I doubt it has not been much understood; I am sure not at all practised, either by our Governours towards the People, in general, or by any dissenting Parties* *of the People towards one another.*

I cannot therefore but hope that this Discourse, *which treats of that Subject, however briefly, yet more exactly than any we have yet seen, demonstrating both the Equitableness and Practicableness of the thing, will be esteemed highly seasonable, by all Men that have Souls large enough to prefer the true Interest of the Publick before that of a Party.*

It is for the use of such as are already so spirited, or to inspire that Spirit into those that are not, that I have Translated it into our Language. But the thing it self is so short, that it will not bear a longer Preface. I leave it therefore to the Consideration of my Countrymen, and heartily wish they may make the use of it that it appears to be designed for.

A LETTER CONCERNING TOLERATION.

Honoured Sir,

Since you are pleased to inquire what are my Thoughts about the mutual Toleration of Christians in their different Professions of Religion, I must needs answer you freely, That I esteem that Toleration to be the chief Characteristical Mark of the True Church.* For whatsoever some People boast of the Antiquity of Places and Names, or of the Pomp of their Outward Worship; Others, of the Reformation of their Discipline; All, of the Orthodoxy of their Faith; (for every one is Orthodox to himself:) these things, and all others of this nature, are much rather Marks of Men striving for Power and Empire over one another, than of the Church of Christ. Let any one have never so true a Claim to all these things, yet if he be destitute of Charity, Meekness, and Good-will in general towards all Mankind; even to those that are not Christians, he is certainly yet short of being a true Christian himself. *The Kings of the Gentiles exercise Lordship over them*, said our Saviour to his Disciples, *but ye shall not be so* (Luke 22: 25–6). The Business of True Religion is quite another thing. It is not instituted in order to the erecting of an external Pomp, nor to the obtaining of Ecclesiastical Dominion, nor to the exercising of Compulsive Force; but to the regulating of Mens Lives according to the Rules of Vertue and Piety. Whosoever will list himself under the Banner of Christ, must in the first place, and above all things, make War upon his own Lusts and Vices. It is in vain for any Man to usurp the Name of Christian, without Holiness of Life, Purity of Manners,* and Benignity and Meekness of Spirit.

Thou when thou art converted, strengthen thy Brethren, said our Lord to *Peter* (Luke 22: 32). It would indeed be very hard for one that appears careless about his own Salvation, to perswade me that he were extreamly concern'd for mine. For it is impossible that those should sincerely and heartily apply themselves to make other People

Christians, who have not really embraced the Christian Religion in their own Hearts. If the Gospel and the Apostles may be credited, no Man can be a Christian without *Charity*, and without *that Faith which works*, not by Force, but by *Love*.* Now I appeal to the Consciences of those that persecute, torment, destroy, and kill other Men upon pretence of Religion, whether they do it out of Friendship and Kindness towards them, or no: And I shall then indeed, and not till then, believe they do so, when I shall see those fiery Zealots correcting, in the same manner, their Friends and familiar Acquaintance, for the manifest Sins they commit against the Precepts of the Gospel; when I shall see them prosecute with Fire and Sword the Members of their own Communion that are tainted with enormous Vices, and without Amendment are in danger of eternal Perdition; and when I shall see them thus express their Love and Desire of the Salvation of their Souls, by the infliction of Torments, and exercise of all manner of Cruelties. For if it be out of a Principle of Charity, as they pretend, and Love to Mens Souls, that they deprive them of their Estates,* maim them with corporal Punishments, starve and torment them in noisome* Prisons, and in the end even take away their Lives; I say, if all this be done meerly to make Men Christians, and procure their Salvation, Why then do they suffer *Whoredom, Fraud, Malice, and such like enormities* (Rom. 1: 28–32); which (according to the Apostle) manifestly rellish* of Heathenish Corruption, to predominate so much and abound amongst their Flocks and People? These, and such like things, are certainly more contrary to the Glory of God, to the Purity of the Church, and to the Salvation of Souls, than any conscientious Dissent from Ecclesiastical Decisions, or Separation from Publick Worship, whilst accompanied with Innocency of Life. Why then does this burning Zeal for God, for the Church, and for the Salvation of Souls; burning, I say, literally, with Fire and Faggot; pass by those moral Vices and Wickednesses, without any Chastisement, which are acknowledged by all Men to be diametrically opposite to the Profession of Christianity; and bend all its Nerves either to the introducing of Ceremonies, or to the establishment of Opinions, which for the most part are about nice* and intricate Matters, that exceed the Capacity of ordinary Understandings? Which of the Parties contending about these things is in the right, which of them is guilty of Schism or Heresie;* whether those that domineer or those that suffer, will then at last be manifest, when the Cause of their Separation comes to be judged of.* He certainly that follows Christ, embraces his Doctrine, and bears his Yoke, tho' he forsake both Father and Mother, separate from the Publick Assembly and Ceremonies of his Country, or whomsoever, or whatsoever else he relinquishes, will not then be judged an Heretick.

Now, tho' the Divisions that are amongst Sects should be allowed to be never so obstructive of the Salvation of Souls; yet nevertheless *Adultery, Fornication, Uncleanness, Lasciviousness, Idolatry, and such like things, cannot be denied to be Works of the Flesh*; concerning which the Apostle has expresly declared, that *they who do them shall not inherit the Kingdom of God* (Gal. 5: 19–21). Whosoever therefore is sincerely sollicitous about the Kingdom of God, and thinks it his Duty to endeavour the Enlargement of it amongst Men, ought to apply himself with no less care and industry to the rooting out of these Immoralities, than to the Extirpation of Sects.* But if any one do otherwise, and whilst he is cruel and implacable towards those that differ from him in Opinion, he be indulgent to such Iniquities and Immoralities as are unbecoming the Name of a Christian, let such a one talk never so much of the Church, he plainly demonstrates by his Actions, that 'tis another Kingdom* he aims at, and not the Advancement of the Kingdom of God.

That any Man should think fit to cause another Man, whose Salvation he heartily desires, to expire in Torments, and that even in an unconverted estate; would, I confess, seem very strange to me; and, I think, to any other also. But no body, surely, will ever believe that such a Carriage can proceed from Charity, Love, or Good-will. If any one maintain that Men ought to be compelled by Fire and Sword to profess certain Doctrines, and conform to this or that exteriour Worship, without any regard had unto their Morals; if any one endeavour to convert those that are Erroneous unto the Faith, by forcing them to profess things that they do not believe, and allowing them to practise things that the Gospel does not permit; it cannot be doubted indeed but such a one is desirous to have a numerous Assembly joyned in the same Profession with himself: But that he principally intends by those means to compose a truly Christian Church, is altogether incredible. It is not therefore to be wondred at, if those who do not really contend for the Advancement of the true Religion, and of the Church of Christ, make use of Arms that do not belong to the Christian Warfare.* If, like the Captain of our

Salvation, they sincerely desired the Good of Souls, they would tread in the Steps, and follow the perfect Example of that Prince of Peace, who sent out his Soldiers to the subduing of Nations, and gathering them into his Church, not armed with the Sword, or other Instruments of Force, but prepared with the Gospel of Peace, and with the Exemplary Holiness of their Conversation.* This was his Method. Tho' if Infidels were to be converted by force, if those that are either blind or obstinate were to be drawn off from their Errors by Armed Soldiers, we know very well that it was much more easie for Him to do it, with Armies of Heavenly Legions, than for any Son of the Church, how potent soever, with all his Dragoons.*

The Toleration of those that differ from others in Matters of Religion, is so agreeable to the Gospel of Jesus Christ, and to the genuine Reason of Mankind, that it seems monstrous for Men to be so blind, as not to perceive the Necessity and Advantage of it, in so clear a Light. I will not here tax the Pride and Ambition of some, the Passion and uncharitable Zeal of others. These are Faults from which Humane* Affairs can perhaps scarce ever be perfectly freed; but yet such as no body will bear the plain Imputation of, without covering them with some specious Colour;* and so pretend to Commendation, whilst they are carried away by their own irregular Passions. But however, that some may not colour their spirit of Persecution and unchristian Cruelty, with a Pretence of Care of the Publick Weal,* and Observation of the Laws; and that others, under pretence of Religion, may not seek Impunity for their Libertinism and Licentiousness; in a word, that none may impose either upon himself or others, by the Pretences of Loyalty and Obedience to the Prince, or of Tenderness and Sincerity in the Worship of God; I esteem it above all things necessary to distinguish exactly the Business of Civil Government from that of Religion, and to settle the just Bounds that lie between the one and the other. If this be not done, there can be no end put to the Controversies that will be always arising, between those that have, or at least pretend to have, on the one side, a Concernment for the Interest of Mens Souls, and, on the other side, a Care of the Commonwealth.*

The Commonwealth seems to me to be a Society of Men constituted only for the procuring, preserving, and advancing of their own *Civil Interests.**

Civil Interests I call Life, Liberty, Health, and Indolency* of Body;

and the Possession of outward things, such as Money, Lands, Houses, Furniture, and the like.

It is the Duty of the Civil Magistrate,* by the impartial Execution of equal Laws, to secure unto all the People in general, and to every one of his Subjects in particular, the just Possession of these things belonging to this Life. If any one presume to violate the Laws of Publick Justice and Equity, established for the Preservation of these things, his Presumption is to be check'd by the fear of Punishment, consisting of the Deprivation or Diminution of those Civil Interests, or Goods, which otherwise he might and ought to enjoy. But seeing no Man does willingly suffer himself to be punished by the Deprivation of any part of his Goods, and much less of his Liberty or Life, therefore is the Magistrate armed with the Force and Strength of all his Subjects, in order to the punishment of those that violate any other Man's Rights.

Now that the whole Jurisdiction of the Magistrate reaches only to these civil Concernments; and that all Civil Power, Right, and Dominion, is bounded and confined to the only care of promoting these things; and that it neither can nor ought in any manner to be extended to the Salvation of Souls; these following Considerations seem unto me abundantly to demonstrate.

First, Because the Care of Souls is not committed to the Civil Magistrate any more than to other Men. It is not committed unto him, I say, by God; because it appears not that God has ever given any such Authority to one Man over another, as to compell any one to his Religion.* Nor can any such Power be vested in the Magistrate by the *Consent of the People*;* because no man can so far abandon the care of his own Salvation, as blindly to leave it to the choice of any other, whether Prince or Subject, to prescribe to him what Faith or Worship he shall embrace. For no Man can, if he would, conform his Faith to the Dictates, of another. All the Life and Power of true Religion consist in the inward and full perswasion of the mind: And Faith is not Faith without believing. Whatever Profession we make, to whatever outward Worship we conform, if we are not fully satisfied in our mind that the one is true, and the other well pleasing unto God; such Profession and such Practice, far from being any furtherance, are indeed great Obstacles to our Salvation. For in this manner, instead of expiating other Sins by the exercise of Religion; I say, in offering thus unto God Almighty such a Worship as we esteem to be displeasing unto him, we add unto the number of our other sins those also of Hypocrisie, and Contempt of his Divine Majesty.

In the second place. The care of Souls cannot belong to the Civil Magistrate, because his Power consists only in outward force: But true and saving Religion consists in the inward perswasion of the Mind; without which nothing can be acceptable to God. And such is the nature of the Understanding, that it cannot be compell'd to the belief of any thing by outward Force. Confiscation of Estate, Imprisonment, Torments, nothing of that Nature can have any such Efficacy as to make Men change the inward Judgment that they have framed of things.

It may indeed be alledged, that the Magistrate may make use of Arguments, and thereby draw the Heterodox into the way of Truth, and procure their Salvation. I grant it.* But this is common to him with other Men. In teaching, instructing, and redressing the Erroneous by Reason, he may certainly do what becomes any good Man to do. Magistracy does not oblige him to put off either Humanity or Christianity. But it is one thing to perswade, another to command: One thing to press with Arguments, another with Penalties. This the Civil Power alone has a Right to do: to the other Goodwill is Authority enough. Every Man has Commission to admonish, exhort, convince another of Error; and by reasoning to draw him into Truth. But to give Laws, receive Obedience, and compel with the Sword, belongs to none but the Magistrate. And upon this ground I affirm, that the Magistrate's Power extends not to the establishing of any Articles of Faith, or Forms of Worship, by the force of his Laws. For Laws are of no force at all without Penalties, and Penalties in this case are absolutely impertinent;* because they are not proper to convince the mind.* Neither the Profession of any Articles of Faith, nor the Conformity to any outward Form of Worship (as has been already said) can be available to the Salvation of Souls; unless the Truth of the one, and the acceptableness of the other unto God, be thoroughly believed by those that so profess and practise. But Penalties are no ways capable to produce such Belief. It is only Light and Evidence that can work a change in Mens Opinions. And that Light can in no manner proceed from corporal Sufferings, or any other outward Penalties.

In the third place. The care of the Salvation of Mens Souls cannot belong to the Magistrate; because, though the rigour of Laws and the force of Penalties were capable to convince and change Mens minds, yet would not that help at all to the Salvation of their Souls. For there being but one Truth, one way to heaven; what hopes is there that more Men would be led into it, if they had no other Rule to follow but the Religion of the Court; and were put under a necessity to quit the Light of their own Reason; to oppose the Dictates of their own Consciences; and blindly to resign up themselves to the Will of their Governors, and to the Religion, which either Ignorance, Ambition, or Superstition had chanced to establish in the Countries where they were born? In the variety and contradiction of Opinions in Religion, wherein the Princes of the World are as much divided as in their Secular Interests, the narrow way would be much straitned.* One Country alone would be in the right, and all the rest of the World would be put under an Obligation of following their Princes in the ways that lead to Destruction. And that which heightens the absurdity, and very ill suits the Notion of a Deity, Men would owe their eternal Happiness or Misery to the places of their Nativity.

These Considerations, to omit many others that might have been urged to the same purpose, seem unto me sufficient to conclude that all the Power of Civil Government relates only to Mens Civil Interests; is confined to the care of the things of this World; and hath nothing to do with the World to come.

Let us now consider what a Church is. A Church then I take to be a voluntary Society* of Men, joining themselves together of their own accord, in order to the publick worshipping of God, in such a manner as they judge acceptable to him, and effectual to the Salvation of their Souls.

I say it is a free and voluntary Society. No body is born a Member of any Church. Otherwise the Religion of Parents would descend unto Children, by the same right of Inheritance as their Temporal Estates, and every one would hold his Faith by the same Tenure he does his Lands; than which nothing can be imagined more absurd. Thus therefore that matter stands. No Man by nature is bound unto any particular Church or Sect, but every one joins himself voluntarily to that Society in which he believes he has found that Profession and Worship which is truly acceptable unto God. The hopes of Salvation, as it was the only cause of his entrance into that Communion, so it can be the only reason of his stay there. For if afterwards he discover any thing either erroneous in the Doctrine, or incongruous in the

Worship of that Society to which he has join'd himself; Why should it not be as free for him to go out, as it was to enter? No Member of a Religious Society can be tied with any other Bonds but what proceed from the certain expectation of eternal Life. A Church then is a Society of Members voluntarily uniting to this end.

It follows now that we consider what is the Power of this Church, and unto what Laws it is subject.

Forasmuch as no Society, how free soever, or upon whatsoever slight occasion instituted, (whether of Philosophers for Learning, of Merchants for Commerce, or of men of leisure for mutual Conversation and Discourse,) No Church or Company, I say, can in the least subsist and hold together, but will presently dissolve and break to pieces, unless it be regulated by some Laws, and the Members all consent to observe some Order. Place, and time of meeting must be agreed on. Rules for admitting and excluding Members must be establisht. Distinction of Officers, and putting things into a regular Course, and such like, cannot be omitted. But since the joyning together of several Members into this Church-Society, as has already been demonstrated, is absolutely free and spontaneous, it necessarily follows, that the Right of making its Laws* can belong to none but the Society it self; or at least (which is the same thing) to those whom the Society by common consent has authorised thereunto.

Some perhaps may object, that no such Society can be said to be a true Church, unless it have in it a Bishop, or Presbyter, with Ruling Authority derived from the very Apostles, and continued down unto the present times by an uninterrupted Succession.*

To these I answer. *In the first place*, Let them shew me the Edict by which Christ has imposed that Law upon his Church. And let not any man think me impertinent, if in a thing of this consequence, I require that the Terms of that Edict be very express and positive. For the Promise he has made us, that *wheresoever two or three are gathered together in his Name, he will be in the midst of them*, seems to imply the contrary (Matt. 18: 20). Whether such an Assembly want any thing necessary to a true Church, pray do you consider. Certain I am, that nothing can be there wanting unto the Salvation of Souls; Which is sufficient to our purpose.

Next, Pray observe how great have always been the Divisions amongst even those who lay so much stress upon the Divine Institution, and continued Succession of a certain Order of Rulers in the Church. Now their very Dissension unavoidably puts us upon a necessity of deliberating, and consequently allows a Liberty of choosing that which upon consideration we prefer.

And in the last place, I consent that these men have a Ruler of their Church, established by such a long Series of Succession as they judge necessary; provided I may have liberty at the same time to join my self to that Society, in which I am perswaded those things are to be found which are necessary to the Salvation of my Soul. In this manner Ecclesiastical Liberty will be preserved on all sides, and no man will have a Legislator imposed upon him, but whom himself has chosen.

But since men are so sollicitous about the true Church, I would only ask them, here by the way, if it be not more agreeable to the Church of Christ, to make the Conditions of her Communion consist in such things, and such things only, as the Holy Spirit has in the Holy Scriptures declared, in express Words, to be necessary to Salvation; I ask, I say, whether this be not more agreeable to the Church of Christ, than for men to impose their own Inventions and Interpretations upon others, as if they were of Divine Authority; and to establish by Ecclesiastical Laws, as absolutely necessary to the Profession of Christianity, such things as the Holy Scriptures do either not mention, or at least not expressly command. Whosoever requires those things in order to* Ecclesiastical Communion, which Christ does not require in order to life Eternal; he may perhaps indeed constitute a Society accommodated to his own Opinion, and his own Advantage; but how that can be called the Church of Christ, which is established upon Laws that are not his, and which excludes such Persons from its Communion as he will one day receive into the Kingdom of Heaven, I understand not. But this being not a proper place to enquire into the marks of the true Church, I will only mind* those that contend so earnestly for the Decrees of their own Society, and that cry out continually the Church, the Church, with as much noise, and perhaps upon the same Principle, as the *Ephesian* Silversmiths did for their *Diana*;* this, I say, I desire to mind them of, That the Gospel frequently declares that the true Disciples of Christ must suffer Persecution; but that the Church of Christ should persecute others, and force others by Fire and Sword, to embrace her Faith and Doctrine, I could never yet find in any of the Books of the New Testament.

The end of a Religious Society (as has already been said) is the Publick Worship of God, and by means thereof the acquisition of

Eternal Life. All Discipline ought therefore to tend to that End, and all Ecclesiastical Laws to be thereunto confined. Nothing ought, nor can be transacted in this Society, relating to the Possession of Civil and Worldly Goods. No Force is here to be made use of, upon any occasion whatsoever. For Force belongs wholly to the Civil Magistrate, and the Possession of all outward Goods is subject to his Jurisdiction.

But it may be asked, By what means then shall Ecclesiastical Laws be established, if they must be thus destitute of all compulsive Power. I answer, They must be established by means suitable to the Nature of such Things, whereof the external Profession and Observation, if not proceeding from a thorow Conviction and Approbation of the Mind, is altogether useless and unprofitable. The Arms by which the Members of this Society are to be kept within their Duty, are Exhortations, Admonitions, and Advices. If by these means the Offenders will not be reclaimed, and the Erroneous convinced, there remains nothing farther to be done, but that such stubborn and obstinate Persons, who give no ground to hope for their Reformation, should be cast out and separated from the Society. This is the last and utmost Force of Ecclesiastical Authority. No other Punishment can thereby be inflicted, than that the relation ceasing between the Body and the Member which is cut off, the Person so condemned ceases to be a part of that Church.

These things being thus determined, let us inquire in the next place, how far the Duty of Toleration extends; and what is required from every one by it.

And first, I hold, That no Church is bound by the Duty of Toleration to retain any such Person in her Bosom, as, after Admonition, continues obstinately to offend against the Laws of the Society. For these being the Condition of Communion, and the Bond of the Society; If the Breach of them were permitted without any Animadversion, the Society would immediately be thereby dissolved. But nevertheless, in all such Cases, care is to be taken that the Sentence of Excommunication,* and the Execution thereof, carry with it no rough usage of Word or Action, whereby the ejected Person may any wise be damnified* in Body or Estate. For all Force (as has often been said) belongs only to the Magistrate; nor ought any private Persons, at any time, to use Force, unless it be in Self-defence against unjust Violence. Excommunication neither does, nor can deprive the excommunicated Person of any of those Civil Goods that he formerly possessed. All those things belong to the Civil Government, and are under the Magistrate's Protection. The whole Force of Excommunication consists only in this, that the Resolution of the Society in that respect being declared, the Union that was between the Body and some Member comes thereby to be dissolved; and that Relation ceasing, the participation of some certain things, which the Society communicated to its Members, and unto which no Man has any Civil Right, comes also to cease. For there is no Civil Injury done unto the excommunicated Person, by the Church-Minister's refusing him that Bread and Wine, in the Celebration of the Lord's Supper, which was not bought with his, but other mens Money.

Secondly, No private Person has any Right, in any manner, to prejudice another Person in his Civil Enjoyments, because he is of another Church or Religion. All the Rights and Franchises* that belong to him as a Man, or as a Denison,* are inviolably to be Preserved to him. These are not the Business of Religion. No Violence nor Injury is to be offered him, whether he be Christian or Pagan. Nay, we must not content our selves with the narrow Measures of bare Justice. Charity, Bounty, and Liberality must be added to it. This the Gospel enjoyns; this Reason directs; and this that natural Fellowship we are born into requires of us. If any man err from the right way, it is his own Misfortune, no Injury to thee: Nor therefore art thou to punish him in the things of this Life, because thou supposest he will be miserable in that which is to come.

What I say concerning the mutual Toleration of private Persons differing from one another in Religion, I understand also of particular Churches; which stand as it were in the same relation to each other as private Persons among themselves; nor has any one of them any manner of Jurisdiction over any other, no not even when the Civil Magistrate (as it sometimes happens) comes to be of this or the other Communion. For the Civil Government can give no new Right to the Church, nor the Church to the Civil Government. So that whether the Magistrate joyn himself to any Church, or separate from it, the Church remains always as it was before, a free and voluntary Society. It neither acquires the Power of the Sword by the Magistrate's coming to it, nor does it lose the Right of Instruction and Excommunication by his going from it. This is the fundamental and immutable Right of a spontaneous* Society; that it has power to remove any of its Members who transgress the Rules of its Institution.

But it cannot, by the accession of any new Members, acquire any Right of Jurisdiction over those that are not joyned with it. And therefore Peace, Equity and Friendship, are always mutually to be observed by particular Churches, in the same manner as by private Persons, without any pretence of Superiority or Jurisdiction over one another.

That the thing may be made yet clearer by an Example; Let us suppose two Churches, the one of *Arminians*, the other of *Calvinists*,* residing in the City of *Constantinople*; Will any one say, that either of these Churches has [a] Right to deprive the Members of the other of their Estates and Liberty, (as we see practised elsewhere) because of their differing from it in some Doctrines or Ceremonies, whilst the *Turks** in the mean while silently stand by, and laugh to see with what inhumane Cruelty Christians thus rage against Christians? But if one of those Churches hath this Power of treating the other ill, I ask which of them it is to whom that Power belongs, and by what Right? It will be answered undoubtedly, That it is the Orthodox Church which has the Right of Authority over the Erroneous or Heretical. This is, in great and specious words, to say just nothing at all. For every Church is Orthodox to it self; to others, Erroneous or Heretical. Whatsoever any Church believes, it believes to be true; and the contrary thereunto it pronounces to be Error. So that the Controversie between these Churches about the Truth of their Doctrines, and the Purity of their Worship, is on both sides equal; nor is there any Judge, either at *Constantinople*, or elsewhere upon Earth, by whose Sentence it can be determined. The Decision of that Question belongs only to the Supream Judge of all men, to whom also alone belongs the Punishment of the Erroneous. In the mean while, let those men consider how hainously they sin; Who, adding Injustice, if not to their Error, yet certainly to their Pride, do rashly and arrogantly take upon them to misuse the Servants of another Master, who are not at all accountable to them.

Nay further: If it could be manifest which of these two dissenting Churches were in the right way, there would not accrue thereby to the Orthodox any Right of destroying the other. For Churches have neither any Jurisdiction in worldly Matters, nor are Fire and Sword any proper Instruments wherewith to convince mens Minds of Error, and inform them of the Truth. Let us suppose, nevertheless, that the Civil Magistrate inclined to favour one of them, and to put his Sword into their Hands; that (by his consent) they might chastise the Dissenters as they pleased. Will any man say, that any Right can be derived unto a Christian Church over its Brethren, from a Turkish Emperor? An Infidel, who has himself no Authority to punish Christians for the Articles of their Faith, cannot confer such an Authority upon any Society of Christians, nor give unto them a Right, which he has not himself. This would be the Case at *Constantinople*. And the Reason of the thing is the same in any Christian Kingdom. The Civil Power is the same in every place; nor can that Power, in the Hands of a Christian Prince, confer any greater Authority upon the Church, than in the Hands of a Heathen; which is to say, just none at all.

Nevertheless, it is worthy to be observed, and lamented, that the most violent of these Defenders of the Truth, the Opposers of Errors, the Exclaimers against Schism, do hardly ever let loose this their Zeal for God, with which they are so warmed and inflamed, unless where they have the Civil Magistrate on their side. But so soon as ever Court favour has given them the better end of the Staff,* and they begin to feel themselves the stronger, then presently Peace and Charity are to be laid aside; otherwise, they are religiously to be observed. Where they have not the Power to carry on Persecution, and to become Masters, there they desire to live upon fair Terms, and preach up Toleration.* When they are not strengthned with the Civil Power, then they can bear most patiently and unmovedly the Contagion of Idolatry, Superstition and Heresie in their Neighbourhood; of which, in other Occasions, the Interest of Religion makes them to be extreamly apprehensive. They do not forwardly attack those Errors which are in fashion at Court, or are countenanced by the Government. Here they can be content to spare their Arguments; which yet (with their leave) is the only right Method of propagating Truth; which has no such way of prevailing, as when strong Arguments and good Reason are joyned with the softness of Civility and good Usage.

No body therefore, in fine,* neither single Persons, nor Churches, nay, nor even Commonwealths, have any just Title to invade the Civil Rights and Worldly Goods of each other upon pretence of Religion. Those that are of another Opinion, would do well to consider with themselves how pernicious a Seed of Discord and War, how powerful a Provocation to endless Hatreds, Rapines, and Slaughters, they thereby furnish unto Mankind. No Peace and Security, no not so much as common Friendship, can ever be established or preserved amongst Men, so long as this Opinion prevails, That *Dominion is* *founded in Grace,** and that Religion is to be propagated by force of Arms.

In the third Place; Let us see what the *Duty of Toleration requires* from those who are distinguished from the rest of Mankind, (from the Laity, as they please to call us)* by some *Ecclesiastical Character and Office*; whether they be Bishops, Priests, Presbyters, Ministers, or however else dignified or distinguished. It is not my Business to enquire here into the Original of the Power or Dignity of the Clergy. This only I say, That whence-soever their Authority be sprung, since it is Ecclesiastical, it ought to be confined within the Bounds of the Church, nor can it in any manner be extended to Civil Affairs; because the Church it self is a thing absolutely separate and distinct from the Commonwealth. The Boundaries on both sides are fixed and immovable. He jumbles Heaven and Earth together, the things most remote and opposite, who mixes these Societies; which are in their Original, End, Business, and in every thing, perfectly distinct, and infinitely different from each other. No man therefore, with whatsoever Ecclesiastical Office he be dignified, can deprive another man, that is not of his Church and Faith, either of Liberty, or of any part of his Worldly Goods, upon the account of that difference which is between them in Religion. For whatever is not lawful to the whole Church, cannot, by any Ecclesiastical Right, become lawful to any of its Members.

But this is not all. It is not enough that Ecclesiastical Men abstain from Violence and Rapine, and all manner of Persecution. He that pretends to be a Successor of the Apostles, and takes upon him the Office of Teaching, is obliged also to admonish his Hearers of the Duties of Peace and Good-will towards all men; as well towards the Erroneous, as the Orthodox; towards those that differ from them in Faith and Worship, as well as towards those that agree with them therein. And he ought industriously to exhort all men, whether private Persons or Magistrates, (if any such there be in his Church) to Charity, Meekness and Toleration; and diligently endeavour to allay and temper all that Heat and unreasonable Averseness of Mind, which either any man's fiery Zeal for his own Sect, or the Craft* of others, has kindled against Dissenters. I will not undertake to represent how happy and how great would be the Fruit, both in Church and State, if the Pulpits every where sounded with this Doctrine of Peace and Toleration; lest I should seem to reflect too severely upon those Men whose Dignity I desire not to detract from, nor would have it diminished either by others or themselves. But this I say, That thus it ought to be. And if any one that professes himself to be a Minister of the Word of God, a Preacher of the Gospel of Peace, teach otherwise; he either understands not, or neglects the Business of his Calling, and shall one day give account thereof unto the Prince of Peace. If Christians are to be admonished that they abstain from all manner of Revenge, even after repeated Provocations and multiplied Injuries;* how much more ought they who suffer nothing, who have had no harm done them, forbear Violence, and abstain from all manner of ill usage towards those from whom they have received none. This Caution and Temper they ought certainly to use towards those who mind only their own Business, and are sollicitous for nothing but that (whatever men think of them) they may worship God in that manner which they are persuaded is acceptable to him, and in which they have the strongest hopes of Eternal Salvation. In private domestick Affairs, in the management of Estates, in the conservation of Bodily Health, every man may consider what suits his own conveniency, and follow what course he likes best. No man complains of the ill management of his Neighbour's Affairs. No man is angry with another for an Error committed in sowing his Land, or in marrying his Daughter.* No body corrects a Spend-thrift for consuming his Substance in Taverns. Let any man pull down, or build, or make whatsoever Expences he pleases; no body murmurs, no body controuls him; he has his Liberty. But if any man do not frequent the Church; if he do not there conform his Behaviour exactly to the accustomed Ceremonies, or if he brings not his Children to be initiated in the Sacred Mysteries of this or the other Congregation; this immediately causes an Uproar; and the Neighbourhood is filled with noise and clamour. Every one is ready to be the Avenger of so great a Crime. And the Zealots hardly have patience to refrain from Violence and Rapine so long till the Cause be heard, and the poor man be, according to Form, condemned to the loss of Liberty, Goods, or Life. Oh that our Ecclesiastical Orators, of every Sect, would apply themselves with all the strength of Arguments that they are able, to the confounding of mens Errors! But let them spare their Persons. Let them not supply their want of Reasons with the Instruments of Force, which belong to another Jurisdiction, and do ill become a Church man's Hands. Let them not call in the Magistrate's Authority to the aid of their Eloquence or Learning; lest, perhaps, whilst they pretend only Love for the Truth, this their intemperate Zeal, breathing nothing but Fire and Sword, betray their Ambition; and shew that what they desire is Temporal Dominion. For it will be very difficult to persuade men of Sence, that he, who with dry Eyes, and satisfaction of Mind, can deliver his Brother unto the Executioner, to be burnt alive, does sincerely and heartily concern himself to save that Brother from the Flames of Hell in the world to come.

In the last place. Let us now consider *what is the Magistrate's Duty* in the Business of Toleration; which certainly is very considerable.

We have already proved, That the Care of Souls does not belong to the Magistrate. Not a Magisterial Care, I mean, (if I may so call it) which consists in prescribing by Laws, and compelling by Punishments. But a charitable Care, which consists in teaching, admonishing, and persuading, cannot be denied unto any man.* The Care therefore of every man's Soul belongs unto himself, and is to be left unto himself. But what if he neglect the Care of his Soul? I answer, What if he neglect the Care of his Health, or of his Estate; which things are nearlier related to the Government of the Magistrate than the other? Will the Magistrate provide by an express Law, That such a one shall not become poor or sick? Laws provide, as much as is possible: That the Goods and Health of Subjects be not injured by the Fraud or Violence of others; they do not guard them from the Negligence or Ill husbandry of the Possessors themselves. No man can be forced to be Rich or Healthful whether he will or no. Nay, God himself will not save men against their wills. Let us suppose, however, that some Prince were desirous to force his Subjects to accumulate Riches, or to preserve the Health and Strength of their Bodies. Shall it be provided by Law, that they must consult none but *Roman* Physicians; and shall every one be bound to live according to their Prescriptions? What, shall no Potion, no Broth be taken, but what is prepared either in the *Vatican*, suppose, or in a *Geneva** Shop? Or, to make these Subjects rich, shall they all be obliged by Law to become Merchants, or Musicians?* Or, shall every one turn Victualler, or Smith; because there are some that maintain their Families plentifully, and grow rich in those Professions? But it may be said, There are a thousand ways to Wealth, but one only way to Heaven. 'Tis well said indeed, especially by those that plead for compelling men into this or the other Way. For if there were several ways that lead thither, there would not be so much as a pretence left for Compulsion. But now if I be marching on with my utmost vigor, in that way which, according to the Sacred Geography, leads streight to *Jerusalem*, Why am I beaten and ill used by others, because, perhaps, I wear not Buskins;* because my Hair is not of the right Cut; because perhaps I have not been dipt* in the right Fashion; because I eat Flesh upon the Road, or some other Food which agrees with my stomach; because I avoid certain By-ways, which seem unto me to lead into Briars or Precipices; because amongst the several Paths that are in the same Road, I chuse that to walk in which seems to be the streightest and cleanest; because I avoid to keep company with some Travellers that are less grave, and others that are more sowr than they ought to be;* or in fine, because I follow a Guide that either is, or is not, cloathed in White,* and crowned with a Mitre? Certainly, if we consider right, we shall find that for the most part they are such frivolous things as these, that (without any prejudice to Religion, or the Salvation of Souls, if not accompanied with Superstition or Hypocrisie) might either be observed or omit-ted; I say they are such like things as these, which breed implacable Enmities amongst Christian Brethren, who are all agreed in the sub-stantial and truly fundamental part of Religion.

But let us grant unto these Zealots, who condemn all things that are not of their Mode, that from these Circumstances arise different Ends. What shall we conclude from thence? There is only one of these which is the true way to Eternal Happiness. But in this great var-iety of ways that men follow, it is still doubted which is the right one. Now neither the care of the Commonwealth, nor the Right of enact-ing Laws, does discover* this way that leads to Heaven more certainly to the Magistrate, than every private mans Search and Study dis-covers it unto himself. I have a weak Body, sunk under a languishing Disease, for which (I suppose) there is one only Remedy, but that unknown: Does it therefore belong unto the Magistrate to prescribe me a Remedy; because there is but one, and because it is unknown? Because there is but one way for me to escape Death, will it there-fore be safe for me to do whatsoever the Magistrate ordains? Those things that every man ought sincerely to enquire into himself, and by Meditation, Study, Search, and his own Endeavours, attain the knowledge of, cannot be looked upon as the peculiar Possession of any sort of Men. Princes indeed are born superior unto other Men in Power, but in Nature equal. Neither the Right, nor the Art of Ruling, does necessarily carry along with it the certain Knowledge of other things; and least of all of the true Religion. For if it were so, how could it come to pass that the Lords of the Earth should differ so vastly as they do in Religious Matters? But let us grant that it is probable the way to Eternal Life may be better known by a Prince than by his Subjects; or at least, that in this incertitude of things, the safest and most commodious way for private Persons is to follow his Dictates. You will say, what then? If he should bid you follow Merchandise for your Livelihood, would you decline that Course for fear it should not succeed? I answer: I would turn Merchant upon the Princes Command, because in case I should have ill success in Trade, he is abundantly able to make up my Loss some other way. If it be true, as he pretends, that he desires I should thrive and grow rich, he can set me up again when unsuccessful Voyages* have broke me. But this is not the Case in the things that regard the Life to come. If there I take a wrong Course, if in that respect I am once undone; it is not in the Magistrates Power to repair my Loss, to ease my Suffering; or to restore me in any measure, much less entirely, to a good Estate. What Security can be given for the Kingdom of Heaven?

Perhaps some will say that they do not suppose this *infallible Judgment*, that all Men are bound to follow in the Affairs of Religion to be in the Civil Magistrate, but *in the Church*. What the Church has determined, that the Civil Magistrate orders to be observed; and he provides by his Authority that no body shall either act or believe, in the business of Religion, otherwise than the Church teaches. So that the Judgment of those things is in the Church. The Magistrate himself yields Obedience thereunto, and requires the like Obedience from others. I answer; Who sees not how frequently the Name of the Church, which was so venerable in time of the Apostles, has been made use of to throw Dust in the Peoples Eyes, in following Ages? But however, in the present case it helps us not. The one only narrow way which leads to Heaven is not better known to the Magistrate than to private persons; and therefore I cannot safely take him for my Guide, who may probably be as ignorant of the way as my self, and who certainly is less concerned for my Salvation than I my self am. Amongst so many Kings of the *Jews*, how many of them were there whom any *Israelite*, thus blindly following, had not fallen into Idolatry, and thereby into Destruction? Yet nevertheless, you bid me be of good courage, and tell me that all is now safe and secure, because the

Magistrate does not now enjoyn the observance of his own Decrees in matters of Religion, but only the Decrees of the Church. Of what Church I beseech you? Of that certainly which likes him best. As if he that compels me by Laws and Penalties to enter into this or the other Church, did not interpose his own Judgment in the matter. What difference is there whether he lead me himself, or deliver me over to be led by others? I depend both ways upon his Will: and it is he that determines both ways of my eternal State. Would an *Israelite*, that had worshipped *Baal** upon the Command of his King, have been in any better condition, because some body had told him that the King ordered nothing in Religion upon his own Head, nor commanded any thing to be done by his Subjects in Divine Worship, but what was approved by the Counsel of Priests, and declared to be of Divine Right by the Doctors of their Church? If the Religion of any Church become therefore true and saving, because the Heads of that Sect, the Prelates and Priests, and those of that Tribe,* do all of them, with all their might, extol and praise it; what Religion can ever be accounted erroneous, false and destructive? I am doubtful concerning the Doctrine of the *Socinians*,* I am suspicious of the way of Worship practised by the *Papists*, or *Lutherans*? Will it be ever a jot the safer for me to joyn either unto the one or the other of those Churches, upon the Magistrates Command; because he commands nothing in Religion but by the Authority and Counsel of the Doctors of that Church?

But to speak the truth, we must acknowledge that the Church (if a Convention of Clergy-men, making Canons, must be called by that Name)* is for the most part more apt to be influenced by the Court, than the Court by the Church. How the Church was under the Vicissitude of Orthodox and Arian Emperors,* is very well known. Or if those things be too remote; The *English* History* affords us fresher Examples, in the Reigns of *Henry* the *8th*, *Edward* the *6th*, *Mary*, and *Elizabeth*, how easily and smoothly the Clergy changed their Decrees, their Articles of Faith, their Form of Worship, every thing, according to the inclination of those Kings and Queens.* Yet were those Kings and Queens of such different minds, in point of Religion, and enjoyed thereupon such different things, that no man in his Wits (I had almost said none but an Atheist) will presume to say that any sincere and upright Worshipper of God could, with a safe Conscience, obey their several Decrees. To conclude. It is the same thing whether a King that prescribes Laws to another mans Religion, pretend to do it by his own Judgment, or by the Ecclesiastical Authority and Advice of others. The Decisions of Churchmen, whose Differences and Disputes are sufficiently known, cannot be any sounder, or safer, than his. Nor can all their Suffrages joyned together add any new strength unto the Civil Power. Tho' this also must be taken notice of, that Princes seldom have any regard to the Suffrages of Ecclesiastics that are not Favourers of their own Faith and way of Worship.

But after all, The *Principal Consideration*, and which absolutely determines this Controversie, is this. Although the Magistrates Opinion in Religion be sound, and the way that he appoints be truly Evangelical, yet if I be not thoroughly perswaded thereof in my own mind, there will be no safety for me in following it. No way whatsoever that I shall walk in, against the Dictates of my Conscience, will ever bring me to the Mansions of the Blessed.* I may grow rich by an Art that I take not delight in; I may be cured of some Disease by Remedies that I have not Faith in, but I cannot be saved by a Religion that I distrust, and by a Worship that I abhor. It is in vain for an Unbeliever to take up the outward shew of another Mans Profession. Faith only, and inward Sincerity, are the things that procure acceptance with God. The most likely and most approved Remedy can have no effect upon the Patient, if his Stomach reject it as soon as taken. And you will in vain cram a Medicine down a sick Mans Throat, which his particular Constitution will be sure to turn into Poison. In a word. Whatsoever may be doubtful* in Religion, yet this at least is certain, that no Religion, which I believe not to be true, can be either true or profitable unto me. In vain therefore do Princes compel their Subjects to come into their Church-communion, under pretence of saving their Souls. If they believe, they will come of their own accord; if they believe not, their coming will nothing avail them. How great soever, in fine, may be the pretence of Good-will and Charity, and concern for the Salvation of Mens Souls; Men cannot be forced to be saved whether they will or no. And therefore, when all is done, they must be left to their own Consciences.

Having thus at length freed Men from all Dominion over one another in matters of Religion, let us now consider *what they are to do*. All men know and acknowledge that God ought to be publickly worshipped. Why otherwise do they compel one another unto the publick Assemblies? Men therefore constituted in this liberty are to enter into some Religious Society; that they may meet together, not only for mutual Edification, but to own* to the World that they worship God, and offer unto his divine Majesty such service as they themselves are not ashamed of, and such as they think not unworthy of him, nor unacceptable to him; and finally that by the purity of Doctrine, Holiness of Life, and decent Form of Worship, they may draw others unto the love of the true Religion; and perform such other things in Religion as cannot be done by each private Man apart.

These Religious Societies I call Churches; and these I say the Magistrate ought to tolerate. For the business of these Assemblies of the People is nothing but what is lawful for every Man in particular to take care of; I mean the Salvation of their Souls. Nor in this case is there any difference between the National Church, and other separated Congregations.* But as in every Church there are two things especially to be considered; *The outward Form and Rites of Worship; And the Doctrines and Articles of Faith*; These things must be handled each distinctly; that so the whole matter of Toleration may the more clearly be understood.

Concerning outward Worship, I say (in the first place) that the Magistrate has no Power to enforce by Law, either in his own Church, or much less in another, the use of any Rites or Ceremonies whatsoever in the Worship of God. And this, not only because these Churches are free Societies; but because whatsoever is practised in the Worship of God, is only so far justifiable as it is believed by those that practise it to be acceptable unto him. Whatsoever is not done with that Assurance of Faith, is neither well in it self, nor can it be acceptable to God. To impose such things therefore upon any People, contrary to their own Judgment, is in effect to command them to offend God; Which, considering that the end of all Religion is to please him, and that Liberty is essentially necessary to that End, appears to be absurd beyond expression.

But perhaps it may be concluded from hence, that I deny unto the Magistrate all manner of Power about *Indifferent things*;* which if it be not granted, the whole Subject matter of Law making is taken away. No; I readily grant that Indifferent Things, and perhaps none but such, are subjected to the Legislative Power. But it does not therefore follow, that the Magistrate may ordain whatsoever he pleases concerning any thing that is indifferent. The Publick Good is the Rule and Measure of all Law-making. If a thing be not useful to the Commonwealth, though it be never so indifferent, it may not presently be established by Law.*

But further: Things never so indifferent in their own nature, when they are brought into the Church and Worship of God, are removed out of the reach of the Magistrate's Jurisdiction; because in that use they have no connexion at all with Civil Affairs. The only business of the Church is the Salvation of Souls: And it no ways concerns the Commonwealth, or any Member of it, that this, or the other Ceremony be there made use of. Neither the Use, nor the Omission of any Ceremonies, in those Religious Assemblies, does either advantage or prejudice the Life, Liberty, or Estate of any Man. For Example: Let it be granted, that the washing of an Infant with Water is in it self an indifferent thing. Let it be granted also, that if the Magistrate understand such washing to be profitable to the curing or preventing of any Disease that Children are subject unto, and esteem the matter weighty enough to be taken care of by a Law, in that case he may order it to be done. But will any one therefore say, that a Magistrate has the same Right to ordain, by Law, that all Children shall be baptized by Priests, in the sacred Font, in order to the Purification of their Souls? The extream difference of these two Cases is visible to every one at first sight. Or let us apply the last Case to the Child of a *Jew*, and the thing will speak it self. For what hinders but a Christian Magistrate may have Subjects that are *Jews*?* Now if we acknowledge that such an Injury may not be done unto a *Jew*, as to compel him, against his own Opinion, to practise in his Religion a thing that is in its nature indifferent; how can we maintain that any thing of this kind may be done to a Christian?

Again: Things in their own nature indifferent cannot, by any human Authority, be made any part of the Worship of God; for this very reason; because they are indifferent. For since indifferent things are not capable, by any Virtue of their own, to propitiate the Deity; no human Power or Authority can confer on them so much Dignity, and Excellency, as to enable them to do it. In the common Affairs of Life, that use of indifferent things which God has not forbidden, is free and lawful: And therefore in those things human Authority has place. But it is not so in matters of Religion. Things indifferent are not otherwise lawful in the Worship of God than as they are instituted by God himself; and as he, by some positive command, has ordain'd them to be made a part of that Worship which he will vouchsafe to accept of at the hands of poor sinful Men. Nor when an incensed Deity shall ask us, (*Who has required these, or such like things, at your hands?*)* will it be enough to answer him; that the Magistrate commanded them. If Civil Jurisdiction extended thus far, what might not lawfully be introduced into Religion? What hodge podge of Ceremonies, what superstitious inventions, built upon the Magistrate's Authority, might not (against Conscience) be imposed upon the Worshippers of God? For the greatest part of these Ceremonies and Superstitions consists in the Religious Use of such things as are in their own nature indifferent: Nor are they sinful upon any other account than because God is not the Author of them. The sprinkling of Water, and the use of Bread and Wine, are both in their own nature, and in the ordinary occasions of Life, altogether indifferent. Will any Man therefore say that these things could have been introduced into Religion, and made a part of Divine Worship, if not by Divine Institution? If any Human Authority or Civil Power could have done this; why might it not also injoyn the eating of Fish, and drinking of Ale, in the Holy Banquet, as a part of Divine Worship? Why not the sprinkling of the Blood of Beasts in Churches, and Expiations by Water or Fire, and abundance more of this kind? But these things, how indifferent soever they be in common uses, when they come to be annexed unto Divine Worship, without Divine Authority, they are as abominable to God, as the Sacrifice of a Dog. And why [is] a Dog so abominable? What difference is there between a Dog and a Goat, in respect of the Divine Nature, equally and infinitely distant from all Affinity with Matter; unless it be that God required the use of the one in his Worship, and not of the other? We see therefore that indifferent things, how much soever they be under the Power of the Civil Magistrate, yet cannot upon that pretence be introduced into Religion, and imposed upon Religious Assemblies; because in the Worship of God they wholly cease to be indifferent. He that Worships God does it with design to please him, and procure his Favour. But that cannot be done by him, Who, upon the command of another, offers unto God that which he knows will be displeasing to him, because not commanded by himself. This is not to please God, or appease his Wrath, but willingly and knowingly to provoke him, by a manifest Contempt; Which is a thing absolutely repugnant to the nature and end of Worship.

But it will be here asked: *If nothing belonging to Divine Worship be left to human Discretion, how is it then that Churches themselves have the*

Power of ordering any thing about the Time and Place of Worship, and the like? To this I answer; That in Religious Worship we must distinguish between what is part of the Worship it self, and what is but a Circumstance. That is a part of the Worship which is believed to be appointed by God, and to be well-pleasing to him; and therefore that is necessary. Circumstances are such things which, tho' in general they cannot be separated from Worship, yet the particular instances or modifications of them are not determined; and therefore they are indifferent. Of this sort are the Time and Place of Worship, the Habit and Posture* of him that worships. These are Circumstances, and perfectly indifferent, where God has not given any express Command about them. For example: Amongst the *Jews*, the Time and Place of their Worship, and the Habits of those that officiated in it, were not meer Circumstances, but a part of the Worship it self; in which if any thing were defective, or different from the Institution, they could not hope that it would be accepted by God. But these, to Christians under the liberty of the Gospel, are meer Circumstances of Worship, which the Prudence of every Church may bring into such use as shall be judged most subservient to the end of Order, Decency, and Edification.* Tho' even under the Gospel also, those who believe the First, or the Seventh Day, to be set apart by God, and consecrated still to his Worship; to them that portion of Time is not a simple Circumstance, but a real Part of Divine Worship, which can neither be changed nor neglected.

In the next place: As the Magistrate has no Power to *impose* by his Laws, the use of any Rites and Ceremonies in any Church; so neither has he any Power to *forbid* the use of such Rites and Ceremonies as are already received, approved, and practised by any Church. Because if he did so, he would destroy the Church it self; the end of whose Institution is only to worship God with freedom, after its own manner.

You will say, by this Rule, if some Congregations should have a mind to *sacrifice Infants*, or (as the Primitive Christians* were falsly accused) *lustfully pollute themselves in promiscuous Uncleanness*,* or practise any other such heinous Enormities, *is the Magistrate obliged to tolerate them*, because they are committed in a Religious Assembly? I answer, No. These things are not lawful in the ordinary course of life,* nor in any private house; and therefore neither are they so in the Worship of God, or in any Religious Meeting. But indeed if any People congregated upon account of Religion, should be desirous to sacrifice a Calf, I deny that That ought to be prohibited by a Law. *Meliboeus,** whose Calf it is, may lawfully kill his Calf at home, and burn any part of it that he thinks fit. For no Injury is thereby done to any one, no Prejudice to another man's Goods. And for the same reason he may kill his Calf also in a Religious Meeting. Whether the doing so be well-pleasing to God, or no, it is their part to consider that do it. The part of the Magistrate is only to take care that the Commonwealth receive no prejudice,* and that there be no Injury done to any man, either in Life or Estate. And thus what may be spent on a Feast, may be spent on a Sacrifice. But if peradventure such were the state of things, that the Interest of the Commonwealth required all slaughter of Beasts should be forborn for some while, in order to the increasing of the Stock of Cattel, that had been destroyed by some extraordinary Murrain;* Who sees not that the Magistrate, in such a case, may forbid all his Subjects to kill any Calves for any use whatsoever? Only 'tis to be observed, that in this case the Law is not made about a Religious, but a Political matter; nor is the Sacrifice, but the Slaughter of Calves thereby prohibited.

By this we see what difference there is between the Church and the Commonwealth. Whatsoever is lawful in the Commonwealth, cannot be prohibited by the Magistrate in the Church. Whatsoever is permitted unto any of his Subjects for their ordinary use, neither can, nor ought to be forbidden by him to any Sect of People for their Religious Uses. If any man may lawfully take Bread or Wine, either sitting or kneeling, in his own house, the Law ought not to abridge him of the same Liberty in his Religious Worship; though in the Church the use of Bread and Wine be very different, and be there applied to the Mysteries of Faith, and Rites of Divine Worship. But those things that are prejudicial to the Common weal of a People in their ordinary use, and are therefore forbidden by Laws, those things ought not to be permitted to Churches in their Sacred Rites. Only the Magistrate ought always to be very careful, that he do not misuse his Authority, to the oppression of any Church, under pretence of publick Good.

It may be said; *What if a Church be* Idolatrous, *is that also to be tolerated by the Magistrate?* In answer, I ask; What Power can be given to the Magistrate for the suppression of an Idolatrous Church, which may not, in time and place, be made use of to the ruine of an Orthodox one? For it must be remembered that the Civil Power is the same every where, and the Religion of every Prince is Orthodox to himself. If therefore such a Power be granted unto the Civil Magistrate in Spirituals, as that at *Geneva* (for Example) he may extirpate, by Violence and Blood, the Religion which is there reputed Idolatrous;* by the same Rule another Magistrate, in some neighbouring Country, may oppress the Reformed Religion; and, in *India*,* the Christian. The Civil Power can either change every thing in Religion, according to the Prince's pleasure, or it can change nothing. If it be once permitted to introduce any thing into Religion, by the means of Laws and Penalties, there can be no bounds put to it; but it will in the same manner be lawful to alter every thing, according to that Rule of Truth which the Magistrate has framed unto himself. No man whatsoever ought therefore to be deprived of his Terrestrial Enjoyments, upon account of his Religion. Not even *Americans*,* subjected unto a Christian Prince, are to be punished either in Body or Goods, for not imbracing our Faith and Worship. If they are perswaded that they please God in observing the Rites of their own Country, and that they shall obtain Happiness by that means, they are to be left unto God and themselves. Let us trace this matter to the bottom.* Thus it is. An inconsiderable and weak number of Christians, destitute of every thing, arrive in a Pagan Countrey. These Foreigners beseech the Inhabitants, by the bowels of Humanity, that they would succour them with the necessaries of Life. Those necessaries are given them; Habitations are granted; and they all joyn together, and grow up into one Body of People. The Christian Religion by this means takes root in that Countrey, and spreads it self; but does not suddenly grow the strongest. While things are in this condition, Peace, Friendship, Faith, and equal Justice, are preserved amongst them. At length the Magistrate becomes a Christian, and by that means their Party becomes the most powerful. Then immediately all Compacts are to be broken, all Civil Rights to be violated, that Idolatry may be extirpated; And unless these innocent Pagans, strict Observers of the Rules of Equity and of the Law of Nature, & no ways offending against the Laws of the Society, I say unless they will forsake their ancient Religion, and embrace a new and strange one, they are to be turned out of the Lands and Possessions of their Forefathers, and perhaps deprived of Life it self. Then at last it appears what Zeal for the Church, joyned with the desire of Dominion, is capable to produce; and how easily the pretence of Religion, and of the care of Souls, serves for a Cloak to Covetousness, Rapine, and Ambition.

Now whosoever maintains that Idolatry is to be rooted out of any place by Laws, Punishments, Fire, and Sword, may apply this Story to himself.* For the reason of the thing is equal, both in *America* and *Europe*. And neither Pagans there, nor any Dissenting Christians here, can with any right be deprived of their worldly Goods, by the predominating Faction of a Court-Church: nor are any Civil Rights to be either changed or violated upon account of Religion in one place more than another.

But *Idolatry* (say some) *is a Sin*, and therefore not to be tolerated. If they said, it were therefore to be avoided, the Inference were good. But it does not follow, that because it is a Sin, it ought therefore to be punished by the Magistrate. For it does not belong unto the Magistrate to make use of his Sword in Punishing every thing, indifferently, that he takes to be a Sin against God. Covetousness, Uncharitableness, Idleness, and many other things are sins, by the consent of all men, which yet no man ever said were to be punished by the Magistrate. The reason is, because they are not prejudicial to other mens Rights, nor do they break the publick Peace of Societies. Nay, even the Sins of Lying, and Perjury, are no where punishable by Laws; unless in certain cases, in which the real Turpitude of the thing, and the Offence against God, are not considered, but only the Injury done unto mens Neighbours, and to the Commonwealth. And what if in another Country, to a Mahumetan, or a Pagan Prince, the Christian Religion seem false and offensive to God; may not the Christians, for the same reason, and after the same manner, be extirpated there?

But it may be urged further, *That by the Law of* Moses, *Idolaters were to be rooted out*.* True indeed, by the Law of *Moses*: But that is not obligatory to us Christians. No body pretends that every thing, generally, enjoyned by the Law of *Moses*, ought to be practised by Christians. But there is nothing more frivolous than that common distinction of Moral, Judicial, and Ceremonial Law, which men ordinarily make use of. For no positive Law, whatsoever, can oblige any People, but those to whom it is given. *Hear O Israel;** sufficiently restrains the Obligation of the Law of *Moses* only to that People: And this Consideration alone is Answer enough unto those that urge the Authority of the Law of *Moses*; for the inflicting of Capital Punishments upon Idolaters. But however, I will examine this Argument a little more particularly.

The Case of Idolaters, in respect of the *Jewish* Commonwealth, falls under a double Consideration. The first is, of those, Who, being initiated in the *Mosaical* Rites, and made Citizens of that Commonwealth, did afterwards apostatize from the Worship of the God of *Israel*. These were proceeded against as Traytors and Rebels, guilty of no less than High Treason. For the Commonwealth of the *Jews*, different in that from all others, was an absolute *Theocracy*; nor was there, or could there be, any difference between that Commonwealth and the Church. The Laws established there concerning the Worship of One Invisible Deity, were the Civil Laws of that People, and a part of their Political Government; in which God himself was the Legislator. Now if any one can shew me where there is a Commonwealth, at this time, constituted upon that Foundation, I will acknowledg that the Ecclesiastical Laws do there unavoidably become a part of the Civil; and that the Subjects of that Government both may, and ought to be kept in strict conformity with that Church, by the Civil Power. But there is absolutely no such thing, under the Gospel, as a Christian Commonwealth. There are, indeed, many Cities and Kingdoms that have embraced the Faith of Christ; but they have retained their ancient Form of Government; with which the Law of Christ hath not at all medled. He, indeed, hath taught men how, by Faith and good Works, they may obtain Eternal Life. But he instituted no Commonwealth. He prescribed unto his Followers no new and peculiar Form of Government; Nor put he the Sword into any Magistrate's Hand, with Commission to make use of it in forcing men to forsake their former Religion, and receive his.

Secondly, Foreigners, and such as were Strangers* to the *Commonwealth* of *Israel*, were not compell'd by force to observe the Rites of the *Mosaical* Law. But, on the contrary, in the very same place, where it is ordered, that *an Israelite, that was an Idolater, should be put to death*, there it is provided, that *Strangers should not be vexed nor oppressed* (Exod. 22: 20–1). I confess, that the Seven Nations, that possest the Land which was promised to the *Israelites*, were utterly to be cut off. But this was not singly because they were Idolaters. For, if that had been the Reason; Why were the *Moabites*, and other Nations to be spared?* No, the Reason is this. God being in a peculiar manner the King of the *Jews*, he could not suffer the Adoration of any other Deity, (which was properly an Act of High Treason against himself) in the Land of *Canaan*, which was his Kingdom. For such a manifest Revolt could no ways consist with his Dominion, which was perfectly Political, in that Country. All Idolatry was therefore to be rooted out of the Bounds of his Kingdom; because it was an acknowledgment of another God; that is say, another King; against the Laws of Empire. The Inhabitants were also to be driven out, that the entire possession of the Land might be given to the *Israelites*. And for the like Reason, the *Emims*, and the *Horims* were driven out of their Countries, by the Children of *Esau* and *Lot*; and their Lands, upon the same grounds, given by God to the Invaders (Deut. 2). But though all Idolatry was thus rooted out of the Land of *Canaan*, yet every Idolater was not brought to Execution. The whole Family of *Rahab*, the whole Nation of the *Gibeonites*, articled with *Joshuah*, and were allowed by Treaty:* and there were many Captives amongst the *Jews*, who were Idolaters. *David* and *Solomon* subdued many Countries without* the Confines of the Land of Promise, and carried their Conquests as far as [the] *Euphrates*. Amongst so many Captives taken, so many Nations reduced under their Obedience, we find not one man forced into the Jewish Religion, and the Worship of the True God; and punished for Idolatry; though all of them were certainly guilty of it. If any one indeed, becoming a Proselyte, desired to be made a Denison of their Commonwealth, he was obliged to submit unto their Laws; that is, to embrace their Religion. But this he did willingly, on his own accord, not by constraint. He did not unwillingly submit, to shew his Obedience; But he sought and sollicited for it, as a Privilege; And as soon as he was admitted, he became subject to the Laws of the Commonwealth; by which all Idolatry was forbidden within the Borders of the Land of *Canaan*. But that Law (as I have said) did not reach to any of those Regions, however subjected unto the *Jews*, that were situated without those Bounds.

Thus far concerning outward Worship. Let us now consider *Articles of Faith*.

The *Articles* of Religion are some of them *Practical*, and some *Speculative*.* Now, tho' both sorts consist in the Knowledge of Truth, yet these terminate simply in the Understanding, Those influence the Will and Manners. Speculative Opinions, therefore, and *Articles of Faith* (as they are called) which are required only to be believed, cannot be imposed on any Church by the Law of the Land. For it is absurd that things should be enjoyned by Laws, which are not in mens power to perform. And to believe this or that to be true, does not depend upon our Will. But of this enough has been said already.

But (will some say) let men at least profess that they believe. A sweet Religion indeed, that obliges men to dissemble, and tell Lyes both to God and Man, for the Salvation of their Souls! If the Magistrate thinks to save men thus, he seems to understand little of the way of Salvation. And if he does it not in order to save them; Why is he so sollicitous about the Articles of Faith as to enact them by a Law?

Further, The Magistrate ought not to forbid the Preaching or Professing of any Speculative Opinions in any Church; because they have no manner of relation to the Civil Rights of the Subjects. If a *Roman Catholick* believe that to be really the Body of Christ, which another man calls Bread, he does no injury thereby to his Neighbour.* If a *Jew* do not believe the New Testament to be the Word of God, he does not thereby alter any thing in mens Civil Rights. If a Heathen doubt of both Testaments, he is not therefore to be punished as a pernicious Citizen. The Power of the Magistrate, and the Estates of the People, may be equally secure, whether any man believe these things or no. I readily grant, that these Opinions are false and absurd. But the business of Laws is not to provide for the Truth of Opinions, but for the Safety and Security of the Commonwealth, and of every particular mans Goods and Person. And so it ought to be. For Truth certainly would do well enough, if she were once left to shift for her Self. She seldom has received, and I fear never will receive, much Assistance from the Power of Great men; to whom she is but rarely known, and more rarely welcome. She is not taught by Laws, nor has she any need of Force to procure her entrance into the minds of men. Errors indeed prevail by the assistance of forreign and borrowed Succours. But if Truth makes not her way into the Understanding by her own Light, she will be but the weaker for any borrowed force Violence can add to her. Thus much for Speculative Opinions. Let us now proceed to *Practical* ones.

A Good Life, in which consists not the least part of Religion and true Piety, concerns also the Civil Government; and in it lies the safety both of Mens Souls, and of the Commonwealth. *Moral Actions* belong therefore to the Jurisdiction both of the outward and inward Court;* both of the Civil and Domestick Governor; I mean, both of the Magistrate and Conscience. Here therefore is great danger, least one of these Jurisdictions intrench upon the other, and Discord arise between the Keeper of the publick Peace, and the Overseers of Souls. But if what has been already said concerning the

Limits of both these Governments be rightly considered, it will easily remove all difficulty in this matter.

Every man has an Immortal Soul, capable of Eternal Happiness or Misery; whose Happiness depending upon his believing and doing those things in this Life, which are necessary to the obtaining of Gods Favour, and are prescribed by God to that end; it follows from thence, 1*st*, That the observance of these things is the highest Obligation that lies upon Mankind, and that our utmost Care, Application, and Diligence, ought to be exercised in the Search and Performance of them; Because there is nothing in this World that is of any consideration in comparison with Eternity.* 2*dly*, That seeing one Man does not violate the Right of another, by his Erroneous Opinions, and undue manner of Worship, nor is his Perdition any prejudice to another Mans Affairs; therefore the care of each Mans Salvation belongs only to himself. But I would not have this understood, as if I meant hereby to condemn all charitable Admonitions, and affectionate Endeavours to reduce Men from Errors; which are indeed the greatest Duty of a Christian. Any one may employ as many Exhortations and Arguments as he pleases, towards the promoting of another man's Salvation. But all Force and Compulsion are to be forborn. Nothing is to be done imperiously. No body is obliged in that matter to yield Obedience unto the Admonitions or Injunctions of another, further than he himself is perswaded. Every man, in that, has the supreme and absolute Authority of judging for himself. And the Reason is, because nobody else is concerned in it, nor can receive any prejudice from his Conduct therein.

But besides their Souls, which are Immortal, Men have also their Temporal Lives here upon Earth; the State whereof being frail and fleeting, and the duration uncertain; they have need of several outward Conveniences to the support thereof, which are to be procured or preserved by Pains and Industry. For those things that are necessary to the comfortable support of our Lives, are not the spontaneous Products of Nature, nor do offer themselves fit and prepared for our use. This part therefore draws on another care, and necessarily gives another Imployment. But the pravity* of Mankind being such, that they had rather injuriously prey upon the Fruits of other Mens Labours, than take pains to provide for themselves; the necessity of preserving Men in the Possession of what honest industry has already acquired; and also of preserving their Liberty and Strength, whereby they may acquire what they further want; obliges Men to enter into Society with one another; that by mutual Assistance,* and joint Force, they may secure unto each other their Properties, in the things that contribute to the Comfort and Happiness of this Life; leaving in the mean while to every Man the care of his own Eternal Happiness, the attainment whereof can neither be facilitated by another Mans Industry, nor can the loss of it turn to another Mans Prejudice, nor the hope of it be forced from him by any external Violence. But for-asmuch as Men thus entring into Societies, grounded upon their mutual Compacts of Assistance, for the Defence of their Temporal Goods, may nevertheless be deprived of them, either by the Rapine and Fraud of their Fellow-Citizens, or by the hostile Violence of Foreigners; the Remedy of this Evil consists in Arms, Riches, and Multitude of Citizens;* the Remedy of the other in Laws; and the Care of all things relating both to the one and the other, is committed by the Society to the Civil Magistrate. This is the Original, this is the Use, and these are the Bounds of the Legislative (which is the Supreme) Power, in every Commonwealth. I mean, that Provision may be made for the Security of each Mans private Possessions; for the Peace, Riches, and publick Commodities* of the whole People; and, as much as possible, for the Increase of their inward Strength, against Forreign Invasions.

These things being thus explain'd, it is easie to understand to what end the Legislative Power ought to be directed, and by what Measures regulated; and that is the Temporal Good and outward Prosperity of the Society; which is the sole Reason of Mens entring into Society, and the only thing they seek and aim at in it. And it is also evident what Liberty remains to Men in reference to their eternal Salvation; and that is, that every one should do what he in his Conscience is perswaded to be acceptable to the Almighty, on whose good pleasure* and acceptance depends his eternal Happiness. For Obedience is due in the first place to God, and afterwards to the Laws.

But some may ask, *What if the Magistrate should enjoyn any thing by his Authority that appears unlawful to the Conscience of a private Person?* I answer, That if Government be faithfully administred, and the Counsels of the Magistrate be indeed directed to the publick Good, this will seldom happen. But if perhaps it do so fall out; I say, that such a private Person is to abstain from the Action that he judges unlawful; and he is to undergo the Punishment, which it is not unlawful for him to bear. For the private Judgment of any Person concerning a Law enacted in Political Matters, for the publick Good, does not take away the Obligation of that Law, nor deserve a Dispensation. But if the Law indeed be concerning things that lie not within the Verge of the Magistrate's Authority; (as for Example, that the People, or any Party amongst them, should be compell'd to embrace a strange Religion, and join in the Worship and Ceremonies of another Church,) men are not in these cases obliged by that Law, against their Consciences. For the Political Society is instituted for no other end but only to secure every mans Possession of the things of this life. The care of each mans Soul, and of the things of Heaven, which neither does belong to the Commonwealth, nor can be subjected to it, is left entirely to every mans self. Thus the safeguard of mens lives, and of the things that belong unto this life, is the business of the Commonwealth; and the preserving of those things unto their Owners is the Duty of the Magistrate. And therefore the Magistrate cannot take away these worldly things from this man, or party, and give them to that; nor change Propriety* amongst Fellow-Subjects, (no not even by a Law) for a cause that has no relation to the end of Civil Government; I mean, for their Religion; which whether it be true or false, does no prejudice to the worldly concerns of their Fellow-Subjects, which are the things that only belong unto the care of the Commonwealth.

But what if the Magistrate believe such a Law as this to be for the publick Good? I answer: As the private Judgment of any particular Person, if erroneous, does not exempt him from the obligation of Law, so the private Judgment (as I may call it) of the Magistrate does not give him any new Right of imposing Laws upon his Subjects; which neither was in the Constitution of the Government granted him, nor ever was in the power of the People to grant; and least of all, if he make it his business to enrich and advance his Followers and Fellow-sectaries, with the Spoils of others. *But what if the Magistrate believe that he has a Right to make such Laws, and that they are for the publick Good; and his Subjects believe the contrary? Who shall be Judge between them?* I answer, God alone. For there is no Judge upon earth between the Supreme Magistrate and the People.* God, I say, is the only Judge in this case, who will retribute unto every one at the last day according to his Deserts; that is, according to his sincerity and uprightness, in endeavouring to promote Piety, and the publick Weal and Peace of Mankind. *But what shall be done in the mean while?* I answer: The principal and chief care of every one ought to be of his own Soul first, and in the next place of the publick Peace: tho' yet there are very few will think 'tis Peace there, where they see all laid waste.*

There are two sorts of Contests amongst Men, the one manag'd by Law, the other by Force: and these are of that nature, that where the one ends, the other always begins.* But it is not my business to inquire into the Power of the Magistrate in the different Constitutions of Nations. I only know what usually happens where Controversies arise, without a Judge to determine them. You will say then the Magistrate being the stronger will have his Will, and carry his point. Without doubt. But the Question is not here concerning the doubtfulness of the Event, but the Rule of Right.

But* to come to particulars. I say, *First*, No Opinions contrary to human Society, or to those moral Rules which are necessary to the preservation of Civil Society, are to be tolerated by the Magistrate. But of these indeed Examples in any Church are rare. For no Sect can easily arrive to such a degree of madness, as that it should think fit to teach, for Doctrines of Religion, such things as manifestly undermine the Foundations of Society, and are therefore condemned by the Judgment of all Mankind: because their own Interest, Peace, Reputation, every Thing, would be thereby endangered.

Another more secret Evil, but more dangerous to the Commonwealth, is, when men arrogate to themselves, and to those of their own Sect, some peculiar Prerogative, covered over with a specious shew of deceitful words, but in effect opposite to the Civil Right of the Community. For Example. We cannot find any Sect that teaches expressly, and openly, that Men are not obliged to keep their Promise; that Princes may be dethroned by those that differ from them in Religion; or that the Dominion of all things belongs only to themselves. For these things, proposed thus nakedly and plainly, would soon draw on them the Eye and Hand of the Magistrate, and awaken all the care of the Commonwealth to a watchfulness against the spreading of so dangerous an Evil. But nevertheless, we find those that say the same things, in other words. What else do they mean, who teach *that Faith is not to be kept with Hereticks*?* Their meaning, forsooth, is that the priviledge of breaking Faith belongs unto themselves: For they declare all that are not of their Communion to be Hereticks, or at least may declare them so whensoever they think fit. What can be the meaning of their asserting that *Kings excommunicated* *forfeit their Crowns and Kingdoms?** It is evident that they thereby arrogate unto themselves the Power of deposing Kings: because they challenge* the Power of Excommunication, as the peculiar Right of their Hierarchy. *That Dominion is founded in Grace,** is also an Assertion by which those that maintain it do plainly lay claim to the possession of all things. For they are not so wanting to themselves as not to believe, or at least as not to profess, themselves to be the truly pious and faithful. These therefore, and the like, who attribute unto the Faithful, Religious and Orthodox; that is, in plain terms, unto themselves; any peculiar Priviledge or Power above other Mortals, in Civil Concernments; or who, upon pretence of religion, do challenge any manner of Authority over such as are not associated with them in their Ecclesiastical Communion; I say these have no right to be tolerated by the Magistrate; as neither those that will not own and teach the Duty of tolerating All men in matters of meer* Religion. For what do all these and the like Doctrines signifie, but that those Men may, and are ready upon any occasion to seise the Government, and possess themselves of the Estates and Fortunes of their Fellow-Subjects; and that they only ask leave to be tolerated by the Magistrate so long, until they find themselves strong enough to effect it?

Again; That Church can have no right to be tolerated by the Magistrate, which is constituted upon such a bottom, that all those who enter into it, do thereby, *ipso facto*, deliver themselves up to the Protection and Service of another Prince.* For by this means the Magistrate would give way to the settling of a foreign Jurisdiction in his own Country, and suffer his own People to be listed, as it were, for Soldiers against his own Government. Nor does the frivolous and fallacious distinction between the Court and the Church* afford any remedy to this Inconvenience; especially when both the one and the other are equally subject to the absolute Authority of the same Person; who has not only power to perswade the Members of his Church to whatsoever he lists,* (either as purely Religious, or in order thereunto) but can also enjoyn it them on pain of Eternal Fire. It is ridiculous for any one to profess himself to be a *Mahumetan** only in his Religion, but in every thing else a faithful Subject to a Christian Magistrate, whilst at the same time he acknowledges himself bound to yield blind obedience to the *Mufti** of *Constantinople*; who himself is intirely obedient to the *Ottoman* Emperor, and frames the feigned Oracles* of that Religion according to his pleasure. But this

Mahumetan living amongst Christians, would yet more apparently renounce their Government, if he acknowledged the same Person to be Head of his Church who is the Supreme Magistrate in the State.

Lastly, Those are not at all to be tolerated who *deny the Being of a God*. Promises, Covenants, and Oaths, which are the Bonds of Humane Society, can have no hold upon an Atheist.* The taking away of God, though but even in thought, dissolves all. Besides also, those that by their Atheism undermine and destroy all Religion, can have no pretence of Religion whereupon to challenge the Privilege of a Toleration. As for other Practical Opinions, though not absolutely free from all Error, yet if they do not tend to establish Domination over others, or Civil Impunity to the Church in which they are taught, there can be no Reason why they should not be tolerated.

It remains that I say something concerning those Assemblies, which being vulgarly called, and perhaps having sometimes been *Conventicles*,* and Nurseries of Factions and Seditions, are thought to afford the strongest matter of Objection against this Doctrine of Toleration. But this has not hapned by any thing peculiar unto the Genius of such Assemblies, but by the unhappy Circumstances of an oppressed or ill-setled Liberty. These Accusations would soon cease, if the Law of Toleration were once so setled, that all Churches were obliged to lay down Toleration as the Foundation of their own Liberty; and teach that Liberty of Conscience is every mans natural Right, equally belonging to Dissenters as to themselves, and that no body ought to be compelled in matters of Religion, either by Law or Force. The Establishment of this one thing would take away all ground of Complaints and Tumults upon account of Conscience. And these Causes of Discontents and Animosities being once removed, there would remain nothing in these Assemblies that were not more peaceable, and less apt to produce Disturbance of State, than in any other Meetings whatsoever. But let us examine particularly the Heads of these Accusations.

You'll say, That *Assemblies and Meetings* endanger the Publick Peace, *and threaten the Commonwealth*. I answer: If this be so, Why are there daily such numerous Meetings in Markets, and Courts of Judicature? Why are Crowds upon the Exchange,* and a Concourse of People in Cities suffered? You'll reply; These are Civil Assemblies; but Those we object against are Ecclesiastical. I answer: 'Tis a likely thing indeed, that such Assemblies as are altogether remote from Civil

Affairs, should be most apt to embroyl them. O, but Civil Assemblies are composed of men that differ from one another in matters of Religion; but these Ecclesiastical Meetings are of Persons that are all of one Opinion. As if an Agreement in matters of Religion, were in effect a Conspiracy against the Commonwealth; or as if men would not be so much the more warmly unanimous in Religion, the less liberty they had of Assembling. But it will be urged still, That Civil Assemblies are open, and free for any one to enter into; whereas Religious Conventicles are more private, and thereby give opportunity to Clandestine Machinations.* I answer, That this is not strictly true: For many Civil Assemblies are not open to every one. And if some Religious Meetings be private, Who are they (I beseech you) that are to be blamed for it? those that desire, or those that forbid their being publick? Again; You'll say, That Religious Communion does exceedingly unite mens Minds and Affections to one another, and is therefore the more dangerous. But if this be so, Why is not the Magistrate afraid of his own Church; and why does he not forbid their Assemblies, as things dangerous to his Government? You'll say, Because he himself is a Part, and even the Head of them. As if he were not also a Part of the Commonwealth, and the Head of the whole People.

Let us therefore deal plainly. The Magistrate is afraid of other Churches, but not of his own; because he is kind and favourable to the one, but severe and cruel to the other. These he treats like Children, and indulges them even to Wantonness: Those he uses as Slaves; and how blamelessly soever they demean themselves, recompenses them no otherwise than by Gallies,* Prisons, Confiscations, and Death. These he cherishes and defends: Those he continually scourges and oppresses. Let him turn the Tables: Or let those Dissenters enjoy but the same Priviledges in Civils as his other Subjects, and he will quickly find that these Religious Meetings will be no longer dangerous. For if men enter into Seditious Conspiracies, 'tis not Religion that inspires them to it in their Meetings; but their Sufferings and Oppressions that make them willing to ease themselves. Just and Moderate Governments are every where quiet, every where safe. But Oppression raises Ferments, and makes Men struggle to cast off an uneasie and tyrannical Yoke. I know that Seditions are very frequently raised, upon pretence of Religion. But 'tis as true that, for Religion, Subjects are frequently ill treated, and live miserably.

Believe me, the Stirs that are made proceed not from any peculiar Temper of this or that Church or Religious Society; but from the common Disposition of all Mankind, who when they groan under any heavy Burthen, endeavour naturally to shake off the Yoke that galls their Necks. Suppose this Business of Religion were let alone, and that there were some other Distinction made between men and men, upon account of their different Complexions, Shapes, and Features; so that those who have black Hair (for example) or gray Eyes, should not enjoy the same Privileges as other Citizens; that they should not be permitted either to buy or sell, or live by their Callings; that Parents should not have the Government and Education of their own Children;* that they should either be excluded from the Benefit of the Laws, or meet with partial Judges; can it be doubted but these Persons, thus distinguished from others by the Colour of their Hair and Eyes, and united together by one common Persecution, would be as dangerous to the Magistrate, as any others that had associated themselves meerly upon the account of Religion. Some enter into Company for Trade and Profit: Others, for want of Business, have their Clubs for Claret:* Neighbourhood joyns some, and Religion others. But there is one only thing which gathers People into Seditious Commotions, and that is Oppression.

You'll say; What, will you have People to meet at Divine Service *against the Magistrate's Will?* I answer; Why, I pray, against his Will? Is it not both lawful and necessary that they should meet? Against his Will, do you say? That's what I complain of, That is the very Root of all the Mischief.* Why are Assemblies less sufferable in a Church than in a Theater or Market? Those that meet there are not either more vicious, or more turbulent, than those that meet elsewhere. The Business in that is, that they are ill used, and therefore they are not to be suffered. Take away the Partiality that is used towards them in matters of common Right; change the Laws; take away the Penalties unto which they are subjected; and all things will immediately become safe and peaceable. Nay, those that are averse to the Religion of the Magistrate, will think themselves so much the more bound to maintain the Peace of the Commonwealth, as their Condition is better in that place than elsewhere; And all the several separate Congregations, like so many Guardians of the Publick Peace, will watch one another,* that nothing may be innovated or changed in the Form of the Government: Because they can hope for nothing better than what they already enjoy; that is, an equal Condition with their Fellow-Subjects, under a just and moderate Government. Now if that Church, which agrees in Religion with the Prince, be esteemed the chief Support of any Civil Government, and that for no other Reason (as has already been shewn) than because the Prince is kind, and the Laws are favourable to it; how much greater will be the Security of a Government, where all good Subjects, of whatsoever Church they be, without any Distinction upon account of Religion, enjoying the same Favour of the Prince, and the same Benefit of the Laws, shall become the common Support and Guard of it; and where none will have any occasion to fear the Severity of the Laws, but those that do Injuries to their Neighbours, and offend against the Civil Peace?

That we may draw towards a Conclusion. The *Sum of all* we drive at is, *That every Man may enjoy the same Rights that are granted to others.* Is it permitted to worship God in the *Roman* manner? Let it be permitted to do it in the *Geneva* Form also. Is it permitted to speak *Latin* in the Market-place? Let those that have a mind to it, be permitted to do it also in the Church. Is it lawful for any man in his own House, to kneel, stand, sit, or use any other Posture; and to cloath himself in White or Black, in short or in long Garments? Let it not be made unlawful to eat Bread, drink Wine, or wash with Water, in the Church. In a Word: Whatsoever things are left free by Law in the common occasions of Life, let them remain free unto every Church in Divine Worship. Let no Mans Life, or Body, or House, or Estate, suffer any manner of Prejudice upon these Accounts. Can you allow of the *Presbyterian* Discipline? Why should not the *Episcopal* also have what they like?* Ecclesiastical Authority, whether it be administred by the Hands of a single Person, or many, is every where the same; and neither has any Jurisdiction in things Civil, nor any manner of Power of Compulsion, nor any thing at all to do with Riches and Revenues.

Ecclesiastical Assemblies, and Sermons, are justified by daily experience, and publick Allowance. These are allowed to People of some one Perswasion: Why not to all? If any thing pass in a Religious Meeting seditiously, and contrary to the Publick Peace, it is to be punished in the same manner, and no otherwise, than as if it had happened in a Fair or Market. These Meetings ought not to be Sanctuaries for Factious and Flagitious* Fellows; Nor ought it to be less lawful for Men to meet in Churches than in Halls;* Nor are one part of the Subjects to be esteemed more blameable, for their meeting together, than others. Every one is to be accountable for his own Actions; and no man is to be laid under a Suspicion, or Odium, for the Fault of another. Those that are Seditious, Murderers, Thieves, Robbers, Adulterers, Slanderers, &c. of whatsoever Church, whether National, or not, ought to be punished and suppressed. But those whose Doctrine is peaceable, and whose Manners are pure and blameless, ought to be upon equal Terms with their Fellow Subjects. Thus if Solemn Assemblies, Observations of Festivals, Publick Worship, be permitted to any one sort of Professors;* all these things ought to be permitted to the *Presbyterians, Independents, Anabaptists, Arminians, Quakers*,* and others, with the same liberty. Nay if we may openly speak the Truth and as becomes one Man to another; neither *Pagan*, nor *Mahumetan*, nor *Jew*,* ought to be excluded from the Civil Rights of the Commonwealth, because of his Religion. The Gospel commands no such thing. The Church, which *judges not those that are without*, wants it not (1 Cor. 5: 12- 13). And the Commonwealth, which embraces indifferently all men that are honest, peaceable, and industrious, requires it not. Shall we suffer a *Pagan* to deal and trade with us, and shall we not suffer him to pray unto, and worship God? If we allow the *Jews* to have private Houses and Dwellings amongst us, Why should we not allow them to have Synagogues?* Is their Doctrine more false, their Worship more abominable, or is the Civil Peace more endangered, by their meeting in publick, than in their private Houses? But if these things may be granted to *Jews* and *Pagans*, surely the condition of any Christians ought not to be worse than theirs in a Christian Commonwealth.

You'll say, perhaps, Yes, it ought to be: Because they are more inclinable to Factions, Tumults, and Civil Wars. I answer: Is this the fault of the Christian Religion? If it be so, truly the Christian Religion is the worst of all Religions, and ought neither to be embraced by any particular Person, nor tolerated by any Commonwealth. For if this be the Genius, this the Nature of the Christian Religion, to be turbulent, and destructive to the Civil Peace; that Church it self which the Magistrate indulges will not always be innocent. But far be it from us to say any such thing of that Religion, which carries the greatest opposition to Covetousness, Ambition, Discord, Contention, and all manner of inordinate Desires; and is the most modest and peaceable Religion that ever was. We must therefore seek another Cause of those Evils that are charged upon Religion. And if we consider right, we shall find it to consist wholly in the Subject that I am treating of. It is not the Diversity of Opinions, (which cannot be avoided) but the Refusal of Toleration to those that are of different Opinions, (which might have been granted) that has produced all the Bustles and Wars that have been in the Christian World, upon account of Religion. The Heads and Leaders of the Church, moved by Avarice and insatiable desire of Dominion, making use of the immoderate Ambition of Magistrates, and the credulous Superstition of the giddy Multitude, have incensed and animated them against those that dissent from themselves; by preaching unto them, contrary to the Laws of the Gospel, and to the Precepts of Charity, That Schismaticks and Hereticks are to be outed of their Possessions, and destroyed. And thus have they mixed together, and confounded two things that are in themselves most different, the Church and the Commonwealth. Now as it is very difficult for men patiently to suffer themselves to be stript of the Goods, which they have got by their honest Industry; and contrary to all the Laws of Equity, both Humane and Divine, to be delivered up for a Prey to other mens Violence and Rapine;* especially when they are otherwise altogether blameless, and that the Occasion for which they are thus treated, does not at all belong to the Jurisdiction of the Magistrate, but entirely to the Conscience of every particular man, for the Conduct of which he is accountable to God only; What else can be expected, but that these men, growing weary of the Evils under which they labour, should in the end think it lawful for them to resist Force with Force, and to defend their natural Rights* (which are not forfeitable upon account of Religion) with Arms as well as they can? That this has been hitherto the ordi-nary course of things, is abundantly evident in History: And that it will continue to be so hereafter, is but too apparent in Reason. It cannot indeed be otherwise, so long as the Principle of Persecution for Religion shall prevail, as it has done hitherto, with Magistrate and People; and so long as those that ought to be the Preachers of Peace and Concord, shall continue, with all their Art and Strength, to excite men to Arms, and sound the Trumpet of War. But that Magistrates should thus suffer these Incendiaries, and Disturbers of the Publick Peace, might justly be wondred at; if it did not appear that they have been invited by them unto a Participation of the Spoil, and have therefore thought fit to make use of their Covetousness and Pride, as Means whereby to increase their own Power. For who does not see that *these Good Men* are indeed more Ministers of the Government, than Ministers of the Gospel; and that by flattering the Ambition, and favouring the Dominion of Princes and Men in Authority, they endeavour with all their might to promote that Tyranny in the Commonwealth, which otherwise they should not be able to establish in the Church?* This is the unhappy Agreement that we see between the Church and State. Whereas if each of them would contain itself within its own Bounds, the one attend ing to the worldly welfare of the Commonwealth, the other to the Salvation of Souls, it is impossible that any Discord should ever have hapned between them. *Sed, pudet haec opprobria. &c.** God Almighty grant, I beseech him, that the Gospel of Peace may at length be Preached, and that Civil Magistrates growing more careful to conform their own Consciences to the Law of God, and less solicitous about the binding of other mens Consciences by Humane Laws, may, like Fathers of their Country, direct all their Counsels and Endeavours to promote universally the Civil Welfare of all their Children; except only of such as are arrogant, ungovernable, and injurious to their Brethren; and that all Ecclesiastical men, who boast themselves to be the Successors of the Apostles, walking peaceably and modestly in the Apostles steps; without intermeddling with State-Affairs, may apply themselves wholly to promote the Salvation of Souls.

Farewel.

POSTSCRIPT.*

Perhaps it may not be amiss to add a few things concerning *Heresie* and *Schism.* A Turk is not, nor can be, either Heretick, or Schismatick to a *Christian*: and if any man fall off from the *Christian Faith* to *Mahumetism*, he does not thereby become a Heretick or Schismatick, but an Apostate, and an Infidel. This no body doubts of. And by this it appears that men of different Religions cannot be Hereticks or Schismaticks to one another.

We are to enquire therefore, what men are of the same Religion. Concerning which, it is manifest that those who have one and the same Rule of Faith and Worship, are of the same Religion; and those who have not the same Rule of Faith and Worship, are of different Religions. For since all things that belong unto that Religion, are contained in that Rule, it follows necessarily, that those who agree in one Rule, are of one and the same Religion: and *vice versa*. Thus *Turks* and *Christians* are of different Religions; because these take the *Holy Scriptures* to be the Rule of their Religion, and those the *Alcoran*. And for the same reason, there may be different Religions also even amongst *Christians*. The *Papists* and the *Lutherans*, though both of them profess Faith in Christ, and are therefore called *Christians*, yet are not both of the same Religion; because These acknowledge nothing but the *Holy Scriptures* to be the Rule and Foundation of their Religion; Those take in also Traditions and the Decrees of Popes,* and of these all together make the Rule of their Religion. And thus the Christians of St. *John** (as they are called) and the Christians of *Geneva*, are of different Religions; because These also take only the Scriptures; and Those, I know not what Traditions, for the Rule of their Religion.

This being setled, it follows; *First*, that Heresie is a Separation made in Ecclesiastical Communion between men of the same Religion, for some Opinions no way contained in the Rule it self. And *Secondly*, That amongst those who acknowledge nothing but the Holy Scriptures to be their Rule of Faith, Heresie is a Separation made in their Christian Communion, for Opinions not contained in the express words of Scripture. Now this Separation may be made in a twofold manner.

1. When the greater part, or (by the Magistrate's Patronage) the stronger part, of the Church separates it self from others, by excluding them out of her Communion, because they will not profess their Belief of certain Opinions which are not to be found in the express words of Scripture. For it is not the paucity of those that are separated, nor the Authority of the Magistrate, that can make any man guilty of Heresie. But he only is an Heretick who divides the Church into parts, introduces Names and Marks of Distinction, and voluntarily makes a Separation because of such Opinions.

2. When any one separates himself from the Communion of a Church, because that Church does not publickly profess some certain Opinions which the Holy Scriptures do not expresly teach.

Both these are *Hereticks*: *because they err in Fundamentals, and they err obstinately against Knowledge*. For when they have determined the Holy Scriptures to be the only Foundation of Faith; they nevertheless lay down certain Propositions as fundamental, which are not in the Scripture; and because others will not acknowledge these additional Opinions of theirs, nor build upon them as if they were necessary and fundamental, they therefore make a Separation in the Church; either by withdrawing themselves from the others, or expelling the others from them. Nor does it signifie any thing for them to say that their Confessions and Symboles* are agreeable to Scripture, and to the Analogy of Faith.* For if they be conceived in the express words of Scripture, there can be no question about them; because those are acknowledged by all Christians to be of Divine Inspiration, and therefore fundamental. But if they say that the Articles which they require to be profess'd, are Consequences deduced from the Scripture; it is undoubtedly well done of them to believe and profess such things as seem unto them so agreeable to the Rule of Faith; But it would be very ill done to obtrude those things upon others, unto whom they do not seem to be the indubitable Doctrines of the Scripture. And to make a Separation for such things as these, which neither are nor can be fundamental, is to become Hereticks. For I do not think there is any man arrived to that degree of madness, as that he dare give out his Consequences and Interpretations of Scripture as Divine Inspirations, and compare the Articles of Faith that he has framed according to his own Fancy with the Authority of Scripture. I know there are some Propositions so evidently agreeable to Scripture, that no body can deny them to be drawn from thence; but about those therefore there can be no difference. This only I say, that however clearly we may think this or the other Doctrine to be deduced from Scripture, we ought not therefore to impose it upon others, as a necessary Article of Faith, because we believe it to be agreeable to the Rule of Faith; unless we would be content also that other Doctrines should be imposed upon us in the same manner; and that we should be compell'd to receive and profess all the different and contradictory Opinions of *Lutherans*, *Calvinists*, *Remonstrants*, *Anabaptists*, and other Sects, which the Contrivers of Symbols, Systems, and Confessions, are accustomed to deliver to their Followers as genuine and necessary Deductions from the Holy Scripture. I cannot but wonder at the extravagant arrogance of those Men who think that they themselves can explain things necessary to Salvation more clearly than the Holy Ghost, the Eternal and Infinite Wisdom of God.

Thus much concerning *Heresie*; which word in common use is applied only to the Doctrinal part of Religion. Let us now consider *Schism*, which is a Crime near akin to it. For both those words seem unto me to signifie an *ill-grounded Separation in Ecclesiastical Communion, made about things not necessary*. But since Use, which is the Supreme Law in matter of Language,* has determined that Heresie relates to Errors in Faith, and Schism to those in Worship or Discipline, we must consider them under that Distinction.

Schism then, for the same reasons that have already been alledged, is nothing else but a Separation made in the Communion of the Church, upon account of something in Divine Worship, or Ecclesiastical Discipline, that is not any necessary part of it. Now nothing in Worship or Discipline can be necessary to Christian Communion, but what Christ our Legislator, or the Apostles, by Inspiration of the Holy Spirit, have commanded in express words.

In a word: He that denies not any thing that the Holy Scriptures teach in express words, nor makes a Separation upon occasion of any thing that is not manifestly contained in the Sacred Text; however he may be nick-named by any Sect of Christians, and declared by some, or all of them to be utterly void of true Christianity, yet indeed and in truth this Man cannot be either a Heretick or a Schismatick.

These things might have been explained more largely, and more advantageously: but it is enough to have hinted at them, thus briefly, to a Person of your parts.*

FINIS.

EXPLANATORY NOTES

SECOND TREATISE OF GOVERNMENT

The notes to the Second Treatise are keyed to paragraph numbers.

The Introduction: this first chapter was probably written as an after-thought, to connect the two treatises. It was omitted in the French transla-tion (Amsterdam, 1691) and in the first American edition (Boston, 1773).

1 *Adam*: whereas Locke regularly discusses biblical figures in the *First Trea-tise*, because commenting on Filmer's scriptural arguments, he rarely does so in the *Second*. Adam appears most often, in eight paragraphs, followed by Jephtha in four, and Noah in three.

Dominion: from the Latin *dominium*, denoting ownership, authority, control.

positive Law: law that is the command of someone having authority, whether God or the earthly ruler. God was held to legislate in two ways, through his Works and his Word: natural law embodied in Creation, and positive law given in the Bible.

Sir Robert F.: Filmer (1588–1653), a Kentish gentleman, the best-known English expositor of monarchical absolutism on patriarchalist founda-tions. He published Royalist tracts during the Civil War, but his chief work, *Patriarcha, or the Natural Power of Kings*, drafted in the 1620s, was not published until 1680, when it became the flagship of the Tory cause. Locke's *First Treatise* is a detailed refutation. Filmer's name appears again in §§ 22 and 61. In the *First Treatise* (§ 5) Locke summarizes Filmer's 'sys-tem' thus: 'Men are not born free, and therefore could never have the liberty to choose either Governors, or Forms of Government. Princes have their Power Absolute, and by Divine Right . . . Adam was an absolute Monarch, and so are all Princes ever since.' For Filmer's argument see the Introduction, pp. ix–xi.

2 *Magistrate*: 'magistrate' refers to civil rulers generally. Later, Locke dis-tinguishes between 'chief' or 'supreme', and 'subordinate' or 'inferior' magistrates. The latter comprise, for example, judges, lords lieutenant, justices of the peace, and parish constables.

Slave: Locke accepts the legitimacy of slavery, an important fact in recent discussion of the problem of reconciling Locke's 'liberalism' with his acceptance of African slavery in America. See § 85.

Common-wealth: 'commonwealth' means 'state' or 'polity'. When refer-ring to political society, Locke uses this word more often than 'state'. By 'state' he generally means 'condition', as in 'state of nature'. See note to § 205.

5 *Hooker*: Richard Hooker (*c.*1554–1600), clergyman and theologian. His multi-volume *Laws of Ecclesiastical Polity* (1594–7; later parts, 1648, 1662) mainly concerned theology and ecclesiology, but includes discussion of politics. The *Second Treatise* has fourteen quotations from Hooker, all but one from Book 1 and mostly from chapter 10. Hooker was Locke's chief exhibit for the claim that Royalist and Tory theories of absolutism were a recent intellectual fashion, no older than the Stuart era. In advice on political reading in 1703, Locke recommended Hooker, Algernon Sidney's *Discourses on Government* (1698), Pufendorf's *De iure naturae et gentium* (*On the Law of Nature and Peoples*, 1672), and *De officio hominis et civis* (*On the Duty of Man and Citizen*, 1673), and his own *Two Treatises* as the best books on 'the original of societies, and the rise and extent of political power'. Locke purchased a copy of Hooker in 1681.

Li. I: Locke uses Latin abbreviations in citations: L., l., or Li. (= Book) and c. (= Chapter).

6 *Liberty . . . Licence*: a fundamental distinction for Locke. Liberty is freedom within the bounds of reason and natural law; license (or 'licentiousness') is the free play of impulse (and hence, not liberty, but slavery to the passions).

Workmanship: for Locke, as he will show in Chapter V, a property and right over a thing arises from labouring upon it. This is a microcosm of the divine economy, for we belong to God and are subject to him because he created us. Hence, as Locke remarks a few lines earlier, man does not have 'liberty to destroy himself'. This ban on suicide is a striking instance of his distance from modern libertarianism.

8 *absolute or arbitrary Power*: Royalists and Tories insisted that 'absolute' is distinct from 'arbitrary' rule, but Locke and the Whigs elided the two, asserting that a benign absolute monarch is in principle as bad as a despotic one, because our liberties would still depend on whim and concession, and not on right.

9 *Prince*: a generic term for any earthly ruler.

Stranger: foreigner.

11 *damnified*: injured, damaged.

whoso sheddeth . . . slay me: Gen. 9: 6; 4: 14.

writ in the Hearts of all Mankind: Locke's claim that the law of nature is innately within us apparently contradicts his denial of innate ideas in Book 1 of his *Essay Concerning Human Understanding*. Early critics of the *Essay* were shocked by his apparent moral relativism, but the stance here is more conventional. A common scriptural citation which 'proved' innate moral knowledge was Prov. 20: 27: 'the spirit of man is the candle of the lord.'

12 *as far forth*: to this extent and no more.

municipal Laws: positive, human laws of a particular country.

13 *God hath . . . Men*: probably an echo of Rom. 13: 3–4: 'Rulers are not a terror to good works, but to the evil . . . He is the minister of God to thee for good . . . he beareth not the sword in vain.' See note to § 237.

Which Men . . . another: this phrase follows the first, second, and third editions; the Christ's Copy has: 'Much better it is in the State of Nature wherein Men are not bound to submit to the unjust will of another'. For the Christ's Copy see the Note on the Text.

14 *Compact*: although Locke is generally described as a 'social contract' theorist, he does not use that phrase; his preferred term is 'compact'.

Body Politick: a familiar metaphor in pre-modern political thought. There were many ways of construing the relationship between the head and organs of a political body.

Truck: barter.

Garcilasso de la Vega: (1539–1616), Peruvian son of a conquistador and an Inca; author of *Commentarios Reales de los Incas* (1609–17), translated into French in *La Commentaire Royale, ou L'Histoire des Yncas, Roys du Peru* (1633). Locke noted the story from de la Vega in his journal in 1687.

between the two Men . . . Indian: in one version of the first edition, this phrase reads 'between the two Men in *Soldania*, in or between, a *Swiss* and an *Indian*', without the reference to Vega. Soldania is Saldanha Bay in South Africa. The phrase marks an important continuity in Locke's thought, for he mentions the atheistic beliefs of the natives of Soldania in his *Essays on the Law of Nature* (1663–4) and his *Essay Concerning Human Understanding* (1689). Perhaps he avoided it here so readers would not detect that the *Essay* and the *Two Treatises* were by the same author.

19 *some Men have confounded*: a reference to the followers of Hobbes; this passage marks a strong difference between the views of the two men concerning the human condition in the state of nature.

20 *both Sides*: in one version of the first edition a lengthy passage is missing, beginning after 'both sides' and continuing to 'army to battle' in the middle of § 21. This involved the text jumping from § 20 to § 22. The Everyman edition of 1924 (not replaced until 1993) followed the faulty version, and arbitrarily renumbered paragraphs to disguise the fault in numeration. It is a good example of the perils of textual editing.

nay where an Appeal to the Law: there follows an angry passage probably directed against the show trials which sent several Whigs to prison or execution between 1681 and 1685 on charges of sedition and treason. The most famous victims were William, Lord Russell, and Algernon Sidney, executed in 1683. When courts of law, which are dedicated to impartial justice, are perverted into instruments of tyranny, then the ruler may truly be said to make war on the people.

21 *Jephtha*: in the Book of Judges, Jephtha intervenes on behalf of Israel and triumphs over the oppressive Ammonites. After 1688 preachers drew parallels between Jephtha and William III.

22 *O. A. 55*: Filmer's *Observations upon Aristotle's Politiques* (1652), cited from the 1679 collection of his tracts, published under the general title *The Free-holders Grand Inquest*.

25 *25*: Chapter V has received more intensive commentary and disagreement in modern times than any other, not least because property has become so central to the economic orientation of modern politics. Since the 1990s, however, a new approach to this chapter has emerged: debate in relation to European colonial empires in America, in which Locke played a personal part. Most mentions of 'America' in the *Second Treatise* occur in this chapter.

a right to their Preservation, and . . . Meat and Drink: Chapter V upholds the rights of the industrious and of private property, but Locke also insists on a universal right to subsistence. He does so in the *First Treatise* (§ 42): 'God hath not left one Man so to the Mercy of another, that he may starve him if he please'; 'his needy Brother [has] a Right to the Surplusage of his Goods . . . when his pressing Wants call for it'; ''twould always be a Sin in any Man of Estate, to let his Brother perish for want of affording him Relief out of his Plenty'.

Commoners: those who share common rights of access and use. In Locke's time there were prolonged struggles to preserve common or community rights to rural fields and woodlands against the enclosure movement, which parcelled up land into private domains. See note to § 36.

26 *Convenience*: commodiousness, well-being.

31 *1 Tim. vi. 12*: '12' is an error for '17'.

32 *subdue the Earth*: Gen. 1: 28.

36 *Nature . . . Property*: the Christ's Copy has: 'The measure of Property, Nature has well set, . . .'

vacant places of America: see note to § 121: 'vacuis locis'.

in Spain . . . use of it: a striking passage, for it endorses squatters' rights. Locke believes that the duty to make the land fruitful through cultivation undergirds claims to private property: a right to land is not fully established unless the land is made productive. In the late eighteenth century a school of Lockean socialists argued for the rights of labourers against landlords.

Propriety: property. Several instances of 'propriety' in the first edition were later amended to 'property'.

37 *To which let me add*: the following important passage of 211 words, to the end of the paragraph, is an addition which first appeared in the fourth edition (1713) and is found handwritten in the Christ's Copy.

40 *Tobacco or Sugar*: a reference to crops recently developed in the slave plantations of the West Indies and North America. Barbados was the economic miracle of the age. A striking instance of Locke's awareness of a growing commercial empire.

41 *And a King . . . England*: this remark captures what will become a fundamental argument for capitalism: advanced economies make everybody richer, albeit at the price of greater inequality.

42 *This shews*: this paragraph, of eighty-nine words, is an addition to the text and first appeared in the fourth edition (1713) and is found handwritten in the Christ's Copy. It is striking that, in the reign of King William III, whom he applauded, Locke is prepared to speak of the best ruler as 'god-like'. This paragraph is Locke's epitome of his own aims and efforts as a member of the Board of Trade and Plantations from 1696 to 1700.

increase of Lands: the use of the word 'lands' has troubled interpreters, for Locke's general view is that governments should aim to increase population and labour productivity rather than merely extend territory. One recent edition (New York, 2005) arbitrarily amends 'lands' to 'hands'. 'Lands' is textually correct, but Locke means not increase of territorial extent but increase of productivity, through the application of labour and technology.

43 *Iron, Wood, . . . reckon up*: Locke gives shipbuilding as his example because it was the most commodity- and capital-intensive of all contemporary industrial enterprises.

50 *Partage*. division.

be hoarded up . . . positive Constitutions: this passage, of eighty words, is an addition to the text which first appeared in the fourth edition (1713) and is found handwritten in the Christ's Copy. Locke extensively reshaped the passage. The version in the Christ's Copy is muddled and can only be clarified in light of the 1713 edition, which is evidence of the existence of a lost master-copy which included most of the Christ's Copy amendments.

52 *52*: Chapter VI is a summary of Locke's critique, in the *First Treatise*, of Filmer's grounding of absolute monarchy on Adam's patriarchy as the archetype of all authority, paternal, marital, domestic, and political.

right of Generation . . . it: in the *First Treatise* Locke rejects Filmer's biological theory that the male is the 'Principal Agent in Generation' (§ 55).

57 *presently*: at that time.

58 *Nonage*: legal infancy, minority.

want: need.

Estate: Locke here means 'condition', but usually 'property'.

61 *Sir R. F.*: Sir Robert Filmer: see note to § 1.

Empire: in pre-modern thought this word denoted sovereignty or supremacy, rather than territorial extent, though the modern usage occurs too (e.g. § 105). From the Latin *imperium*.

65 *leave Father . . . Wife*: Gen. 2: 24, Matt. 19: 5.

68 *Children . . . Parents*: Eph. 6: 1.

74 *Latins call Piety*: *pietas*, loyalty and devotion to parents and relations.

74 [*Footnote*] *Arch-Philosopher*: Aristotle, the most influential of the ancient Greek philosophers, especially in ethics and politics. His *Politics* was cited by all sides in pre-modern thought: Tories emphasized the familial origins of commonwealths, from Book 1, and Whigs the idea of the mixed polity, from Book 3.

[*Footnote*] *Regiment*: polity. This usage ceased around the mid-seventeenth century.

Fact: crime.

76 *Priest . . . Houshold*: a reference to Hooker's point (§ 74 n.), and in turn to Melchizedek, the first person in the Bible described as king and priest: Gen. 14: 18. Theorists in the 'Erastian' tradition assigned quasi-sacerdotal authority to kings, which most Anglican Royalists were anxious to avoid.

80 *Hymen*: in Greek mythology, the god of marriage.

uncertain Mixture . . . Solutions: the first phrase means polygamy; 'solutions' means dissolutions.

81 *81*: in this paragraph Locke offers (albeit guardedly) a defence of divorce. The courts did, however, allow separation (see next paragraph).

85 *Family of his Master*: like his contemporaries, Locke treats servants and apprentices as belonging to a 'family'. Locke himself was said to belong to the 'family' of his patron, the Earl of Shaftesbury. Despite his anti-patriarchalism, he accepts the family as the basic unit of society. Families were understood in terms of the classical notions of the *oikos* or *domus*, meaning 'household' (from which we derive 'economy' and 'domestic').

Slaves . . . just War: Locke does not endorse a naturalistic account of (racial) slavery, but a juridical account: those who are defeated in a war of self-defence may be killed or enslaved.

89 *Judge . . . by it*: where we would expect to see reference to judicial power, Locke subsumes it under legislative and executive power. He treats judges in courts of law as magistrates acting under the society's general legislative power.

90 *some Men*: Royalist and Tory defenders of absolute monarchy. Although Locke formally wrote to refute Filmer, he says in the Preface that he would not have troubled to answer Filmer, 'had not the Pulpit, of late Years, publickly owned his Doctrine, and made it the Currant Divinity of the Times'.

91 *Grand Signior*: the Sultan of the Ottoman Empire.

[*Footnote*] *Commodity*: commodiousness, utility, well-being.

92 *late Relation of Ceylon*: Robert Knox (*c.*1640–1720), *An Historical Relation of the Island of Ceylon in the East Indies* (1681), the first account of Ceylon (Sri Lanka) published in England. Locke bought a copy in 1681. This is the most recent book cited in the *Second Treatise*: James Tyrrell's *Patriarcha non Monarcha* (1681) is cited in the *First*.

94 *amuze*: mislead, divert attention from.

Deference: the 1713/14 editions have 'difference'; I have corrected it from the Christ's Copy.

98 *Cato's . . . again*: Martial, *Epigrams*, Bk 1. Cato of Utica was a politician who opposed Julius Caesar; he was lionized by Cicero, who makes him the martyr-hero of the dying Roman Republic.

Leviathan: given that the word inevitably pointed to Hobbes's much-maligned book of 1651, it seems oddly risqué, and unnecessary, of Locke to use it at this point.

99 *unless they . . . greater than the Majority*: political societies sometimes, for some purposes, institute a 'supermajority', e.g. a two-thirds majority. 'Agreed on' would be clearer than 'agreed in'.

100 *Story*: history.

101 *Salmanasser, or Xerxes*: respectively, an Assyrian conqueror ('Shalmaneser', ninth century BCE), and king of Persia, who conquered Greece (fifth century BCE). Known from the Bible and Herodotus.

Letters: literacy.

102 *beginning of Rome and Venice . . . Subjection*: Livy and Plutarch were the standard sources for the early history of Rome; medieval chroniclers narrated the founding of Venice in 421 by refugees from Padua and elsewhere.

Josephus Acosta's . . . c. 25: José de Acosta (1539–1600), Jesuit priest, naturalist, and explorer; author of *Historia natural y moral de las Indias* (1590), translated as *The Natural and Moral History of the Indies* (1590). Locke read Acosta in 1681.

Politicians: Locke's only use of the word, here meaning writers on politics. Those engaged in politics were generally called 'statesmen'.

103 *Palantus . . . Justin*: Palantus was a Spartan leader who founded Tarentum in Italy in the eighth century BCE; the story is told in Justin's epitome of Trogus Pompeius' *Historiae Philippicae*, which dates from the second or third century CE.

105 *Empires of Peru and Mexico*: the Inca and Aztec.

ceteris paribus: other things being equal.

107 *The Equality . . . Justice*: this passage, of forty-nine words, is an addition to the text which first appeared in the fourth edition (1713), and is found, in shorter form, handwritten in the Christ's Copy. The latter has simply 'and there wanted not justice' instead of 'or Variety of Officers . . . Execution of Justice'.

109 *going out and in . . . People*: Num. 27: 17.

in: at.

article: treat, agree.

Also (say they) . . . Israel: 2 Sam. 5: 2.

111 *amor sceleratus habendi*: the accursed love of possessing.

111 [*Footnote*] . . . : Locke here supplies the identical quotation as appears in the footnote to § 94; it is pertinent in both places; I have omitted it here.

112 *Jure Divino*: by divine right.

Divinity of this last Age: the treatises and sermons of the clergy during the Stuart century.

113 *Demonstration*: beyond doubt.

114 *owned*: acknowledged.

116 *bating*: excepting.

119 *express and a tacit Consent*: commentators have variously interpreted the significance of Locke's distinction in §§ 119–22. Some say it is Locke's device for restricting citizenship to an elite. It is unclear what actions count as express consent. Locke's contemporaries relied on oaths of allegiance. After 1688 there was furious controversy over the oath required by the new regime.

121 *vacuis locis*: empty places. Locke probably means that such places are 'empty' not literally, because they were inhabited by native peoples, but in the sense that those peoples failed to cultivate the land, so that, rightly speaking, the land is nobody's property, until others arrive to cultivate it. This passage is important in recent claims that Locke seeks to justify European colonialism.

123 *Lives, Liberties, and Estates*: a number of phrases which we think of as quintessentially Lockean were in fact common in contemporary Whig pamphleteering.

132 *compounded and mixed Forms of Government*: Locke's analysis of three primary forms of government, and of a fourth, mixed form, is standard in pre-modern political thought, and derives from Greek and Roman, and Renaissance, sources. His acceptance of 'mixed' polities goes sharply against Hobbes's contempt for 'mixarchy' and Filmer's 'anarchy of a limited or mixed monarchy'. Compare § 213.

133 *King James the first*: the first edition referred simply to 'K. James' and was corrected in later editions. Since, from 1685, there was a 'James II', this is evidence that Locke drafted the *Two Treatises* prior to 1685. There is another instance at § 200, not corrected until the third edition (1698).

134 *fundamental positive Law*: some commentators, with an eye to the American Constitution, try to extract from Locke a doctrine of a 'written constitution' that stands outside and above the ordinary laws of the legislative assembly. Whigs did often talk of 'fundamental laws', speaking of Magna Carta and the Bill of Rights as standing superior to ordinary law, and regularly claimed that all human positive law is subordinate to natural law; but they rarely envisaged a formal written constitution.

137 *Liberty to defend . . . Combination*: American theorists who today defend the right to bear arms make use especially of this phrase and paragraph.

138 *The supream Power . . . Consent*: in the 1760s and 1770s the American

revolutionaries, and their British supporters, repeatedly quoted from §§ 138–40 to defend the principle of 'no taxation without representation'.

141 *The Power of the Legislative . . . hands*: this passage, of fifty-seven words, is an addition to the text which first appeared in the second edition (1694).

143 *143*: in this chapter Locke's discussion of the three powers of the commonwealth leads some commentators to find the modern doctrine of 'separation of powers'. Locke holds that the powers are conceptually distinct, but he does not envisage them as necessarily being held by separate persons. Also, his typology does not match the modern triad of legislative, executive, and judicial.

149 *Fiduciary Power*: a power held in trust, delegated to a trustee who may act only within the terms of the trust. Locke makes extensive use of the concept of trust.

154 *That either . . . People*: Locke is agnostic about the regularity of parliaments, whereas many contemporary Whigs held that annual, or at least fixed-term, parliaments should be constitutionally prescribed.

156 *Constant frequent . . . People*: a nice instance of Locke's assumptions predating the Glorious Revolution, since even defenders of parliament had not envisaged it necessarily sitting for more than a few weeks each year. After 1689 parliament became a permanent institution, sitting annually for many months, and the amount of legislation multiplied rapidly.

157 *Representation becomes . . . disproportionate*: Locke is unusual in proposing franchise reform, for there was little discussion of it between the Civil War and the late eighteenth century. Locke proposes a fairer distribution of parliamentary seats to reflect the growth of new commercial towns.

To what gross Absurdities . . . Riches: the reference is to the ancient borough of Old Sarum in Wiltshire, later notorious in campaigns for parliamentary reform because, although having no inhabitants, it sent two MPs to parliament.

158 *Salus Populi Suprema Lex*: 'the safety [or well-being] of the people is the supreme law.' This epigram, from Cicero's *De legibus*, is perhaps the most ubiquitously quoted piece of classical wisdom in the history of pre-modern political thought.

in Proportion . . . Publick: Locke shares the standard assumption of contemporaries that the franchise should depend on a property qualification. By 'equal Representative', a few lines later, he means proportionate equality.

The Power . . . had it: Locke is concessive to royal prerogative, here the crown's power to charter boroughs, awarding rights to send MPs. In fact, the enfranchisement of Newark in 1673 was the final instance of this practice, and all later franchise changes were made by parliament.

159 *159*: in this chapter Locke is strikingly supportive of prerogative power.

Where a ruler has the trust of the people, it is prudent to allow consider-able discretionary action.

166 *that saying*: not traced.

publick Disorders . . . so: probably an allusion to King John's reign and the signing of Magna Carta—in contrast to the rule of the 'God-like' St Edward the Confessor. See Locke's remarks on recovery of ancestral right and on the Norman Conquest in §§ 176–7.

172 *the common bond . . . Security*: this passage, of 110 words, is an addition to the text which first appeared in the fourth edition (1713) and is found handwritten in the Christ's Copy. The Christ's Copy has two versions of the final phrase; the alternative reads: 'Noxious brute that is destructive to their being'.

175 *175*: some Royalists and Tories argued for the absolute power of monarchs as derived from conquest: see note to § 177.

176 *176*: in *The Case of Ireland* (1698), William Molyneux of Dublin cited this paragraph and chapter to argue that England's conquest conferred no right over Ireland. It was the first occasion on which Locke's book was used by a colonial writer to challenge imperial dominion. However, Moly-neux accepted that Ireland's monarch was the same as England's: Ireland was a free and independent monarchy, equal and not subject to the Eng-lish parliament. Molyneux was later cited by American Revolutionaries.

Pyrates . . . Empire: an echo of a famous passage in Augustine's *City of God*, where a pirate tells Alexander the Great that his rule is but piracy writ large (bk. 4, ch. 4).

Submission: Locke distinguishes submission (forced assent) from (free) consent.

177 *Draw-can-Sirs*: violent swaggerers, ready to draw their swords and slay their opponents, 'without . . . justice'. From the Duke of Buckingham's play *The Rehearsal* (1672). Locke may be recollecting Andrew Marvell's description of the Royalist author Samuel Parker, as 'the ecclesiastical Draw-Can-Sir' who 'kills whole nations', in *The Rehearsal Transpros'd* (1672).

William: King William I, usually called 'the Conqueror' (1027–84), who became king of England after the Battle of Hastings in 1066. Royalists and Tories argued that parliament's rights and the people's liberties were gracious concessions by absolute monarchs whose title derives, in part, from conquest. Whigs, conversely, denied that 1066 marked a conquest; rather, the Anglo-Saxon ('Ancient' or 'Gothic') free constitution per-sisted, albeit often suppressed and in need of periodic renovation.

184 *Wampompeke*: wampum (*wampumpeag*), bead money of the Native Ameri-can Algonquin people.

disseiz'd: dispossessed.

five hundred: this read 'five thousand' in the first edition. The difference is between 'five years product' and 'perpetual'.

192 *Opportunity to do it*: the Christ's Copy has 'power to do it'.

196 *Hingar, or Hubba*: Ingware and Ubba, supposed leaders of the first Danish invasion of England in the 860s. They are mentioned in the contemporary *Anglo-Saxon Chronicle* and by the chronicler Roger of Wendover (d. 1236). Whig historians argued that, like the coming of William I, the advent of the Danes did not mark a conquest in the sense of the subjugation of the English people and destruction of their liberties.

Spartacus: Roman gladiator who led a slave revolt in 73 BCE.

198 *For the Anarchy . . . Monarch*: in the 1713/14 editions this passage occurs twice, first a couple of lines earlier, after 'people'. I have excised the first instance, which is the intention in the Christ's Copy.

200 *Hereafter, Seed-time . . . remaineth*: Gen. 8: 22.

Speech to the Parliament . . . Commonwealth: James VI of Scotland and I of England (1566–1625) became the first Stuart monarch of England in 1603. Locke's citation of James belongs to a common Whig ploy of showing that even absolutists distinguish true monarchy from tyranny. The ploy is not, however, very useful, since the real issues are whether liberties exist by right or merely by a gracious monarch's will; and what a people was entitled to do in the face of tyranny. The latter of the two speeches cited here in fact belongs to 1610.

201 *Thirty Tyrants . . . Syracuse . . . Decemviri at Rome*: respectively, oligarchs who briefly overthrew democracy and ruled Athens, 404–403 BCE; Hiero, tyrant of Syracuse (third century BCE); and the ten patricians of Rome overthrown in 449 BCE.

202 *Country*: probably here meaning 'county'.

205 *Neighbour . . . Example*: apparently in fact a reference to England, inserted in 1689.

Republick: state or commonwealth. In pre-modern usage, 'republic' was generic, and so included monarchies; from the Latin *res publica*, the public entity. However, by Locke's time the word was tainted by regicide and the Cromwellian republic, and Locke otherwise avoids it.

206 *As is plain . . . not*: Locke alludes to a vibrant oppositional legal culture in which law officers were regularly challenged over procedural defects in warrants or in their execution.

210 *Religion underhand favoured*: an allusion to Catholicism, but presumably to Charles II's crypto-, rather than James II's open, popery.

Algiers: entrepôt for the trade in Christians captured into slavery by the Moors.

211 *211*: this chapter contains the polemical culmination of the *Second Treatise*, the defence of a community's right of armed resistance against a tyrannical monarch.

213 *Let us suppose . . . Persons*: what follows is a description of the English 'mixed' constitution. A commonwealth may choose any form of

government it thinks good, but historically the English have chosen this particular form. Compare § 132.

213 *pro tempore*: for a period.

214 *First*: in §§ 214–17 Locke comes closest to providing a commentary on the actions of Charles II and James II during the 1680s: laws disregarded, parliaments suspended, elections manipulated, the nation subjected to foreign power.

217 *Subjection of a foreign Power*: Locke means the Stuart kings' craven submission to Louis XIV's France, the epitome of despotism and with aspirations to dominate all Europe, and/or to Roman Catholicism, since the papacy was regarded as a hostile foreign power.

225 *a long train of Abuses*: the phrase occurs in the American Declaration of Independence.

228 *Polyphemus's Den*: in Greek mythology, Polyphemus is a one-eyed Cyclops who traps and eats companions of Ulysses: Homer, *Odyssey*, bk. 9.

passive Obedience: an allusion to Tory exponents of the duty of 'passive obedience and non-resistance' in the face of tyranny.

230 *more disposed . . . Resistance*: the phrase is echoed in the American Declaration of Independence: 'mankind are more disposed to suffer, while evils are sufferable, than to right themselves.'

232 *Barclay*: William Barclay (*c.*1546–1608), Scottish absolutist who settled in France. Author of *De regno et regali potestate* (*On Kings and Royal Power*) (1600) which attacked theorists of resistance, for whom he coined the word 'monarchomachs', king-killers. Locke cites Barclay to show that even absolutists allow resistance *in extremis*. He bought a copy of Barclay in 1680.

His words are these: Locke first gives the quotation in Latin, which I have omitted.

233 *Buchanan*: George Buchanan (1506–68), humanist scholar, tutor to King James VI and I, and heir of John Knox in the intellectual leadership of the Scottish Reformation. Royalists and Tories deplored, and Whigs applauded, his *De jure regni apud Scotos* (*The Powers of the Crown in Scotland*) (1579).

235 *Juvenal*: (*c.*60–140 CE), Roman satirist. The following quotes are from *Satires*, 3.

ubi . . . tantum: when you strike, I'm just a punchbag.

Libertas . . . reverti: such is the poor man's freedom: after being beaten to a pulp, he may beg, as a special favour, to be left with his few remaining teeth.

His Words are: Locke first gives the quotation in Latin, which I have omitted. The quotation also occupies § 236.

237 *Honour the King . . . God*: Exod. 20: 12, Rom. 13: 2. In pre-modern political thought Romans 13 was the most frequently quoted scriptural text in

defence of obedience to civil authority: 'Let every soul be subject unto the higher powers. For . . . the powers that be are ordained of God. Whosoever therefore resisteth . . . shall receive to themselves damnation.' Locke does not pause to extricate resistance theory from the standard absolutist reading of Romans 13.

Interregnum: English absolutists repudiated the possibility of an interregnum, but the matter was more ambiguous in Scottish constitutional thought.

Winzerus: Ninian Winzet (1518–92), Scottish Catholic priest, who published attacks on the architects of the Scottish Reformation, Knox and Buchanan. 'Winzerus' is an error for 'Winzetus'.

Nero . . . Caligula: Roman emperors (reigned 54–68 and 37–41 CE), notorious for their cruelty.

And he . . . blow: Suetonius, *Caligula*, 30.

238 *One Example . . . Annals*: probably John Balliol, king of Scots (reigned 1292–6), whose submission to Edward I of England provoked the Scottish War of Independence.

239 *This farther I desire . . . Offence*: this passage, of 240 words, is an addition to the text which first appeared in the second edition (1694).

Bilson: Thomas Bilson (1547–1616), bishop of Worcester and then Winchester; enemy of Puritanism and defender of monarchical and episcopal authority; author of *The True Difference between Christian Subjection and Unchristian Rebellion* (1585).

Bracton, Fortescue . . . Mirrour: a trio of medieval lawyers and political writers, much quoted by Whigs: Henry de Bracton (c.1210–68), believed to be the author of *De legibus et consuetudinibus Angliae* (*On the Laws and Customs of England*); Sir John Fortescue (c.1395–c.1477), author of *De laudibus legum Angliae* (*In Praise of the Laws of England*) (c.1460s); and the anonymous *Mirror of Justices* (publ. 1640), perhaps by Andrew Horne (d.1328). In advice on reading in 1703, Locke distinguishes two aspects of the study of politics, 'the one containing the original of societies, and the rise and extent of political power', and 'the other, the art of governing men in society'. The first is universal, pertaining to all humans, under the law of nature; the second pertains to the laws and customs of particular societies. For books under the first head see note to § 5. For the second, he recommended such authors as here cited, together with recent Whig writers on the 'Ancient Constitution': William Atwood, William Petyt, and James Tyrrell.

Egyptian Under-Taskmasters: the image of the Israelites suffering under Egyptian taskmasters (Exod. 1: 11) has been one of the most ubiquitous in Christian rhetoric of liberation from tyranny.

243 *erect a new Form . . . new Hands*: this is how the phrase appears in the Christ's Copy, and in the 1713/14 editions. Earlier editions had read: 'place it in a new form, or new hands'. By introducing the phrase 'old

form', Locke clarifies the passage in a conservative direction. In a letter to Edward Clarke, written in the midst of the Revolution in January 1689, he urged the settlement of the nation 'by restoring our ancient government, the best possibly that ever was'.

A LETTER CONCERNING TOLERATION

The notes to the Letter are keyed to page numbers.

123   TO THE READER: the preface was written by the translator, William Popple, but most eighteenth-century readers assumed it was by Locke.

Translated . . . Dutch and French: although no copy is extant, a Dutch edition was published in 1689; a French was planned, but none appeared until 1710. Not many Continental Europeans read English: Latin and French were the international languages. This opening sentence would lead readers to assume that this anonymous tract was written by either a Huguenot exile or a Dutch Arminian.

so much . . . Ours: toleration had been intensively discussed since the Civil Wars. Among earlier English books in defence of toleration were Roger Williams's *Bloudy Tenent of Persecution* (1644), Jeremy Taylor's *Liberty of Prophesying* (1646), William Walwyn's *Toleration Justified* (1646), and William Penn's *Great Case of Liberty of Conscience* (1670).

narrow Principles . . . Sects: the principle that 'true religion' should be enforced by 'the godly ruler' was so widespread that many apparent defences of toleration were in fact cases by particular claimants to 'true religion' for toleration of *them*, when in a minority, until they achieved power.

Declarations of Indulgence: royal edicts (such as those issued in 1672 and 1687) suspending the penal laws which enforced membership of the Church of England. Although tolerationist, the Declarations made illegal use of the royal prerogative.

Acts of Comprehension: there were several unsuccessful Bills, between the 1670s and 1689, for 'comprehension', which would have relaxed the doctrinal and liturgical requirements of the Church of England in order to readmit moderate Puritans, but which would have left other groups no better, and perhaps worse, off.

Absolute . . . Liberty: this ringing phrase was quoted as a slogan by later tolerationists, who believed it was Locke's. Scholars have pointed out that Locke, elsewhere, rejects 'absolute' liberty, but this is scarcely relevant, since the phrase is rhetorical and refers to the need to go further than the Toleration Act of 1689. Popple's preface puzzlingly does not mention the Act. He perhaps thought it an interim measure, because a project for comprehension was due for debate by the Church's Convocation. Or, more likely, he regretted that the Act left untouched the Test Acts which excluded non-Anglicans from public office; and it did not tolerate

Unitarians. The Act's title was begrudging: 'An Act for Exempting their Majesties Protestant Subjects Dissenting from the Church of England from the Penalties of Certain Laws.' It merely suspended the punishments rather than repealing old laws for uniformity, and nowhere contained the word 'toleration'.

dissenting Parties: since the Restoration in 1660 the Puritan denominations, which had flourished during the Civil Wars, had been excluded from the Church of England. The largest and most influential were the Presbyterians; other leading groups were the Congregationalists (or Independents), Baptists (or Anabaptists), and Quakers. The term 'Dissenter' did not include Catholics, whom most Protestants regarded as beyond the pale. 'Dissenters' were also called 'Nonconformists'.

124 *Characteristical Mark . . . Church*: theologians had long written of the 'marks' of the church: criteria for identifying Christ's true church. Thus Locke opens with a powerful *theological* claim on behalf of tolerance.

Manners: morals.

125 *Charity . . . Love*: Gal. 5: 6.

Estates: property. Occasionally 'estate' means 'condition'.

noisom: noxious, foul.

rellish: smell.

nice: subtle.

Schism or Heresie: schism is separation from (or renunciation of) ecclesiastical authority; heresy is deviation from orthodox doctrine.

126 *judged of*: at the Last Judgement.

rooting out . . . Sects: it was a characteristic claim of the 'Reformation of Manners' movement in the 1690s that the Restoration church had been wrongly preoccupied with enforcing conformity in worship rather than with suppressing immorality, thus prioritizing liturgical correctness over virtuous living.

another Kingdom: earthly clerical supremacy.

Christian Warfare: 2 Cor. 10: 4: 'the weapons of our warfare are not carnal'.

127 *Conversation*: consorting or engaging with others.

Dragoons: an allusion to Louis XIV's persecution of French Protestants, the Huguenots, through military *dragonnades*. Popple is elaborating, for Locke's Latin has 'cohorts' (*cohortes*).

Humane: human.

Colour: appearance, plausibility.

Weal: welfare.

Commonwealth: civil society. This is the standard translation of *res publica*, although Popple occasionally uses 'state' or 'civil government'.

The Commonwealth . . . Interests: this is the first of several passages which parallel Locke's *Second Treatise of Government*.

127 *Indolency*: freedom from pain.

128 *Magistrate*: a generic term for ruler: usually the 'supreme' magistrate, but it can include 'lesser' or 'subordinate' magistrates.

compell . . . Religion: Locke had in mind Luke 14: 23, where Jesus said 'compel them to come in' to the marriage feast, which theologians had (by holding the feast to be symbolic of the church) quoted for centuries in order to sanction persecution. Locke's contemporary Pierre Bayle entitled his defence of toleration, *A Philosophical Commentary on these Words of the Gospel, Luke 14: 23, Compel them to Come in* (1686).

by the Consent of the People: Popple out-Lockes Locke, for the Latin simply has 'by men' (*ab hominibus*).

129 *It may . . . grant it*: Locke allows that civil rulers may evangelize. See note to p. 139.

impertinent: irrelevant, beside the point.

Penalties . . . mind: the chief argument of Locke's contemporary adversary Jonas Proast was that, while it is true that force cannot *convince* the mind of a belief, it can lead to *consideration* of beliefs. The Restoration Anglican position was that compulsion *can* be efficacious in so far as forced attendance at religious teaching can encourage rethinking of habitual and unreflective beliefs.

130 *much straitned*: made yet narrower: Matt. 7: 14.

Society: this follows the Latin (*societatem*), but the sense might better be captured by 'association'. Locke means that a church is not the religious aspect of society as a whole, but a private organization within the plurality of civil society.

131 *Right of making its Laws*: 'laws' are not only the legislative acts of the state, but also the injunctions by any civil association making rules governing its own members.

derived . . . Succession: a standard claim of hierarchical Christian churches was that the authority of their leaders (variously pope, bishops, presbyters) derived from the 'Apostolic Succession', a continuous transmission of the 'power of the keys' which Christ gave to Peter and the first Apostles: Matt. 16: 18–19. A 'presbyter' is a priest or minister, but here denotes the Calvinist or Presbyterian system of clerical authority without bishops.

132 *in order to*: for.

mind: remind.

Ephesian . . . Diana: Acts 19: 24–41. The silversmiths, who depended for their livelihoods on the cult of Diana, set up the cry of 'Great is Diana' against the Christians. 'Great is Diana' was invoked by anticlericals to imply that clerical self-interest lurks behind the mask of godliness.

133 *Excommunication*: Locke asserts the conventional right of churches to cut off members from their body, temporarily or permanently, but rejects

the no less conventional claim that the 'godly ruler' should enforce spiritual excommunications with civil punishments.

damnified: harmed.

134 *Franchises*: privileges conferred by civil laws, in contrast to natural rights.

Denison: citizen.

spontaneous: voluntary, self-created.

135 *Arminians . . . Calvinists*: Locke's Latin has 'Remonstrants' and 'Anti-Remonstrants', two factions in the Dutch Reformed church. The latter were Calvinist, believing in divine predestination to salvation or damnation, while the former allowed a role for human moral effort in God's judgement upon humankind. Arminius (1560–1609) was a Dutch theologian; the term 'Arminian' had entered the English language to denote the rejection of predestination.

Turks: Muslims. Islam was chiefly identified with the Ottoman Empire.

136 *the better end of the Staff*: proverb: the right end of the stick.

Where they . . . Toleration: sentence added by Popple, an example of his occasional amendments. He may be referring to the Church of England which, deprived of its power of coercion under the Catholic and tolerationist James II in 1687–8, suddenly began to court the Dissenters.

in fine: in sum.

137 *Dominion is founded in Grace*: the belief, attributed especially to Catholics but also to extreme Protestants, that earthly rule should be grounded on spiritual righteousness, and hence that God's chosen should rule and should overthrow those who lack divine grace. The doctrine was invoked in the papal claim to depose heretical rulers, but also by advocates of the Puritan 'Rule of the Saints'. Today, 'dominion in grace' sanctions many varieties of religious violence.

Laity, as they please to call us: anticlericals echoed radical Protestant distaste for the separation of 'priests' and 'laity'. Luther had pronounced 'the priesthood of all believers'.

Craft: during the 1690s a new word became fashionable among anticlerical authors: priestcraft.

138 *repeated . . . Injuries*: Popple's translation misses Locke's allusion to Matt. 18: 22: 'seventy times seven'.

marrying his Daughter: Locke apparently shares the patriarchal view that a daughter's marriage is her father's decision.

139 *charitable Care . . . man*: although Locke rejects religious coercion by the ruler, he does not confine religious belief to the private sphere, for he insists there is a general duty to evangelize.

Geneva: as Rome was symbolic of Catholicism, so Geneva was of Calvinism.

Or, to make . . . Musicians: this remark makes sense if we note that Locke's Latin refers not only to being rich but also to being elegant or cultured.

140 *Buskins*: elaborate boots or stockings.

dipt: baptized.

more sowr than they ought to be: a delicate phrase, for it deprecates the rigid solemnity of some Puritans and their shunning of outsiders, while condemning ill-treatment of them.

cloathed in White: a reference to the white surplice, worn in the Anglican church, which Puritans rejected as 'popish', preferring the 'black Geneva gown'.

discover: reveal.

141 *unsuccessful Voyages*: the Latin is more general: bad investments. Buying shares in overseas mercantile voyages was the clearest example of a high-risk investment.

142 *Baal*: a pagan god, often referred to in the Old Testament.

Tribe: a contemptuous anticlerical word for a fraternity of followers.

Socinians: followers of the Italian theologian Faustus Socinus (1539–1604), who denied the doctrines of the Trinity and divinity of Christ: Unitarians.

the Church . . . Name: another anticlerical slight against the presumption of priests in monopolizing 'the Church' to themselves. A 'convention' of the church is, variously, a council, synod, or (in the Church of England) Convocation. 'Canons' are church laws.

Orthodox and Arian Emperors: in the third century and after, the Christian church was torn apart by theological disputes between Athanasians and Arians concerning the nature of the unity between God the Father and God the Son.

The English History: the first edition had 'our' English history, which indicated that, even though the tract was published in Holland, the author was English.

Henry the 8th . . . Queens: the Tudor monarchs enforced several religious revolutions, in which the clergy largely acquiesced. Henry's Reformation separated England from Rome but remained Catholic in theology; Edward pursued a thoroughgoing Reformation; Mary reverted to Catholicism; Elizabeth entrenched an ambiguously Protestant settlement. Later, the phrase 'Vicar of Bray' was coined to denote time-serving clergy.

143 *Mansions of the Blessed*: proverb, derived from John 14: 2.

doubtful: Locke silently amended this to 'doubted' when he quoted it in his *Second Letter Concerning Toleration*.

144 *own*: witness.

National Church . . . Congregations: Locke has 'Court Church' (*aulicam*) and 'others' (*diversas*). Popple anglicizes this, particularly in specifying 'separated congregations', the Dissenters. The term 'Established Church' was not common until the eighteenth century.

Indifferent things: theologians distinguished 'things necessary' for salvation from 'things indifferent', the latter being matters which were not pre-scribed in Scripture. Some held that 'things indifferent' (also technically called *adiaphora*) could be imposed by earthly authority, without offend-ing conscience; others that they should not be, because not required by Christ.

145   *useful . . . Law*: many Restoration Anglicans argued that religious coercion *was* useful to the commonwealth, in preserving society from violent reli-gious conflict among rival factions. Locke had himself argued this in his youthful early tracts on government. Hence, a tolerationist stance did not necessarily follow from a stress on the broad ambit of 'things indifferent'.

Jews: the Jews were readmitted to England by Oliver Cromwell in 1656.

146   *Who . . . hands*: Isa. 1: 12.

147   *Habit and Posture*: 'habit' here means attire, and points to controver-sies over the godliness or 'popery' of vestments; 'posture' points to con-troversies over the propriety of standing or kneeling to receive the euchar-ist. A little later Locke refers to 'sitting or kneeling'.

Order, Decency, and Edification: 1 Cor. 14: 26, 40. A standard citation by those who defended liturgical conformity.

Primitive Christians: those of the early church. 'Primitive' was not a pe-jorative term; it denoted the purity of the earliest times, closest to Christ.

falsly accused . . . Uncleanness: the second-century Christian apologists, such as Justin Martyr, parried pagan attacks on the immorality of Christians.

not lawful . . . life: note that Locke does not extend tolerance to matters of sexual immorality, which ought to be punished by law.

148   *Maliboeus*: an allusion to Virgil's *Eclogues*, 3. 1.

take care . . . prejudice: an echo of Cicero, *Against Catiline*, 1. 2. 4.

Murrain: disease.

149   *Geneva . . . Idolatrous*: Geneva was a Calvinist theocracy. Notoriously, Cal-vin burnt Servetus for heresy in 1553. Locke is just as hostile to theocratic Calvinism as to domineering Catholicism or Anglicanism.

in India: perhaps an allusion to persecutions by the Mughal emperor Aurangzeb (1618–1707); but Locke's *in Indiis* may refer to either the East-ern or American Indies.

Americans: native peoples. The encounter between European colonists and pagan nations in the New World prompted extensive controversy. In Protestant legend, the Spanish Empire epitomized Catholic cruelty in its dealings with native peoples. But it is not Catholicism Locke has in mind here. The apparently hypothetical story in this paragraph is an allusion to the experience of Native Americans under the impact of English settlers in New England. The early settlers could not have survived without native support, yet the settlers latterly became intolerant of pagan natives and Christian dissenters alike. Massachusetts was a Congregationalist polity, and this passage is striking proof that Locke's targets are not only Catholics, Anglicans, and Dutch Calvinists, but also Puritan theocracies.

149 *Let . . . bottom*: Locke has 'This is how it began': he is beginning a narrative.

150 *this Story to himself*: Horace, *Satires*, 1. 1. 69–70.

    Idolaters . . . rooted out: Exod. 22: 20–1. Locke now embarks on an analysis of Mosaic law concerning heathens.

    Hear O Israel: Deut. 5: 1.

151 *Strangers*: foreigners. The propriety of tolerating and integrating immigrants was hotly debated. Huguenot refugees were themselves divided between those willing to conform to the Church of England and those not.

    Moabites . . . spared?: Num. 33: 50–2; Deut. 7: 1, 2: 9.

152 *Gibeonites . . . Treaty*: Josh. 2: 9. *Articled*: made a pact. *Allowed*: reprieved. *without*: outside.

    Practical . . . Speculative: moral and doctrinal. 'Speculative' does not here mean doubtful, but pertaining to belief rather than action.

153 *Roman Catholick . . . Neighbour*: a reference to the doctrine of transubstantiation. Locke holds that it is not the absurdity of such beliefs that makes Catholics intolerable: it is their other, political beliefs that rule them out. His Latin has 'Papist' (*Pontificius*) rather than 'Roman Catholic'.

    outward and inward Court: public judgement and private conscience.

154 *Because . . . Eternity*: Rom. 8: 18.

    pravity: wickedness.

155 *honest industry . . . mutual Assistance*: these phrases are also found in *Second Treatise*, §§ 19, 42.

    Arms . . . Citizens: Locke's triad of the fundamental desiderata of governments. Like his contemporaries, he assumed that demographic growth was a necessity for flourishing societies, and he feared depopulation.

    Commodities: benefits, welfare.

    good pleasure: Eph. 1: 9.

156 *Propriety*: property.

    For there . . . People: compare *Second Treatise*, §§ 21, 168, 141.

157 *Peace . . . waste*: an echo of Tacitus, *Agricola*, 5: 'they make a desert and call it peace.'

    where the one . . . begins: compare *Second Treatise*, § 202: 'Wherever law ends, tyranny begins.'

    But: the following four paragraphs, giving reasons for not tolerating Catholics, were omitted from an edition published in 1788, by which time opinion was becoming more favourable toward Catholics, whose worship was made lawful in 1791.

    Faith . . . Hereticks: it was commonly held that Catholics, or at least Jesuits, taught that it was permissible to lie to heretics. The Oath of Allegiance imposed after the Gunpowder Plot of 1605 included the phrase, 'without . . . equivocation or mental . . . reservation'.

158 *Kings excommunicated . . . Kingdoms*: the papacy claimed the right to excommunicate and depose heretic monarchs. This is what Pope Pius V had done to Queen Elizabeth in 1570, which underpinned the Gunpowder Plot against her successor.

challenge: claim.

Dominion . . . Grace: see note to p. 137.

meer: pure, unalloyed.

deliver themselves . . . Prince: this refers to the Catholic church. Locke shares the standard Protestant view that Catholics not only hold false theological beliefs but also owe their civil allegiance to the papacy.

frivolous . . . Church: anxious for toleration and often willing to give civil allegiance to Protestant monarchs, English Catholics argued that their religion can be distinguished from the politics of 'the Court of Rome'.

lists: pleases.

Mahumetan: Locke may be using Islam here as a metaphor for a continuing discussion of Catholic allegiance, but it is not clear. The ensuing passage is today hotly debated by those seeking to determine Locke's position regarding Islam.

Mufti: an Islamic scholar. Locke has in mind the Grand Mufti, a state official.

Oracles: this follows Locke's Latin (*oracular*), but a recent translation (Cambridge, 2010) renders this as 'fatwas'.

159 *Atheist*: Locke believes atheists could not be tolerated, for these, too, had no reason to keep faith with the social order. His contemporaries Pierre Bayle and Baruch Spinoza did allow toleration of atheists.

Conventicles: illegal meetings for worship. The Conventicle Act of 1670 forbad all gatherings for worship other than those of the Church of England. The phrase explaining 'Assemblies' is Popple's addition.

Meetings: religious meetings. Dissenters were sometimes called 'meeters'.

Courts of Judicature . . . Exchange: the principal law-courts sat in Westminster Hall, a crowded place of public resort; the Royal Exchange in the City of London was a great concourse of merchants and shoppers, and, like the Hall, of newsmongers. Popple's translation again anglicizes Locke's more cosmopolitan Latin, which has not 'Exchange', but 'guild' or 'corporation' (*collegiis*).

160 *Conventicles . . . Machinations*: to assuage the fear that conventicles were a cover for conspiracy, the Toleration Act of 1689 required that all licensed Dissenting meeting-houses must have their doors unlocked during worship.

160 *Gallies*: another allusion to France, where Huguenot heretics were sent to the galleys. Locke has 'forced labour' (*ergastulum*).

161 *Education . . . Children*: French edicts against the Huguenots ordered the seizing of children to enforce a Catholic upbringing.

Clubs for Claret: the likening of churches to drinking-clubs was shocking. Locke's point is that both are voluntary associations within civil society, and not part of the fabric of political rule. The precise phrase is Popple's (who had been a wine merchant); Locke's Latin has *hilaritatem otium:* 'leisure' or 'amusement'.

all the Mischief: Locke has 'the disaster that has fallen on our condition' (*fundi nostri calamitas*), from Terence, *Eunuchus*, 1. 1. 34.

And all . . . another: Locke here deploys a *politique* or prudential argument for toleration: a plurality of denominations will provide mutual checks and balances.

162 *Presbyterian Discipline . . . like*: in the 1640s and 1650s, under the dominance of the Puritans, Anglicanism was suppressed. In 1689 Scotland adopted a different religious settlement from England, abolishing episcopacy and establishing Presbyterianism: episcopalian worship was not legalized until 1711.

Flagitious: vicious.

Halls: Popple alludes to the fact that some London Dissenters met in merchant guilds' halls. The Pinners Hall Lecture was a prestigious Presbyterian sermon.

163 *Professors*: those who follow a particular religion.

Presbyterians . . . Quakers: the list in Locke's Latin is different: Remonstrants, Anti-Remonstrants, Lutherans, Anabaptists, Socinians. Note that Locke here includes Socinians (anti-Trinitarians) within the ambit of toleration. Scholars have often suggested that Locke was himself a Socinian.

Mahumetan, nor Jew: Locke insists that Muslims and Jews should be tolerated. In his *Second Letter* he hopes for their conversion to Christianity, which was often the motive for tolerating non-Christians.

Why . . . Synagogues?: Jewish services were held in England from the 1660s, but the first purpose-built synagogue was Bevis Marks in London in 1701.

164 *honest Industry . . . Rapine*: perhaps an allusion to the gangs of informers who secured convictions of Dissenters in Restoration England, arranged for the exaction of fines, often through sequestration, and pocketed some of the proceeds.

natural Rights: Locke has 'rights which God and nature have given' (*jura sibi a Deo et natura concessa*).

165 *Tyranny . . . Church*: a common Whig charge was that churchmen preached up the divine right of kings, expecting, as a *quid pro quo*, that the absolute monarch would in turn support their power in religious matters.

Sed . . . &c.: 'I am ashamed to say something so scandalous and yet which could not be answered.' Ovid, *Metamorphoses*, 1. 758–9.

POSTSCRIPT: Popple's insertion: the Latin does not have a heading. The Postscript appears to be intended to defend Dutch Arminians from charges of heresy and schism.

166 *Rule . . . Popes*: contemporaries debated the 'rule of faith', the criterion by which religious doctrine was to be adjudged true. Some insisted on 'Scripture alone', some the pronouncements of the papacy, some the traditions or received wisdom of the church over time.

Christians of St. John: the reference is unclear: either the Catholic order of the Knights of St John of Malta; or an ancient Mesopotamian sect.

167 *Symboles*: creeds.

Analogy of Faith: a principle of interpretation by which an obscure passage in Scripture can be understood by analogy with a clearer one. From Rom. 12: 3.

168 *Use . . . Language*: echoing Horace, *Art of Poetry*, 71–2: 'use, which is the law that decides what is correct in speech.'

parts: talents, abilities.

INDEX

It may be useful to list a number of terms in the *Second Treatise* that occur too frequently to index: *Authority, Commonwealth, Earth, Force, Free, Freedom* (but see *Freemen, Natural liberty*), *God* (but see *Godlike princes*), *Government* (but see *Art of government*), *Judge, Judgement, Just, Justice* (but see *Just war*), *King, Kingdom, Law* (but see *Common law, Law of God, Law of nature, Law of reason, Positive law*), *Liberty* (but see *Natural liberty*), *Life* (but see *Lives, liberties, estates*), *Magistrate, Mankind, Nature* (but see *Law of nature, Natural liberty, Natural right*), *People, Person, Power* (but see *Absolute power*), *Preservation, Prince, Reason* (but see *Rational*), *Right* (but see *Common right, Natural right, Right reason*), *Society* (but see *Civil society*), *Subjects, Supreme, War* (but see *State of war, War leaders*), *Will, World*. Likewise in the *Letter Concerning Toleration*: *Church, Civil, Commonwealth, Conscience, Doctrine, Ecclesiastical, Faith, Force, God, Magistrate, Opinion, Persecution* (but see *Punishment*), *Public, Religion, Salvation, Soul, Toleration, Truth, Worship*.

The Oxford World's Classics Website

www.worldsclassics.co.uk

- Browse the full range of Oxford World's Classics online

- Sign up for our monthly e-alert to receive information on new titles

- Read extracts from the Introductions

- Listen to our editors and translators talk about the world's greatest literature with our Oxford World's Classics audio guides

- Join the conversation, follow us on Twitter at OWC_Oxford

- Teachers and lecturers can order inspection copies quickly and simply via our website

www.worldsclassics.co.uk

American Literature

British and Irish Literature

Children's Literature

Classics and Ancient Literature

Colonial Literature

Eastern Literature

European Literature

Gothic Literature

History

Medieval Literature

Oxford English Drama

Philosophy

Poetry

Politics

Religion

The Oxford Shakespeare

A complete list of Oxford World's Classics, including Authors in Context, Oxford English Drama, and the Oxford Shakespeare, is available in the UK from the Marketing Services Department, Oxford University Press, Great Clarendon Street, Oxford OX2 6DP, or visit the website at www.oup.com/uk/worldsclassics.

In the USA, visit www.oup.com/us/owc for a complete title list.

Oxford World's Classics are available from all good bookshops. In case of difficulty, customers in the UK should contact Oxford University Press Bookshop, 116 High Street, Oxford OX1 4BR.

Bhagavad Gita

The Bible Authorized King James Version
   With Apocrypha

The Book of Common Prayer

Dhammapada

The Gospels

The Koran

The Pañcatantra

The Sauptikaparvan (from the
   Mahabharata)

The Tale of Sinuhe and Other Ancient
   Egyptian Poems

The Qur'an

Upanisads

ANSELM OF CANTERBURY   The Major Works

THOMAS AQUINAS   Selected Philosophical Writings

AUGUSTINE   The Confessions
   On Christian Teaching

BEDE   The Ecclesiastical History

KĀLIDĀSA   The Recognition of Śakuntalā

LAOZI   Daodejing

RUMI   The Masnavi

ŚĀNTIDEVA   The Bodhicaryāvatāra

Classical Literary Criticism
**The First Philosophers: The Presocratics
  and the Sophists**
Greek Lyric Poetry
Myths from Mesopotamia

APOLLODORUS   **The Library of Greek Mythology**

APOLLONIUS OF RHODES **Jason and the Golden Fleece**

APULEIUS   **The Golden Ass**

ARISTOPHANES   **Birds and Other Plays**

ARISTOTLE   **The Nicomachean Ethics**
                      Politics

ARRIAN   **Alexander the Great**

BOETHIUS   **The Consolation of Philosophy**

CAESAR   **The Civil War**
                      The Gallic War

CATULLUS   **The Poems of Catullus**

CICERO   **Defence Speeches**
                      The Nature of the Gods
                      On Obligations
                      Political Speeches
                      The Republic and The Laws

EURIPIDES   **Bacchae and Other Plays**
                      Heracles and Other Plays
                      Medea and Other Plays
                      Orestes and Other Plays
                      The Trojan Women and Other Plays

HERODOTUS   **The Histories**

HOMER   **The Iliad**
                      The Odyssey